THE ULTIMATE BARBECUE COOKBOOK

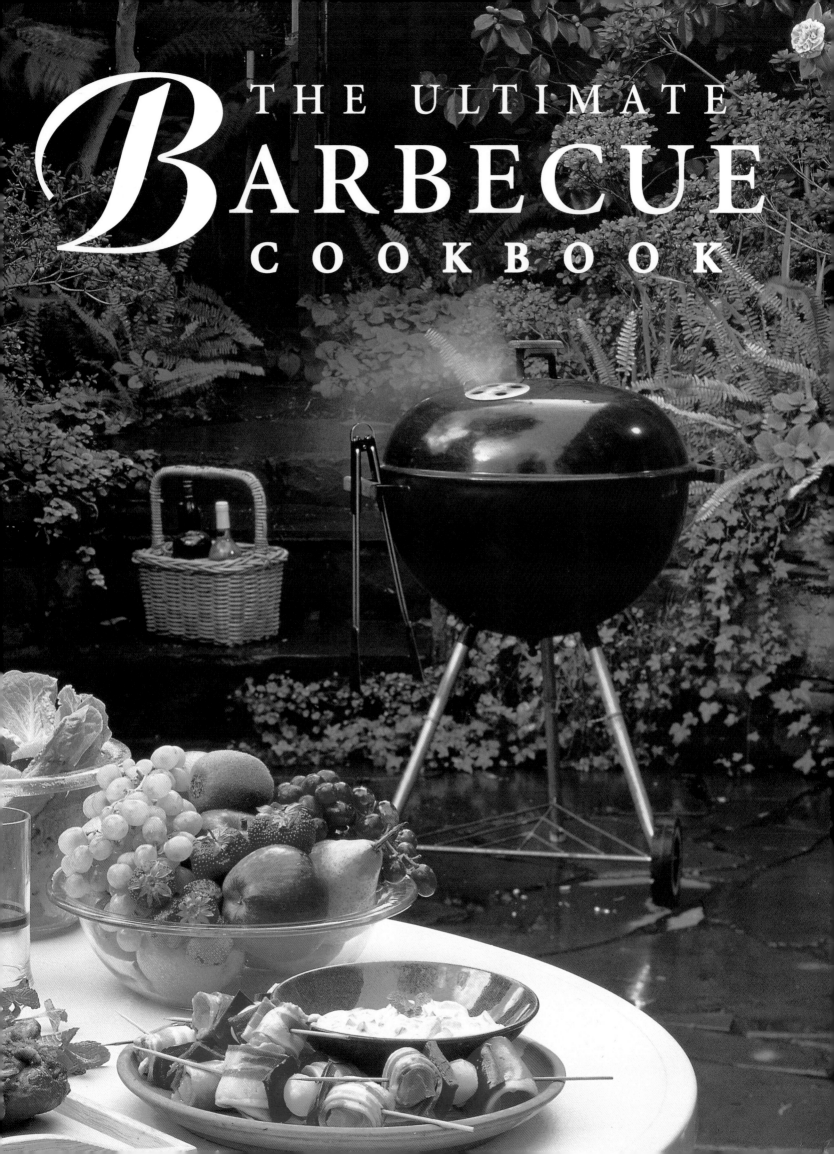

THE ULTIMATE
BARBECUE
COOKBOOK

Contents

Barbecue basics

*S*ome *barbecues can be as formal as a dinner party, others as relaxed as a picnic on the beach. Whatever the case, you will need to be prepared — choose the barbecue that suits you best, light the perfect fire and prepare the food to its maximum advantage.*

Types of barbecues

Fuel-burning

Fixed barbecue Many gardens contain some sort of fixture for barbecuing; they are relatively simple constructions, usually made from bricks or cement and featuring two grills — the bottom for building the fire, the top for cooking the food. These grills are not generally height-adjustable, so cooking can only be regulated by adjusting the fire, or moving the food away from or towards the fire. Being fixed these barbecues cannot, of course, be put out of high winds or moved to shelter in the event of rain. Despite this, fixed barbecues are easy to use and maintain, and quite often are large enough to cater for big gatherings.

Weber (kettle) barbecue One of the most popular styles of portable barbecue, the Weber features a close-fitting lid and air vents at top and bottom which allow for greater versatility and accuracy in cooking. Webers can function either as a traditional barbecue, as an oven or as a smoker (see page 13 for preparation techniques). Weber barbecues only burn charcoal or heat beads (wood is not recommended) and are relatively small. The standard diameter is 57 cm, so if barbecuing for large groups more than one Weber is probably required.

Brazier This is the simplest style of fuel-burning barbecue, of which the small, cast-iron hibachi is probably best known. A brazier consists of a shallow fire-box for burning fuel with a grill on top. Some grills

A Weber barbecue, although compact, can prepare a variety of foods

7

are height adjustable or can rotate. Braziers are best fitted with a heat-reflecting hood, so that food will cook at an even temperature.

Fuel

Although traditional, wood is not an ideal fuel for cooking. It can be difficult to light and burns with a flame. Charcoal or heat beads are preferable. They will create a bed of glowing heat which is perfect for cooking. They do not smell, smoke or flare and are readily available in supermarkets or hardware shops. (Heat beads are sometimes known as barbecue briquettes and should not be confused with heating briquettes, which are not suitable for cooking.)

Firelighters are essential for lighting charcoal or heat bead fires. They are soaked in kerosene so will ignite instantly. Do not attempt to cook while firelighters are still burning, as they give off kerosene fumes. Generally one or two firelighters will light about twenty pieces of charcoal or heat beads.

A 'normal' fire consists of about 50–60 heat beads or pieces of charcoal and will last for several hours. All recipes in this book can be cooked over a normal fire.

Don't be put off by the pungent smell. It takes 20 minutes to get coals glowing and even longer for heat beads. By then the fire starters have served their purpose and are quite odourless. When briquets (made of compressed coal dust) and charcoal are well alight the flames will die down and a grey ash will appear all over the red-hot glowing coals. If preparing a Weber (kettle) barbecue, leave off the lid while the fire is developing.

Build the fire in the middle of the grate, so that

Coals ready for cooking — the beads have developed a fine ash coating

cooked food can be moved to the edge of the grill and kept warm.

A good way to find out if the heat is right is to hold the palm of your hand about 10 cm above the glowing coals. If you pull it away within two seconds, you know the barbecue is ready for the food. Likewise, when cooking over a wood fire, make certain that the flames have died down completely to leave glowing coals, covered with ash, before starting to cook. The flavour is unique. Some leaves and twigs from certain trees, especially anything with a milky white sap, are not suitable to use on the barbecue so, if in doubt, leave it out. If you'd rather collect than buy wood, just be sure that what you're gathering isn't going to make your family barbie front page news!

Smoke flavour can be achieved on even the humblest barbecue with the addition of water-soaked mesquite or hickory chips just prior to cooking. However, to smoke-cook foods the indirect way, you will need to use some kind of covered barbecue. This method needs a drip pan (a baking dish will do) containing 4 cups of water to be positioned beneath food for smoking (see page 13 for details).

With indirect cooking on a gas barbecue, keep the burner lit under the wood chips and turn off the burner that's under the food. It's a slow-cooking method, but the smoke flavour will be much stronger than in direct smoke-cooked foods.

If cooking whole joints, check for 'doneness' with a meat thermometer or, in the case of poultry, by inserting a metal skewer in the thigh and making sure that the juices that run out are clear. If the juices are pink, longer cooking time is needed.

If using a kettle barbecue arrange the coals so that they are to the sides of the drip pan and place wood chips over coals. Place food to be smoked on a grill or wire rack over the drip pan, but not touching the water. The steam helps to keep the food moist.

Temperature control

A fire's temperature can be lowered by damping down with a spray of water. (A trigger-style plastic spray-bottle is ideal.) Damping also produces steam which puts moisture back in the food.

The best and safest way to increase the heat of a fire is to add more fuel and wait for the fire to develop. Do not fan a fire to increase its heat; this will only produce a flame. Never pour flammable liquids on a fire.

Gas or electric barbecues

Although often more expensive, these barbecues are very simple to use. They do not require an open flame, only connection to their fuel source. In most cases, the gas or electricity heats a tray of reusable volcanic rock. Hickory chips can be placed over the rock-bed to produce a smoky flavour in the food, if desired. Sizes of models vary, the largest being the wagon style, which usually features a workbench, reflecting hood and, often, a bottom shelf for storage. While small portable gas models, which require only the connection of a gas bottle, are greatly manoeuvrable, electric models are, of course, confined to areas where mains electricity is available. Most gas or electric barbecues have temperature controls; their accuracy is their primary advantage. Electric models can be fitted with rotisseries or spit turners for spit roasting.

A gas-filled wagon barbecue featuring hood and work areas

Building your own barbecue

Basically, a brick barbecue consists of a metal plate and/or grill suspended above a hearth that is bordered on three sides by brickwork. The design can be as simple or as grand as your outdoor setting can accommodate. Some elaborate barbecues incorporate a chimney but, unless you're a competent bricklayer, it's best to keep it all simple.

Decide on the size of grill you need; this will be governed by your partying ambitions. Cast iron is the best material. A flat, tiled area on one side of the barbecue to hold plates, drinks and general paraphernalia is also useful.

If the grill is to fit inside the barbecue, make sure you have 10 mm clearance from the tray or grill to the brickwork. This allows for expansion in the metal. The height can be adjusted to what is most comfortable for you.

Correct siting of the barbecue is important. Think of the neighbours: smoke, and noise that you consider convivial, are usually perceived as a nuisance by others. If at all possible, locate it in a protected place — one in close proximity to the kitchen.

Brick quantities

Draw your barbecue to scale, say 1:5 or 1:10. Show a front view and a side view. You can then measure the area of brickwork and calculate how many bricks you'll need. Allow 48 bricks per square metre in a single skin (110 mm thick), stretcher bond brickwork (assuming a 10 mm joint). If the wall is 230 mm thick (as the centre wall in the sketch is), you'll need 96 bricks per square metre. You must allow at least 10 per cent extra for chips and breakages (just multiply the total number by 1.1 if you want to add 10 per cent).

Note how the diagram shows the hearth has a brick skin which is infilled with rubble and covered with a layer of concrete 75 mm thick. Alternatively, if you have some old bricks, you could lay the whole thing in solid brickwork.

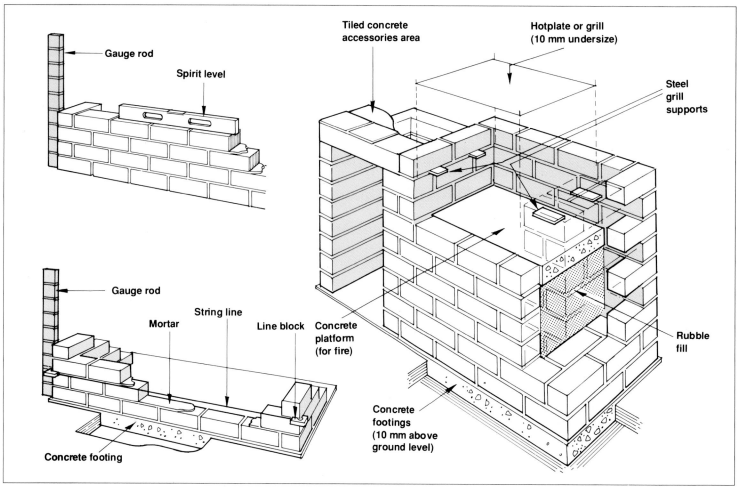

Barbecue construction, showing the back wall bricklaying

Mortar

The mortar in a barbecue should not be too strong or it will crack. A one part cement to one part lime to nine parts sand mix (with a bit of plasticiser in it to make laying easier) is ideal. Colour the mortar with oxide to suit the bricks. The joints can be finished in a number of ways: made flush with the brick faces; raked out 5 mm and left square; or ironed, which leaves the joint slightly concave.

Tools

Tape; pencil; lump hammer; a bolster for cutting the bricks; a shovel; a wheelbarrow; trowel; level; string line and blocks; a tool for ironing (making a rounded joint) or raking (making a square joint).

The footing

Ideally, the barbecue should be built on a level, 100 mm thick, reinforced concrete slab. Make the width and length of the slab to suit brick sizes. It should project 10 mm above ground level so that the bricks are not touching the soil and getting wet all the time, which could lead to staining and mould.

Laying the bricks

1 Prepare a gauge rod by drawing on a 50 x 25 mm batten, to the full size, a series of 76 mm bricks with 10 mm joints. This rod will help you maintain even courses. Remember to start with a joint.

2 After wetting the bricks, measure out the mortar ingredients and mix them together with the shovel. If possible, select a waterproof surface on which to do your mixing; in a wheelbarrow is ideal. Mix ingredients thoroughly to a thick paste.

3 Starting on one of the back corners of the slab, lay a bed of mortar with the trowel. Lay the first corner brick in the mortar. Lightly tap it down with the handle of the trowel and cut away the excess mortar. Buttering the end of the next brick, repeat the procedure until the first course of one corner is laid and level. Start the next course, bearing in mind that the brickwork overlaps on the corners (check the brickwork on your house if you're unsure). Use the gauge rod periodically to check the joint sizes (see diagram) and constantly use your spirit level to check for plumb and level.

4 When one back corner is done, build the one at the opposite end. Once both corners are complete, use two line blocks or pins and a nylon line to work to when filling in the middle (but make sure you get the line on two opposite courses!).

5 The grill may be laid on top of the bricks. Alternatively, the grill may be suspended using four pieces of 25 x 10 mm flat steel (or 100 x 100 mm thick stainless steel rod). These are built into the brick joints at an appropriate height. Ensure that 50 mm projects out of the brick joints.

When laying the bricks, make sure you finish the joints before the mortar hardens. Brush off any excess mortar before it dries. If staining occurs, use a mix of one part hydrochloric acid to 10 parts water to clean the bricks. Then rinse with plenty of water.

6 The tiled top can easily be done if you cover the area where the bench is to be with 25 mm thick compressed fibre cement which can be screwed to the brickwork using plugs. Once it is fixed securely, glue glazed tiles (they are more easy to clean) to the top, making sure you have 5–10 mm joints. When the glue has dried, grout between them with a 3:1 sand and cement mix.

Give the mortar two weeks to cure. Then you're ready to go ahead and call your friends round to give the barbecue a test run.

Equipment and accessories

If you know an avid barbecue chef, you'll never be stuck for ideas when it comes to birthday and Christmas gifts. Don't be intimidated by the list of utensils; you can make a good start with even the first half dozen.

❏ A stiff wire brush/scraper — for brushing and scraping away burnt-on food from grill bars and flatplate.

❏ Gas lighter — a must for gas barbecues without automatic lighter.

❏ Long-handled tongs — for turning and moving food and coals while cooking (help to prevent singed hands and arms).

❏ Metal frying slice — good for lifting hamburgers, onion rings, fried eggs, fish fillets etc.

❏ Long, sharp knife — for carving large pieces of meat or poultry.

❏ Heatproof mitts — especially for handling skewers and cast iron pans.

❏ Water spray — to subdue flare-ups.

❏ A fire blanket — keep one on hand wherever you cook.

❏ Skewers — long and flat metal are preferable, although bamboo works well if thoroughly soaked in water before use.

❑ Bristle basting brush or bulb baster — for coating with sauce or marinade.

❑ Wire fish frame — to hold fish together as it cooks and for easy turning.

❑ Rotisserie — for cooking large joints of meat evenly.

❑ Meat thermometer — to test if large cuts of meat are done.

❑ Non-stick baking paper and heavy duty foil — non-stick baking paper is an ideal cooking medium, perfect for roasting and baking. It's best not to cook directly in foil; sweet things are more prone to sticking or burning, while acid marinades can react with the aluminium.

Cooking techniques

Most recipes in this book call for the food to be cooked over a direct flame. Indirect cooking is only possible on Weber (kettle) barbecues. (See page 13 for how to prepare a barbecue for indirect cooking.)

Retain moistness in the meat by searing quickly and turning once only

A barbecue flatplate can be used to stir-fry vegetables

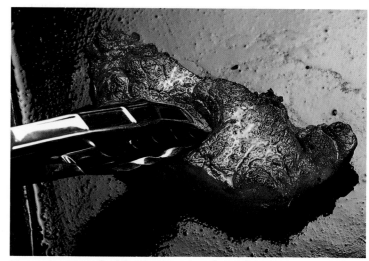

Test meat is cooked by pressing gently with tongs

Fish is ready when the flesh has turned opaque and flakes easily

Direct cooking

As with grilling or frying in the kitchen, the less turning or handling of the food the better. Once the fire is ready, lightly brush the grill or flatplate with oil. Place the food over the hottest part of the fire and sear quickly on both sides; this retains moisture. Once seared move the food to a cooler part of the grill or flatplate to cook for a few more minutes. Barbecuing is a fast-cooking process so even well-done food will not take very long. Techniques such as stir-frying are ideal for the barbecue flatplate.

Test that meat is done by firmly pressing it with tongs or the flat edge of a knife. Meat that is ready to serve should 'give' slightly but not resist pressure too easily. At first, it may be difficult to judge when it is ready, but try to resist cutting or stabbing the meat; this not only reduces its succulence, but releases juices which may cause the fire to flare. Pork and chicken should not be served rare, so if in any doubt remove to a separate place and make a slight cut in the thickest part of the meat. If the juices do not run clear, return to the heat for further cooking. Test if fish is cooked by gently flaking back the flesh in the thickest part with a fork. Cooked flesh should be white and opaque, but still moist.

Smoking

Smoking chips or chunks come from hickory wood, mesquite, dried mallee root, red gum or acacia trees and are available from barbecue specialists and some hardware or variety stores. Their smoke provides an extra and unusual flavour to the food.

Smoking is best done on a covered barbecue (see below for technique) but can also be done on an open fire. Scatter some smoking wood throughout the coals. Once the wood is burning, damp down with a little water to create more smoke. Smoking wood is available in chips and chunks; chips burn quickly so should be added towards the end of the cooking process. Chunks should last through the entire cooking process.

If glazing meat, such as ham, and smoking it, always glaze before adding wood. (Please note that some woods, such as pine, cedar or eucalyptus produce acrid smoke and are unsuitable for cooking. Use only wood sold specifically for smoking.)

Indirect cooking

Indirect cooking roasts or bakes food more slowly than direct cooking. It also allows for adding fragrant wood chips to the coals which introduces extra flavour to the food.

To prepare a Weber for indirect cooking:
1 Remove lid; open bottom vent.
2 Position bottom grill inside bowl and attach charcoal rails. Heap coals in rails; position firelighters inside coals.
3 Light fire and allow coals to develop to fine-ash stage.

(Leave lid off while fire develops.) Place a drip tray or baking dish on bottom grill. Position top grill; add food.

To prepare a Weber for smoking:
1 Prepare barbecue as above.
2 When coals reach fine-ash stage, add wood chips; fill drip tray or baking dish with 4 cups hot water. Cover with lid until fragrant smoke develops.
3 Remove lid; centre food on top grill. Cover with lid.

Planning your menu

Now you have the barbecue, and the necessary equipment to get started, it's time to invite people round. Design your menu to take full advantage of the barbecue — vegetables, kebabs, breads, even desserts can be cooked or warmed easily.

Serve at least one salad with the cooked food. Salad dressings and special sauces can be made in advance and stored in a screw-top jar in the refrigerator. (See page 219 for salad dressing recipes.) Assemble salads up to one day in advance, but dress just before serving.

Light the fire about an hour before using it. Check the fire occasionally — it can easily go out if unattended.

Assemble all necessary utensils and accessories, for example, tongs, forks, knives, plates and basting brushes, before cooking.

Have plenty of snacks and drinks available for your guests, but place them well away from the fire.

Have a hose or water bottle standing by in case of emergencies. (As a general safety rule, do not attempt to barbecue in strong winds.) A torch may be useful if barbecuing at night.

Always extinguish a fire once you have finished cooking on it. If possible, clean out the barbecue as soon as it has cooled down, brush or scrape grills and flatplates, and discard ash and embers.

Place two or three firelighters in the coals; light fire, allow to develop

Place a drip tray underneath the top grill when coals are ready

Spoon a generous quantity of smoking wood over the hot coals

Beef, lamb and pork

*b*eef is always popular at a barbecue. Tender steaks, juicy roasts and burgers all play an important role. Choose good quality lean meat. The best beef cuts for barbecue roasting are whole pieces of rib eye, a thick slice of rump and boneless sirloin. If you're marinating beef for the barbecue, economical cuts which give good results include the first 4–5 slices of round, topside and silverside. Rib steak, bone-in-blade, oyster blade and beef spare ribs are also good choices.

Succulent and tender, lamb lends itself perfectly to barbecue cooking, either pink or well done. But be careful to avoid mutton, the older relative, which may prove tougher and takes much longer to cook. Lamb lends itself wonderfully to all kinds of marinades — from a yoghurt-based tandoori mixture, to an oriental ginger-chilli base.

Pork, too, is a good choice when barbecuing. It marries well with Asian-style ingredients like soy sauce, ginger and sesame oil to produce tender satays and finger lickin' ribs. Try some of the 'new fashioned' cuts.

Nowadays there's no excuse for serving 'burnt offerings'. With a little practice you can monitor when the meat is done with the touch of a finger. Choose steaks of an even thickness — about 3 cm is best — and remove the excess fat. Make small nicks on the edges of each steak to prevent the meat curling on the barbecue. If it has been refrigerated, allow the meat to come back to room temperature before barbecuing — this ensures the even cooking of the meat.

Always preheat the flatplate or grill and brush lightly with oil before cooking your barbecue food to prevent the meat from catching. Sear the meat for one minute each side to firm the surface and retain the natural juices. Turn the meat once only and remember to always use tongs — never use a fork, as it may puncture the meat and release the juices, causing flare-ups and toughening the meat. Continue cooking the steaks on a flatplate (you may need to move the meat to a cooler part of the barbecue to continue cooking).

For rare meat, cook only a further minute or two each side. To test if the meat is done, press the steak with your index finger. A rare steak should be soft and yielding to the touch. The inside of the steak should still be red with a thin edge of cooked meat around it.

For a medium rare result, cook a few minutes longer or until slightly springy to the touch. The steak will be very moist and have a slightly thicker edge of cooked meat and a paler red centre.

For a medium steak, cook for a further two minutes each side. The meat should be firm to the touch with only a little pinkness in the centre and a crisp brown outside. It should still be quite juicy inside.

Well done steak needs a little more time and the meat will be firm to the touch, with a rich brown outside and an evenly cooked centre.

Rare

Medium rare

Medium

Well done

Breakfast Skewers with Quick Tomato Sauce

Serve this dish with scrambled eggs and English muffins for a hearty breakfast.

PREPARATION TIME:
25 MINUTES
COOKING TIME:
35 MINUTES
SERVES 4

4 beef sausages
16 small button mushrooms
4 rashers bacon
4 lamb kidneys
30 g butter, melted
4 large tomatoes, halved

QUICK TOMATO SAUCE
1 tablespoon oil
1 small onion, finely chopped
3 medium tomatoes, peeled, finely chopped
1/4 cup barbecue sauce

1   Prepare and heat the barbecue. Place the sausages in a large pan, cover with cold water and bring slowly to simmering point. Leave to cool. Drain well and cut each sausage into six pieces.

2   Wipe the mushrooms clean with absorbent paper. Chop the bacon into bite-sized pieces. Trim the kidneys, remove the core and cut into quarters.

3   Thread the sausage, bacon, kidney and mushrooms alternately on skewers. Place the skewers on a hot lightly oiled barbecue flatplate, brush with melted butter and cook for 15 minutes, turning occasionally, or until browned and cooked through.

4   Place the tomatoes on a hot grill cut-side down and cook for 5 minutes. Serve skewers with tomatoes and Quick Tomato Sauce.

5   To make Quick Tomato Sauce: Heat the oil in a small pan. Cook the onion over a medium low heat for 5 minutes until soft. Add the tomatoes and sauce. Cook for 10 minutes, stirring occasionally. Serve warm or at room temperature.

Steaks with Lemon Mustard Butter

PREPARATION TIME:
5 MINUTES
COOKING TIME:
6–16 MINUTES
SERVES 6

6 fillet steaks, about 150 g each
1 tablespoon olive oil
2 cloves garlic, crushed
1 teaspoon ground rosemary

LEMON MUSTARD BUTTER
125 g butter
1 tablespoon French mustard
1 tablespoon lemon juice
2 teaspoons finely grated lemon rind
1 tablespoon finely chopped fresh chives

1 Trim the meat of excess fat and sinew. Flatten the steaks to an even thickness and nick the edges to prevent curling. Combine the oil, garlic and rosemary. Rub evenly over each steak.

2 Place the meat on a lightly oiled grill or flatplate. Cook over a high heat for 2 minutes each side to seal, turning once. For a rare result cook a further minute each side. For medium and well done results, move meat to a cooler part of the barbecue and cook for a further 2–3 minutes each side for medium and 4–6 minutes each side for well done. Serve steaks topped with a slice of Lemon Mustard Butter.

3 To make Lemon Mustard Butter: Cream the butter with the mustard, lemon juice and rind. Stir in the chives. Shape into a log, wrap in plastic wrap and refrigerate until required.

Best-ever Burger with Homemade Barbecue Sauce

The barbecue sauce in this recipe can be made up to a week in advance and stored in the refrigerator.

PREPARATION TIME: 20 MINUTES +
30 MINUTES REFRIGERATION
COOKING TIME: 25 MINUTES
SERVES 6

750 g beef mince
250 g sausage mince
1 small onion, finely chopped
1 tablespoon Worcestershire
  sauce
2 tablespoons tomato sauce
1 cup fresh breadcrumbs
1 egg, lightly beaten
2 large onions, extra, thinly
  sliced in rings
6 wholemeal rolls
6 small lettuce leaves
1 large tomato, sliced

HOMEMADE BARBECUE SAUCE
2 teaspoons oil
1 small onion, finely chopped
3 teaspoons brown vinegar
1 tablespoon soft brown sugar
1/3 cup tomato sauce
2 teaspoons Worcestershire
  sauce
2 teaspoons soy sauce

1   Place the beef mince and sausage mince in a large bowl. Add the onion, sauces, breadcrumbs and egg. Using hands, mix until thoroughly combined. Divide the mixture into six equal portions and shape into 1.5-cm thick patties. Refrigerate the patties for at least 30 minutes. Prepare and heat the barbecue.

2   Place the patties on a hot lightly oiled barbecue grill or flatplate. Barbecue over the hottest part of the fire for 8 minutes each side, turning once. While the patties are cooking, fry the onions on an oiled flatplate until golden.

3   To assemble burgers: Split the rolls in half and place the bases on individual serving plates. Top each base with a lettuce leaf, patty, tomato slice and fried onions. Top with a generous quantity of Homemade Barbecue Sauce. Cover with the remaining bun half.

4   To make Homemade Barbecue Sauce: Heat the oil in a small pan. Cook the onion for 5 minutes or until soft. Add the vinegar, sugar and sauces. Stir to combine and bring to the boil. Reduce the heat and simmer 3 minutes. Leave to cool.

Hot Dogs *with* Creamy Slaw

PREPARATION TIME:
20 MINUTES
COOKING TIME:
10 MINUTES
SERVES 6

6 large thick, spicy frankfurts
1 tablespoon oil
6 hot dog rolls
6 small lettuce leaves

CREAMY SLAW
100 g red cabbage
100 g green cabbage
2 spring onions
1/2 cup whole egg mayonnaise
1 tablespoon German mustard

1 Prepare and heat the barbecue. Make four diagonal cuts in each frankfurt, slicing halfway through. Brush them with oil, and cook on a hot lightly oiled barbecue flatplate for 7–10 minutes or until cooked through.

2 Split the rolls lengthways through the centre top and line with a lettuce leaf. Place the Creamy Slaw on the lettuce, and top with a frankfurt. Serve immediately.

3 To make Creamy Slaw: Finely shred the cabbage and finely chop the spring onions. Combine the mayonnaise with the mustard. Place all ingredients in a medium mixing bowl and toss to combine thoroughly.

Barbecued Mustard-coated Rib Steaks

Use any fresh herbs you prefer in the Herbed Cream.

PREPARATION TIME:
5 MINUTES +
2 HOURS
MARINATING
COOKING TIME:
10–16 MINUTES
SERVES 6

6 rib eye steaks, about
200 g each, or 6 T-bone
steaks
1/3 cup seeded mustard
2 tablespoons bottled salad
dressing
1 tablespoon lemon juice
1 tablespoon chopped fresh
chives
1 tablespoon honey
1 clove garlic, crushed
dash Tabasco sauce

HERBED CREAM
2/3 cup sour cream
1 tablespoon finely chopped
fresh chives
2 tablespoons finely chopped
bottled pimiento

1 Trim the meat of excess fat and sinew. Flatten the steaks to an even thickness and nick the edges to prevent curling.

2 Combine the mustard, salad dressing, lemon juice, chives, honey, garlic and Tabasco in a small bowl and whisk for 1 minute or until well combined. Place the meat in a shallow dish and pour the marinade over. Store in the refrigerator, covered with plastic wrap, for 2 hours or overnight, turning occasionally.

3 Place the meat on a lightly oiled grill or flatplate. Cook over a high heat for 2 minutes each side to seal, turning once. For a rare result, cook a further 2–3 minutes each side. For medium and well done results, move meat to a cooler part of the barbecue, cook a further 2–3 minutes each side for medium and 4–6 minutes each side for well done. Serve steaks with the Herbed Cream.

4 To make Herbed Cream: Mix all the ingredients until well combined; the mixture should be fairly thick.

Spicy Beef and Mint Barbecued Sausages

For a less spicy sausage, leave out the sambal oelek.

PREPARATION TIME: 15 MINUTES
COOKING TIME: 10 MINUTES
MAKES 12 SAUSAGES

750 g minced beef
250 g sausage mince
2 tablespoons cornflour
1 egg, lightly beaten
1 medium onion, finely chopped
2 cloves garlic, crushed
2 tablespoons chopped fresh mint
1 teaspoon sambal oelek
1 teaspoon ground cumin
1 teaspoon garam masala
1/2 teaspoon ground cardamom
1/2 cup mango chutney, to serve

1 Combine the minced beef and sausage mince in a bowl and add the cornflour, egg, onion, garlic, mint, sambal oelek, cumin, garam masala and cardamom; mix well.

2 Divide the mixture into twelve even-sized portions. Using wet hands, mould each portion into sausage shapes.

3 Place the sausages on a lightly oiled grill or flatplate. Cook over a medium heat for 10 minutes or until cooked through, turning the sausages occasionally during cooking. Serve with chutney.

Barbecued Mustard-coated Rib Steaks (above). Spicy Beef and Mint Barbecued Sausages

Mustard Beef Kebabs

PREPARATION TIME:
10 MINUTES +
STANDING TIME
COOKING TIME:
10 MINUTES
SERVES 4

2 tablespoons grainy mustard

1 teaspoon prepared horseradish

2 teaspoons brown sugar

2 tablespoons brandy (or orange juice)

1/2 cup low-fat yoghurt

500 g lean rump steak, cut into 2.5-cm cubes

2 medium onions, cut into wedges

1   Combine the mustard, horseradish, sugar, brandy or juice and yoghurt. Toss the beef in the yoghurt mixture. Leave, covered, in the refrigerator for at least 30 minutes (or overnight).

2   Thread the meat and onion onto eight skewers (soaked in water to prevent burning) and cook on a preheated lightly greased barbecue flatplate for 5–10 minutes, brushing several times with yoghurt mixture. Serve immediately.

Barbecued Chilli Beef Burgers with Mustard Butter

This is a tasty variation of an old favourite.

PREPARATION TIME:
25 MINUTES +
2 HOURS
MARINATING
COOKING TIME:
8 MINUTES
MAKES 18

1 kg minced beef

3 medium onions, grated

1/4 cup finely chopped parsley

1 1/2 cups packaged breadcrumbs

1 egg, lightly beaten

1 tablespoon milk

1 tablespoon malt vinegar

1 tablespoon tomato paste

2 tablespoons soy sauce

1 tablespoon chilli sauce

3 teaspoons dried oregano leaves

MUSTARD BUTTER
125 g butter, softened
2 tablespoons sour cream
2 tablespoons German mustard

1 Place the minced beef in a large bowl and add the onion, parsley, breadcrumbs, egg, milk, vinegar, tomato paste, sauces and oregano leaves; mix well. Store in refrigerator, covered with plastic wrap, for 2 hours.

2 Divide the mixture into eighteen even-sized portions; shape each portion into a burger about 1.5-cm thick.

3 Place burgers on a lightly oiled grill or flatplate. Cook over a high heat for 4 minutes each side or until well browned and cooked through. Serve the burgers with salad and dollops of Mustard Butter.

4 To make Mustard Butter: Beat the butter, sour cream and mustard in a small bowl for 2 minutes or until well combined. Leave the mixture, uncovered, for 20 minutes to allow the flavours to blend.

Apricot-glazed Sausages and Onions

Use a barbecue flatplate for this recipe.

PREPARATION TIME:
20 MINUTES
COOKING TIME:
15–20 MINUTES
SERVES 4–6

3 onions
8 thick beef sausages
1 teaspoon seeded mustard
1 cup dried apricot halves
3/4 cup apricot nectar

1 Prepare and heat the barbecue. Cut the onions in half and slice thinly. Cook the onions on a lightly greased barbecue flatplate for 5 minutes or until soft. Transfer to a plate to keep warm.

2 Place sausages on the flatplate and cook for 5 minutes or until well browned, turning frequently.

3 Slice the sausages lengthways, three-quarters of the way through. Cook, cut-side down, a further 5 minutes or until browned. Add the mustard, apricots and onions to sausages; stir.

4 Add the nectar to the sausage, apricot and onion mixture, a little at a time. Stir until the nectar coats the sausages and begins to thicken. Repeat this process until all the nectar is used. Serve the sausages cut-side up, topped with onion and apricot mixture.

Focaccia and Piquant Steak

PREPARATION TIME:
5 MINUTES +
30 MINUTES
STANDING
COOKING TIME:
15 MINUTES
SERVES 4

500 g rump steak
1/4 teaspoon ground black
    pepper
1 small red onion
1 tablespoon balsamic vinegar
1 tablespoon chopped fresh
    parsley
1 large red capsicum
2 pieces focaccia, about 12 x
    10 cm
butter for spreading
10 lettuce leaves
4 anchovies, chopped
1 tablespoon capers, chopped
3 tablespoons mayonnaise
1 tablespoon Dijon mustard

1 Trim the meat of excess fat and sinew and sprinkle with pepper. Cook the meat on a preheated lightly greased barbecue flatplate for 3 minutes on each side or until tender. Cool to room temperature, then slice across the grain evenly into long, thin strips.

2 Slice the onion very thinly and mix with the vinegar and parsley. Leave for 30 minutes. Halve the capsicum lengthways and remove the membrane and seeds. Place skin-side down on the hot flatplate, cook under high heat for 5 minutes or until skin lifts off and blackens slightly; cool. Remove the skin and slice the capsicum thinly.

3 Split focaccia in half and toast on both sides until brown and crisp. Spread with butter.

4 To assemble, place the lettuce on the focaccia, top with capsicum, meat, anchovies, capers and drained onion and parsley mixture. Finish off with a dollop of the combined mayonnaise and mustard.

Herb Burger

PREPARATION TIME: 20 MINUTES
COOKING TIME: 15–20 MINUTES
MAKES 8

750 g minced beef or lamb
2 tablespoons chopped fresh
   basil
1 tablespoon chopped fresh
   chives
1 tablespoon chopped fresh
   rosemary
1 tablespoon chopped fresh
   thyme
2 tablespoons lemon juice
1 cup stale breadcrumbs
1 egg
pinch salt
pinch pepper
2 long crusty bread sticks
lettuce leaves
2 tomatoes, sliced
bottled tomato sauce

1   Prepare and heat the barbecue. Place mince in bowl and combine with the herbs, juice, breadcrumbs, egg, salt and pepper. Mix with your hands until well combined. Divide mixture into eight portions.

2   Shape the portions into thick rectangular patties about 15 cm long. Place on a hot barbecue flatplate or grill. Cook for 5–10 minutes each side until well browned and just cooked through.

3   Cut each bread stick into four sections. Cut each piece in half, horizontally. Top each half with lettuce, tomato, a herb burger and tomato sauce. Place the remaining half of bread on top. Serve immediately.

Teriyaki Beef Kebabs

Serve these kebabs with a crisp green salad.

PREPARATION TIME:
15 MINUTES +
2 HOURS
MARINATING
COOKING TIME:
6–16 MINUTES
SERVES 6

- **6 topside steaks, about 350 g each**
- **1 cup beef stock**
- **1/4 cup teriyaki sauce**
- **2 tablespoons hoisin sauce**
- **2 tablespoons lime juice**
- **1 tablespoon honey**
- **2 spring onions, finely chopped**
- **2 cloves garlic, crushed**
- **1 teaspoon finely grated ginger**

1 Trim the meat of excess fat and sinew and slice it across the grain evenly into long, thin strips. Thread the meat on skewers, 'weaving' them in place.

2 Combine the stock, sauces, lime juice, honey, spring onion, garlic and ginger in a small bowl and whisk for 1 minute or until well combined. Place the skewered meat in a shallow dish and pour marinade over. Store in the refrigerator, covered with plastic wrap, for 2 hours or overnight, turning occasionally. Drain, reserving marinade.

3 Cook the skewered meat on a preheated lightly greased barbecue grill or flatplate for 2 minutes each side to seal, turning once. For a rare result, cook a further 1 minute each side. For medium and well done results, cook a further 2–3 minutes each side for medium and 4–6 minutes each side for well done. Brush occasionally with the reserved marinade during cooking.

Beef Satays with Peanut Sauce

PREPARATION TIME:
30 MINUTES + 3 HOURS MARINATING
COOKING TIME:
10–15 MINUTES
SERVES 4

800 g rump steak
1/3 cup soy sauce
2 tablespoons oil
2 cloves garlic, crushed
1 teaspoon grated ginger

PEANUT SAUCE
1 cup pineapple juice
1 cup peanut butter
1/2 teaspoon garlic powder
1/2 teaspoon onion powder
2 tablespoons sweet chilli sauce
1/4 cup soy sauce

1 Trim the steak of excess fat and sinew. Cut the meat into 1-cm cubes and thread them onto soaked bamboo skewers. Place the satays in a shallow, non-metal dish.

2 Combine the soy sauce, oil, garlic and ginger in a small jug and pour over the satays. Store in the refrigerator, covered with plastic wrap, for several hours or overnight, turning occasionally.

3 Prepare and heat the barbecue 1 hour before cooking. Place the skewers on a hot lightly oiled grill or flatplate. Barbecue 8–10 minutes or until tender, turning occasionally. Serve with Peanut Sauce.

4 To make Peanut Sauce: Combine juice, peanut butter, garlic and onion powders and sauces in a small pan and stir over medium heat 5 minutes or until smooth. Serve warm.

Beef Teriyaki with Onion Rings

PREPARATION TIME:
20 MINUTES +
15 MINUTES
MARINATING
COOKING TIME:
15 MINUTES
SERVES 8

8 x 1.5-cm slices Scotch fillet or fillet steak
1/2 cup mirin or dry sherry
1/2 cup soy sauce
1 clove garlic, crushed
1 teaspoon grated fresh ginger
1/2 teaspoon ground pepper

ONION RINGS
4 large white onions
2 tablespoons sunflower oil
2 tablespoons beef marinade

1　Marinate the beef slices in the combined mirin, soy, garlic, ginger and pepper for 15 minutes. Preheat the barbecue.

2　Peel the onions and cut into 1.5-cm thick slices. Drizzle oil on the flatplate. Cook the onion rings until golden, sprinkle with marinade and continue to cook until caramelised — about 5 minutes. Remove to a cooler part of the flatplate and keep warm.

3　Oil the flatplate and cook the beef on a high heat for 5 minutes on one side and 3 minutes on the reverse, cooking for an increased time if a well done steak is preferred. Serve the meat with barbecued onion rings.

Note: Mirin is available from good delicatessens and Japanese food outlets. Use dry sherry instead.

Korean Beef Ribs

PREPARATION TIME:
20 MINUTES +
4–6 HOURS
MARINATING
COOKING TIME:
15 MINUTES
SERVES 6

2 kg beef short ribs or pork ribs
1/2 cup soy sauce
1/2 cup water
1 onion, grated
3 cloves garlic, crushed
1 teaspoon grated fresh ginger
1 tablespoon sugar
2 teaspoons oriental sesame oil (see note)
2 tablespoons toasted sesame seeds, crushed
1/2 teaspoon ground pepper

Beef Satays with Peanut Sauce (left). Beef Teriyaki with Onion Rings

1　When purchasing the meat, ask the butcher to cut the ribs into 5-cm squares. Using a sharp knife, cut through the flesh of each piece to allow the marinade to penetrate.

2　Place the ribs in a pan and cover with water, bring to the boil, cover and simmer for 5 minutes. Drain well. This runs off some of the fat.

3　Combine the remaining ingredients in a bowl and add the ribs, mix well, cover and marinate refrigerated for 4–6 hours or overnight. Turn the ribs occasionally while marinating, so that the flavours are evenly distributed.

4　Cook the ribs over a hot oiled grill, allowing each side to brown and become crisp. Serve warm.

Note: Most supermarkets have oriental sesame oil (which is made from dark roasted sesame seeds) on their Asian shelves. Or look for it at your local Asian food outlet. Light sesame oil from the health food store will not do.

Burger with the Works

Serve this classic with potato chips and a salad.

PREPARATION TIME: 40 MINUTES
COOKING TIME: 10–15 MINUTES
SERVES 6

750 g lean beef mince
1 onion, finely chopped
1 egg
1/2 cup fresh breadcrumbs
2 tablespoons tomato paste
1 tablespoon Worcestershire
** sauce**
2 tablespoons chopped fresh
** parsley**
salt and cracked pepper,
** to taste**
3 large onions
30 g butter
6 slices cheddar cheese
6 eggs, extra
6 rashers bacon
6 large hamburger buns, lightly
** toasted**
6 lettuce leaves
2 tomatoes, thinly sliced
6 large slices beetroot,
** drained**
6 pineapple rings,
** drained**
tomato sauce

1   Prepare and heat the barbecue. Combine the mince, onion, egg, breadcrumbs, tomato paste, Worcestershire sauce, parsley, salt and pepper in a large bowl. Mix with your hands until well combined.

2   Divide mixture into six portions. Shape each portion into round patties 1.5 cm thick. Cover and set aside.

3 Slice the onions into thin rings. Heat the butter on a hot barbecue flatplate. Cook the onions, turning often until well browned. Move the onions towards the outer edge of flatplate to keep warm. Brush barbecue grill or flatplate liberally with oil.

Cook the meat patties for 3–4 minutes each side or until browned and cooked through. Move them to a cooler part of the barbecue or transfer to a plate and keep warm. Place a slice of cheese on each patty. (The heat of the burger will be enough to partially melt the cheese.)

4 Heat a small amount of butter in a large frying pan. Fry the eggs and bacon until the eggs are cooked through and the bacon is golden and crisp. Remove from heat.

5 To assemble burgers: Place toasted bun bases on individual serving plates. Top each with lettuce, tomato, beetroot and pineapple. Place cooked meat patty on top, followed by cooked onions, egg, bacon and tomato sauce. Place remaining bun halves on top.

1 Trim the meat of excess fat and sinew and combine with the lemon juice and thyme. Store in the refrigerator, covered with plastic wrap, for 2 hours or overnight, turning occasionally.

2 Place the meat on a lightly oiled grill or flatplate. Cook over a high heat for 2 minutes each side to seal, turning once. For a rare result, cook a further minute each side. For medium and well done results, move the meat to a cooler part of the barbecue and cook a further 2–3 minutes each side for medium and for 4–6 minutes each side for well done. Serve with Vegetable Relish.

3 To make Vegetable Relish: Heat oil in a small pan. Add the onion and stir over a high heat for 2 minutes or until well browned and soft. Add the capsicum and mustard seeds to the pan and stir over a medium heat for 2 minutes. Add the cucumber, tomato, vinegar, sultanas and sugar. Bring to the boil, reduce heat to a simmer. Cook for 15 minutes, uncovered, stirring occasionally.

Steak with Vegetable Relish

The Vegetable Relish is delicious served warm or cold.

PREPARATION TIME:
15 MINUTES +
2 HOURS
MARINATING
COOKING TIME:
6–16 MINUTES
SERVES 6

6 sirloin steaks, about 200 g each
2 tablespoons lemon juice
1 teaspoon dried thyme leaves

VEGETABLE RELISH
2 tablespoons olive oil
1 medium onion, sliced
1 medium red capsicum, sliced
1/2 teaspoon yellow mustard seeds
1 thin-skinned cucumber, sliced
1 large tomato, peeled, chopped
2 tablespoons malt vinegar
1 tablespoon sultanas
2 teaspoons soft brown sugar

Whole Fillet of Beef with Mustard Coating

PREPARATION TIME: 1 HOUR 5 MINUTES
+ 15 MINUTES STANDING
COOKING TIME: 40 MINUTES
SERVES 6–8

2 kg scotch fillet of beef
1/4 cup brandy

MUSTARD COATING
1/3 cup wholegrain mustard
1/4 cup cream
3/4 cup black pepper, coarsely
ground

1 Prepare the Weber (kettle) barbecue for indirect cooking at moderate heat (normal fire). Trim the meat of excess fat and sinew.
2 Tie the meat securely with string at regular intervals to retain its shape. Brush it all over with the brandy and leave to stand for 1 hour.
3 To make Mustard Coating: Combine the mustard, cream and pepper in a small bowl. Spread evenly over the top and sides of the fillet
4 Place the meat on a large greased sheet of foil. Grasp the corners of foil and pinch securely to form a tray. (This will hold in the juices.) Place the lid on the barbecue and cook for 30–40 minutes for medium rare meat. Stand for 10–15 minutes before carving into thick slices. Serve warm with barbecued or grilled vegetables.

Tangy Beef Ribs

Ribs are ideal finger food — make sure you have plenty of napkins available!

PREPARATION TIME:
20 MINUTES +
3 HOURS
MARINATING
COOKING TIME:
15–20 MINUTES
SERVES 4

1 kg beef ribs
1/2 cup tomato sauce
2 tablespoons Worcestershire sauce
2 tablespoons soft brown sugar
1 teaspoon paprika
1/4 teaspoon chilli powder
1 clove garlic, crushed

1 Chop the ribs into individual serving pieces, if necessary. Bring a large pan of water to the boil. Cook the ribs in boiling water for 5 minutes; drain.

2 Combine the tomato sauce, Worcestershire sauce, sugar, paprika, chilli powder and garlic in a large bowl and mix well. Add ribs to sauce. Cover and marinate, in the refrigerator, for several hours or overnight. Prepare and heat the barbecue 1 hour before cooking.

3 Cook the ribs on a hot lightly greased barbecue grill or flatplate for 10–15 minutes, brushing frequently with marinade, or until the ribs are well browned and cooked through. Serve with barbecued vegetables or slices of grilled fresh pineapple.

Thai Beef Salad

The herbs in this salad give it a lovely fresh flavour. Fresh kaffir lime leaves, if you can get them, make it really special.

PREPARATION TIME:
10 MINUTES
COOKING TIME:
3–5 MINUTES
SERVES 4–6

500 g rump or fillet steak

DRESSING
1 clove garlic, crushed
2 teaspoons palm sugar or brown sugar
1 tablespoon fish sauce
1 tablespoon white vinegar
2 teaspoons grated lemon or lime rind
2 tablespoons lime juice

SALAD
2 spring onions, sliced
1 small red capsicum, diced
2 small seedless cucumbers, thickly sliced
1/2 cup finely chopped coriander leaves and stems
1/2 cup shredded mint
1/2 cup shredded basil
1 tender stem of lemongrass, thinly sliced
or 2 teaspoons grated lemon rind
1 red chilli, finely shredded
3 fresh kaffir lime leaves, cut into threads (optional)

1 Trim any excess fat from the steak.
2 To make the dressing: Combine all the ingredients in a screw-top jar and shake well.
3 To make the Salad: Combine all the prepared salad ingredients in a large bowl, cover tightly with plastic wrap and chill until serving time.
4 To cook the meat: Sear over a high heat on a lightly oiled barbecue flatplate. Cook to your taste. Best results with this salad are with moist, juicy rare to medium rare steak. Remove from the barbecue, allow to rest for 10 minutes and slice thinly. Combine the meat slices with the salad and dressing and toss well to distribute the flavours. Serve immediately.

Note: If kaffir lime leaves are not available, use very tender citrus leaves — either lemon or Tahitian lime — instead, though the fragrance is not quite the same.

Moroccan Beef Koftas

This recipe may be cooked on an open-style barbecue or a kettle barbecue. Allow slightly longer cooking time if using an open-style barbecue.

PREPARATION TIME:
15 MINUTES
COOKING TIME:
8 MINUTES
SERVES 6

750 g premium minced beef
1 egg
1/2 cup finely chopped fresh coriander or parsley
salt and pepper, to taste
2 teaspoons ground coriander
2 teaspoons ground cumin
1 teaspoon chilli powder
2 teaspoons ground sweet paprika
1/2 teaspoon ground turmeric
1 medium onion, grated
1/2 teaspoon ground cinnamon
water-soaked grape or cherry wood (optional)

1 Combine all the ingredients together and form into sausage shapes around skewers, or make into patties.
2 Heat the kettle barbecue on medium-high. Place the soaked grape or cherry wood over grill, if using, and oil the flatplate.
3 Place the skewered koftas on the flatplate and cook for 4 minutes each side, covered, making sure the fruit wood burns and gives off its particular aroma. Serve with lavash or Middle Eastern bread, sliced tomatoes and raw onion rings.

Note: Turmeric, a member of the onion family, is an orange-yellow coloured spice used to add colour and flavour. Like all spices and herbs, store in an airtight container away from direct sunlight.

Thai Beef Salad (above). Moroccan Koftas

Roast Beef with Pecan Sauce

With a kettle or hooded barbecue you can prepare a wonderful roast. Serve with jacket potatoes hot from the coals, and barbecued corn cobs.

PREPARATION TIME:
25 MINUTES +
30 MINUTES
STANDING
COOKING TIME:
1½ HOURS
SERVES 8

ROAST
2.5-kg rib of roasting beef
1 medium onion, grated
1 clove garlic, crushed
1/2 teaspoon ground pepper
1 teaspoon ground dried oregano

SAUCE
1/2 cup pecans, toasted (see note)
1 cup water
2 teaspoons beef stock powder
1/4 teaspoon ground pepper
30 g unsalted butter
2 tablespoons plain flour
1 cup soaked hickory wood chips (optional)

1 Slash the rib meat, mix all the ingredients together and spread over roast. Let stand for 30 minutes while making the sauce.

2 To make the sauce: Place the toasted pecans in a blender jar together with water, stock powder and pepper. Blend to a paste.

3 Melt the butter in a small pan, add the flour and mix to a paste. Cook, stirring occasionally for 5–6 minutes or until golden. Remove from the heat and add the pecan mixture gradually. Return to the heat and stir until the mixture simmers and thickens.

4 To cook the roast: Heat the barbecue kettle, place rib on a rack in a dish, with 1½ cups water. Place on the grill plate, cover and cook for about 1½ hours, basting every 30 minutes with the sauce. The time allowed should result in a rare roast. For medium or well done result, allow extra cooking time. If using hickory chips add the chips to the barbecue during the final ½ hour of cooking time.

5 When done to your preference, remove the roast to a serving dish and serve with the remaining sauce and jacket potatoes.

Note: To toast pecans: Place on a baking tray and heat in a moderate 180°C oven for 10 minutes or until crisp. Shake the tray occasionally to avoid burning.

Beef Balls in Barbecue Sauce

These tasty beef morsels are great with fresh bread rolls and salad. If preferred, place two or three onto short bamboo skewers and cook, turning the skewers occasionally. For a quick appetiser, place on toothpicks and serve with extra barbecue sauce as a dip.

PREPARATION TIME:
15 MINUTES
COOKING TIME:
6 MINUTES
SERVES 6

500 g premium minced beef
1 egg
1 medium onion, finely chopped
1 clove garlic, crushed
1 teaspoon grated fresh ginger
salt and pepper, to taste
1 cup bottled barbecue sauce (see note)

1 Place the mince, egg, onion, garlic, ginger, salt and pepper in a bowl. Combine thoroughly by hand. Take level tablespoonsful of the mince mixture and roll into balls.

2 Place on a well oiled, hot barbecue flatplate and cook for 5–6 minutes, moving them around occasionally.

3 Brush the meatballs liberally with barbecue basting sauce 1 minute before the end of cooking. Serve immediately with the remaining barbecue sauce.

Note: Bottled barbecue sauce is available in most supermarkets. It has a mild hickory smoked flavour. If not available, use your favourite homemade barbecue sauce.

Beef Balls in Barbecued Sauce (above). Roast Beef with Pecan Sauce

Steak in Red Wine

Substitute 2 tablespoons of fresh oregano for dried oregano, if you wish.

PREPARATION TIME:
10 MINUTES +
3 HOURS
MARINATING
COOKING TIME:
5–10 MINUTES
SERVES 4

750 g rump steak
1 cup good red wine
2 teaspoons garlic salt
1 tablespoon dried oregano
leaves
cracked black pepper, to taste

1 Cut the steaks into large, even-sized serving pieces and trim meat of excess fat and sinew.
2 Combine the wine, salt, oregano leaves and pepper in a jug. Place the steak in a large, shallow non-metal dish. Cover and refrigerate for several hours or overnight. Prepare and heat the barbecue 1 hour before cooking.
3 Cook the steak on a hot lightly greased barbecue grill or flatplate for 3–4 minutes each side or until cooked as desired, brushing with the wine mixture frequently. Serve immediately.

Hint: Choose a basting brush with pure bristles. Nylon bristles can melt in the heat and introduce an unpleasant flavour to cooked foods.

Barbecued Beef with Sesame and Ginger

PREPARATION TIME:
15 MINUTES +
2 HOURS
MARINATING
COOKING TIME:
25 MINUTES
SERVES 4–6

500 g beef fillet
1/4 cup sesame oil
1/4 cup soy sauce
2 cloves garlic, crushed
2 tablespoons grated fresh ginger
1 tablespoon lemon juice
2 tablespoons chopped spring onions
1/4 cup firmly packed soft brown sugar

1   Trim the beef of any excess fat or sinew.
2   Combine the sesame oil, soy sauce, garlic, ginger, lemon juice, spring onion and brown sugar in a non-metallic bowl. Add the fillet of beef and coat well with the marinade. Cover and refrigerate for 2 hours, or overnight if possible.
3   Preheat a lightly oiled barbecue grill or flatplate. When very hot, add the beef and brown on all sides until the meat is sealed. Remove, wrap in foil and cook on the barbecue, turning occasionally, for a further 15–20 minutes, depending on how rare or well done you like your meat.
4   Allow the beef to stand for 10 minutes before slicing. Serve with a fresh mixed salad.

Note: Individual steaks can be used and cooked on the barbecue or in a chargrill pan; however, there is no need to wrap them in foil. The marinade is delicious as a sauce for the beef. Boil in a small pan for about 5 minutes and drizzle over the beef just before serving.

Fillet Steak with Onion Marmalade

PREPARATION TIME:
20 MINUTES
COOKING TIME:
1 HOUR
SERVES 4

4 thick rib-eye steaks

ONION MARMALADE
30 g butter
2 red onions, thinly sliced
2 tablespoons soft brown sugar
1 tablespoon balsamic vinegar

1   Trim any fat from the steaks, then sprinkle liberally with freshly ground black pepper. Cover and refrigerate until ready to cook.

2   To make the Onion Marmalade: Heat the butter in a heavy-based pan. Add the onion and cook, stirring occasionally, for about 10 minutes over low heat, or until the onion is soft but not brown. Stir in the brown sugar and balsamic vinegar and continue to cook for about 30 minutes, stirring frequently. The mixture will become thick and glossy.

3   Place the steaks on a lightly oiled preheated chargrill pan or barbecue grill or flatplate and cook for 3 minutes each side to seal, turning once only. For rare steaks, cook a further minute. For medium, cook for another few minutes and for well done, about 5 minutes. Serve at once with the Onion Marmalade and a fresh green salad.

Beef with Fennel Beans and Parsnip Purée

PREPARATION TIME: 15 MINUTES
TOTAL COOKING TIME: 25 MINUTES
SERVES 4

PARSNIP PUREE
4 parsnips
30 g butter
1 tablespoon cream

FENNEL BEANS
50 g butter
1–2 cloves garlic, crushed
1 small red chilli, seeded and
  chopped
1 medium fennel bulb, thinly
  sliced
310 g can cannellini beans,
  drained and rinsed
310 g can chickpeas, drained
  and rinsed
1/4 cup chopped fresh
  parsley

4 rib-eye fillet steaks

1   To make the Parsnip Purée: Cut the peeled parsnips into pieces and cook in salted boiling water for 6–8 minutes, or until they are tender. Drain well, then purée in a food processor until just smooth. Return to the hot pan and beat in the butter and cream with a wooden spoon. Season to taste with salt and freshly ground black pepper. Set aside and keep the purée warm until ready to serve.

2   To make the Fennel Beans: Melt the butter in a heavy-based frying pan and add the garlic, chilli and fennel. Cook for 5 minutes over medium heat, stirring frequently, until the fennel softens. Stir in the beans and chickpeas and continue to cook for a further 3–4 minutes before adding the parsley. Set aside and keep warm.

3   Preheat a lightly oiled chargrill pan or barbecue grill or flatplate. Brush the steaks with a little olive oil and cook over medium to high heat, turning once, until they are tender and done to your liking. Arrange the steaks on warm plates and serve immediately with the Parsnip Purée and the Fennel Beans.

Note: Pork chops or medallions are also suitable for this recipe.

T-Bone Steak with Sweet Onions

PREPARATION TIME:
10 MINUTES
COOKING TIME:
20 MINUTES
SERVES 4

4 tablespoons oil
6 onions, sliced into rings
3 tablespoons barbecue sauce
4 T-bone steaks

1 Heat 2 tablespoons of the oil on a preheated chargrill pan or barbecue grill or flatplate. Add the onions and barbecue sauce and cook for 10 minutes, or until very soft and brown. Push to one side of hot plate to keep warm.

2 Brush the T-bone steaks with the remaining oil and add to the hot plate. Cook over high heat, turning once or twice, until tender and cooked to your liking. Arrange the steaks on warm plates, spoon over some of the sweet onions and serve immediately.

Scotch Fillet with Stuffed Pears

PREPARATION TIME:
25 MINUTES

COOKING TIME:
15 MINUTES

SERVES 4

- **4 medium-firm pears**
- **100 g mild, soft blue cheese**
- **2 slices smoked honey-cured ham, finely chopped**
- **1 tablespoon finely chopped fresh chives**
- **2 tablespoons chopped mixed nuts**
- **4 Scotch fillet steaks**

1 Cut each pear in half and remove the core and a little of the flesh to make a deep dip in the middle.

2 In a bowl, mix together the cheese, ham, chives and nuts. Pack the mixture firmly into the pear halves and round off the tops.

3 Preheat a chargrill pan or barbecue flatplate and brush with a little oil. Add the steaks and cook over high heat until tender and done to your liking. Keep warm.

4 Add the pears to the hot plate, filling-side-up, and cook for 2–3 minutes. Cover loosely with foil and steam for a further 2 minutes. Then remove the foil and turn the pears over for about 10 seconds to quickly sear the filling. Serve with the steaks.

Steak with Capsicum Relish and Creamy Mash

PREPARATION TIME: 30 MINUTES
TOTAL COOKING TIME: 50 MINUTES
SERVES 4

4 thick New York cut steaks
2–3 cloves garlic, crushed
2 teaspoons olive oil

CAPSICUM RELISH
1 large red capsicum
1 large yellow capsicum
1 tablespoon balsamic vinegar
1 teaspoon soft brown sugar

CREAMY MASH
600 g potatoes
2 tablespoons cream
30 g butter

1 Trim the steaks of any excess fat or sinew. Combine the garlic and olive oil, coat the steaks with the mixture and cover and refrigerate.
2 To make the Capsicum Relish: Halve the capsicums, remove the seeds and cut into strips. Heat some olive oil in a chargrill pan or on a barbecue flatplate, add the capsicum strips and cook over low heat, stirring frequently, for about 20 minutes. Partially cover the pan or flatplate during this cooking time and take care not to burn. Stir through the balsamic vinegar and brown sugar and continue to cook for a further 10 minutes. Set aside and keep warm.
3 To make the Creamy Mash: Cut the peeled potatoes into cubes.

Bring a pan of salted water to the boil, add the potatoes and boil for 10–15 minutes, or until just tender. Drain, then mash with a fork or potato masher. Beat in the cream and butter and season with some salt and freshly ground black pepper.
4 Heat a chargrill pan or barbecue grill or flatplate.

When very hot, add the steaks. For rare steaks, cook for 2–3 minutes each side. For medium and well-done steaks, cook for another 3–4 minutes each side for medium and 5–6 minutes each side for well done. Arrange on warm plates and serve with the Creamy Mash and Capsicum Relish.

Hot Peppered Steaks with Horseradish Sauce

PREPARATION TIME: 15 MINUTES
COOKING TIME: 10 MINUTES
SERVES 4

4 medium-sized sirloin steaks
1/4 cup seasoned, cracked
  pepper

HORSERADISH SAUCE
2 tablespoons brandy
1/4 cup beef stock
1/3 cup cream
1 tablespoon horseradish cream
1/2 teaspoon sugar
salt and pepper, to taste

1   Prepare and heat the barbecue. Lightly grease the barbecue grill. Trim the meat of excess fat and sinew and coat on both sides with pepper, pressing it firmly into the meat.

2   Cook the meat over a high heat for 2 minutes each side to seal, turning once. For a rare result, cook a further minute each side. For medium and well done results, move the meat to a cooler part of the barbecue and cook a further 2–3 minutes each side for medium and 4–6 minutes each side for well done. Serve with Horseradish Sauce.

3   To make Horseradish Sauce: Combine the brandy and stock in a pan. Bring to the boil, reduce heat. Add the cream, horseradish and sugar and stir until heated through. Season to taste.

Herbed Lamb

This is best cooked on a kettle barbecue. If using an open-style barbecue, allow extra time for cooking.

PREPARATION TIME:
15 MINUTES + 30 MINUTES MARINATING
COOKING TIME:
8 MINUTES
SERVES 4–6

12 rib loin cutlets

MARINADE
1 clove garlic, crushed
salt and pepper, to taste
1 medium onion, grated
2 tablespoons finely chopped fresh oregano
2 tablespoons lemon juice
4 tablespoons olive oil
1 cup hickory or cherry wood chips, soaked (optional)

1   Snip the edges of the cutlets to prevent them from curling.

2   To make the marinade: Combine all the ingredients in a large shallow non-metal dish and add the cutlets. Turn the cutlets over in the marinade and allow them to marinate for 30 minutes, turning once.

3   Place the cutlets on a preheated barbecue grill plate, add water-soaked wood chips to the glowing coals, if using, and cook over a medium heat, hood down, for 4 minutes. Turn and continue to cook for 3 minutes to give a medium rare result and continue to cook if well done is preferred. Serve with a crisp green salad or barbecued vegetables.

Lamb Fillets with Ginger (above). Herbed Lamb

Lamb Fillets with Ginger

PREPARATION TIME:
20 MINUTES +
30 MINUTES
MARINATING
COOKING TIME:
10 MINUTES
SERVES 6

12 small lamb loin fillets

MARINADE
2 cloves garlic, crushed
2 teaspoons grated fresh ginger
2 spring onions, finely chopped
1 tablespoon Korean chilli paste
2 tablespoons toasted sesame seeds, crushed
1 teaspoon ground pepper
1 tablespoon water
2 teaspoons oriental sesame oil

1   Use a sharp knife to remove the silvery sinew from the outside of each lamb fillet. Split the fillets almost in half lengthways, leaving them joined, and open them out so they are flat.

2   To make the marinade: Combine all the ingredients thoroughly. Pour over the fillets, mix and leave to marinate for 30 minutes or overnight in the refrigerator.

3   Cook on a preheated barbecue grill, over a medium high heat for 3 minutes on each side or until done. Serve with your favourite salad.

Note: Adjust the quantity of chilli paste to suit your taste.

Lamb Kebabs with Golden Pilaf

PREPARATION TIME:
25 MINUTES
COOKING TIME:
30 MINUTES
MAKES 8

750 g lamb mince
1 small onion, finely chopped
2 tablespoons finely chopped fresh coriander
1 tablespoon ground cumin
1 teaspoon grated lemon rind

GOLDEN PILAF
3 tablespoons oil
1 teaspoon turmeric
1 medium onion, sliced
2 cups Basmati or jasmine rice
4 cups vegetable stock

1   Place the mince, onion, coriander, cumin and lemon rind in a large mixing bowl and combine thoroughly. Divide the mixture into eight equal portions and form into sausage shapes around large metal or soaked wooden skewers. Refrigerate until required.

2   To make Golden Pilaf: Heat the oil in a large pan. Add the turmeric and onion and stir over a medium heat for 2 minutes or until the onion is soft. Add the rice and continue stirring for 1 minute, until grains of rice are coated in oil.

3   Add the stock and cover the pan with a tight-fitting lid. Bring slowly to the boil, stirring once. Reduce heat and simmer, covered, for 10 minutes or until almost all the water is absorbed. Remove from the heat and leave covered for 5 minutes or until the water is absorbed and the rice is just tender. Stir the rice with a fork to separate the grains before serving.

4   Place the kebabs on a preheated lightly greased barbecue grill or flatplate. Cook for 12 minutes, turning occasionally to brown all over. Serve on a bed of Golden Pilaf.

Spicy Rotisserie Leg of Lamb

PREPARATION TIME:
10 MINUTES +
1 HOUR
MARINATING
COOKING TIME:
1½ HOURS
SERVES 8

2-kg leg of lamb

MARINADE
2 teaspoons ground turmeric
1 teaspoon ground sweet paprika
salt and pepper, to taste
2 large cloves garlic, crushed
1 teaspoon grated fresh ginger
3 tablespoons yoghurt
1 teaspoon ground cardamom

1   Trim off excess fat and score the leg of lamb with shallow diagonal cuts 3 cm apart on both sides.

2   To make the marinade: Combine all the ingredients and spread over the lamb, making sure to fill the criss-cross cuts. Marinate for 1 hour or overnight in the refrigerator.

3   Heat covered barbecue. Skewer the lamb and attach to the rotisserie, taking care to balance the leg of lamb so the weight is evenly distributed or the rotisserie will not turn smoothly. Cook 1½ hours over a low heat until done to your liking. Baste with the remaining marinade every 15 minutes.

Barbecued Spicy Lamb Koftas

Serve these koftas with barbecued vegetables such as eggplant and capsicum.

PREPARATION TIME:
10 MINUTES +
1 HOUR
STANDING
COOKING TIME:
10 MINUTES
SERVES 6

500 g minced lamb
1 medium onion,
 finely chopped
1 clove garlic, crushed
2 tablespoons chopped fresh
 mint
1 teaspoon ground coriander
1 teaspoon ground cardamom
1/4 teaspoon curry powder
pinch cayenne pepper
1/2 cup packaged breadcrumbs
1 egg, lightly beaten
1 cup packaged breadcrumbs,
 extra

YOGHURT DRESSING
2/3 cup plain yoghurt
1 tablespoon chopped fresh
 coriander
2 teaspoons chopped fresh mint
1/2 teaspoon grated lemon rind

1 Place the minced lamb in a medium bowl and add the onion, garlic, herbs, spices and breadcrumbs. Mix together well using your hands. Divide the meat mixture into twelve even portions. Mould into sausage shapes around oiled, metal skewers.

2 Brush lightly with egg; roll in extra breadcrumbs to coat evenly. Store in the refrigerator, covered with plastic wrap, for 1 hour or overnight.

3 Place skewers on a lightly greased barbecue grill or flatplate. Cook over a medium heat for 10 minutes or until cooked through, turning occasionally. Serve with Yoghurt Dressing.

4 To make Yoghurt Dressing: Beat all the ingredients in a small bowl until well combined. Refrigerate.

49

Fragrant Leg of Lamb

This recipe is best cooked on a kettle barbecue.

PREPARATION TIME: 15 MINUTES
COOKING TIME: 1 HOUR 30 MINUTES
SERVES 6

2-kg leg of lamb
4 cloves garlic
6–8 sprigs rosemary
2 tablespoons olive oil
2 tablespoons freshly ground
**   black pepper**

1   Prepare the Weber (kettle) barbecue for indirect cooking at moderate heat (normal fire). Place a drip tray on the bottom grill.

2   Trim the meat of excess fat and sinew. Cut narrow, deep slits all over top and sides of meat.

3   Cut the garlic cloves in half lengthways. Push the garlic and rosemary sprigs into slits. Brush all over with oil and sprinkle with black pepper.

4   Place the lamb on the barbecue grill over a drip tray, cover and cook for 1 hour 30 minutes for medium rare meat. Brush with olive oil occasionally. Stand lamb in a warm place, covered with foil for 10–15 minutes before carving.

Fragrant Leg of Lamb. Baked Vegetables (see page 179)

Oriental Lamb Fillets

PREPARATION TIME:
20 MINUTES +
30 MINUTES
MARINATING

COOKING TIME:
10 MINUTES

SERVES 6

12 small lamb fillets

MARINADE
1 clove garlic, crushed
1 teaspoon grated fresh ginger
1 small onion, peeled and roughly chopped
1 tablespoon fresh curry leaves (see note)
1/4 teaspoon turmeric
salt and pepper, to taste
1 tablespoon lemon juice
1 tablespoon water
1 teaspoon oriental sesame oil

1 Trim the lamb fillets and remove all the silvery sinews using a sharp knife. Split each of the fillets in half lengthways starting at the tip and leaving the fillet jointed at the thick end.

2 To make the marinade: Combine all the ingredients in a blender until smooth. If a blender is not available, grate the onion and finely chop the curry leaves. Combine all the ingredients in a small bowl. Pour the marinade over the fillets, mix and leave to marinate for 30 minutes.

3 Thread the meat onto metal skewers ribbon fashion. Cook on a preheated barbecue grill over a medium high heat for 5 minutes each side or until done. Serve with your favourite salad.

Note: Fresh curry leaves can be found in Asian food stores. If not available, substitute fresh oregano or marjoram leaves. The taste is just as delicious.

Barbecued Lamb Shanks

Try this recipe with other cuts of meat on the bone, such as lamb neck chops, osso bucco, pieces of ox tail and chicken drumsticks.

PREPARATION TIME: 5 MINUTES +
OVERNIGHT MARINATING
COOKING TIME: 45 MINUTES
SERVES 6

2 cloves garlic, halved
1/3 cup olive oil
6 lamb shanks
salt and pepper, to taste

1   Combine the garlic and oil in a small bowl, cover and marinate, at room temperature, overnight.
2   Prepare the Weber (kettle) barbecue for indirect cooking at moderate heat (normal fire). Place a drip tray under the top grill.
3   Trim the shanks of excess fat and sinew. Brush the garlic oil generously over the shanks and sprinkle with salt and pepper.
4   Place the lamb shanks on the top grill of the barbecue, cover with a lid and roast for 35–45 minutes or until the meat is tender when pierced with a fork. Serve with barbecued vegetables, such as capsicum, and thick slices of chargrilled potato, scattered with herbs.

Barbecued Lamb with Chermoula

Marinate this dish overnight for best results.

PREPARATION TIME:
25 MINUTES +
3 HOURS
MARINATING
COOKING TIME:
1 HOUR
SERVES 6

1 medium onion, grated
2 cloves garlic, crushed
4 tablespoons chopped flat-leaved parsley
4 tablespoons chopped fresh coriander
1/2 teaspoon ground cumin
1/2 teaspoon ground saffron
1/2 teaspoon harissa (see note)
1/2 cup olive oil
2 tablespoons lemon juice
1 x 1/2-kg leg of lamb

1 To make Chermoula: Mix the onion, garlic, flat-leaved parsley, coriander, cumin, saffron, harissa, olive oil and lemon juice together; stand for 1 hour.

2 Starting at the thicker end of the leg of lamb, cut down and around bone. Scrape away as much meat as possible. Remove bone. Cut down into, not through, the thickest part of the meat; open out flat.

3 Spread the Chermoula mixture onto both sides of the lamb and marinate for at least 3 hours.

4 Prepare the kettle barbecue for indirect cooking. Place a drip tray on the bottom grill. Place the lamb on the grill, cover and cook for 1 hour for a medium rare result. Brush with oil frequently during cooking. Stand the lamb for 10–15 minutes before carving. Cut in thick slices across the grain and serve.

Note: Harissa is a fiery condiment widely used in Morocco. The basic ingredients are red chillies, cayenne, olive oil and garlic. It is delicious served with poached eggs or sausages.

Lamb Chops Indienne

PREPARATION TIME:
10 MINUTES +
1 HOUR
MARINATING
COOKING TIME:
6–8 MINUTES
SERVES 6

12 lamb chops, excess fat removed

MARINADE
2 teaspoons curry powder
1 teaspoon garam masala
1 teaspoon garlic powder
2 teaspoons onion powder
1 tablespoon white vinegar
salt, to taste
3 tablespoons water
2 tablespoons oil

1   To make the marinade: Combine all the ingredients and spread evenly over the lamb chops. Allow the meat to marinate for 1 hour or overnight in refrigerator.

2   Heat the barbecue to medium and place the marinated lamb chops on an oiled flatplate or grill. Cook for 5 minutes, turn and cook for a further 3 minutes. Cook further according to taste if required. Serve with mango chutney.

Note: Garam masala can be purchased in supermarkets and Indian food stores.

Lamb Kebabs

A real change from roasts and chops, and quick to cook too, either grilled or barbecued.

PREPARATION TIME:
20 MINUTES +
3 HOURS
MARINATING
COOKING TIME:
8–10 MINUTES
SERVES 4–6

1 kg lean boned lamb
1 clove garlic, crushed
1 teaspoon salt
1/2 teaspoon black pepper
1 teaspoon finely grated fresh ginger
1/2 teaspoon ground turmeric
1 teaspoon ground coriander
1 teaspoon ground cumin
1 tablespoon lemon juice
1 tablespoon sesame oil
1 tablespoon peanut oil

1   Cut the lamb into large cubes and place in a bowl.

2   Combine all the other ingredients and mix well. Pour over the lamb and stir thoroughly, ensuring all pieces of lamb are coated with marinade. Cover and refrigerate overnight, if possible, or for at least 3 hours.

3   Thread four pieces of lamb on each skewer (make sure you soak the skewers beforehand) and cook over glowing coals. Cubes of lamb should be crusty brown all over. Serve hot with rice or flat breads.

Butterflied Leg of Lamb

Ask the butcher to bone and butterfly the leg of lamb to make the preparation of this dish much easier.

PREPARATION TIME:
20 MINUTES +
30 MINUTES
MARINATING
COOKING TIME:
25 MINUTES
SERVES 6–8

1.5-kg leg of lamb, boned and butterflied

MARINADE
2 teaspoons ground dried mint
2 cloves garlic, crushed
1 tablespoon olive oil
1 tablespoon pickled green peppercorns, mashed (see note)
salt and pepper, to taste

1 Trim off excess fat and lay the boned leg of lamb on a flat surface. Score the inside, criss-cross fashion. Turn the lamb and repeat with the other side.

2 To make the marinade: Combine all the ingredients and rub into the scored surfaces. Allow the meat to marinate, covered, for at least 30 minutes or overnight.

3 Place the lamb on a lightly oiled preheated barbecue grill and cook for 20–25 minutes, turning once during cooking for a rare result. Increase the cooking time if you prefer lamb well done. Allow the meat to stand for 15 minutes before slicing.

Note: Pickled green peppercorns are available at delicatessens and some supermarkets. Store the remaining peppercorns and brine in an airtight jar, refrigerated. To reduce flare-ups, place a foil tray directly under the lamb to catch melted fat.

Smoked Leg of Lamb

This recipe calls for a kettle or covered barbecue. If cooked by any other method it will not have quite the same wonderful results.

PREPARATION TIME:
10 MINUTES +
1 HOUR
MARINATING
COOKING TIME:
1½ HOURS
SERVES 6–8

1.5-kg leg of lamb, excess fat removed

3 cups mesquite or hickory chips, soaked (optional)

MARINADE
2 teaspoons ground sweet paprika
1/2 teaspoon ground pepper
salt, to taste
1 teaspoon ground dried mint flakes
3 cloves garlic, crushed
1 teaspoon ground cumin
1 tablespoon ground rice
2–3 tablespoons water

1 Put the mesquite or hickory chips, if using, to soak in cold water before starting preparation of the food.

2 To make the marinade: Combine all the ingredients. Score the lamb with shallow diagonal slashes to form diamond shapes and spread the marinade, making sure it gets into all the slashes. Cover and let stand for 1 hour or overnight in the refrigerator.

3 Heat the barbecue, skewer the lamb securely and attach to the rotisserie.

4 Bake with the hood down on a low heat for about 1½ hours, basting with the leftover marinade. Add two handfuls of soaked chips to the glowing coals every 30 minutes, if using.

5 When the meat is done to your liking remove the rotisserie spit from the barbecue and let the meat stand for 10 minutes before serving. Serve the smoked leg of lamb with vegetables of your choice, or spiced rice.

Note: Marinated meats should be at room temperature before barbecuing to allow for even cooking, and for the meat to absorb extra flavour. If not, the outside may be overcooked while the inside is still raw.

Spicy Lamb Kebabs

Fresh grated ginger adds a distinct flavour to this recipe.

PREPARATION TIME:
30 MINUTES +
OVERNIGHT
MARINATING
COOKING TIME:
10 MINUTES
SERVES 6

1.5-kg leg of lamb, boned

MARINADE
2 teaspoons grated fresh ginger
2 cloves garlic, crushed
salt and pepper, to taste
3 teaspoons ground coriander
2 teaspoons ground cumin
2 teaspoons ground turmeric
1/2 teaspoon ground nutmeg
1/2 teaspoon ground cardamom
1 teaspoon white vinegar
2 tablespoons peanut oil

1 Trim any excess fat from the lamb and cut into 2.5-cm cubes.

2 To make the marinade: Combine all the ingredients in a medium-sized bowl.

3 Add the lamb, and stir to coat with spice mix. Cover and refrigerate overnight.

4 Thread each skewer with four to five pieces of lamb and barbecue on a lightly oiled preheated barbecue grill or flatplate. Cook until well browned, turning gradually. Serve with pita bread or rice and a sauce of finely chopped cucumber and yoghurt.

Smoked Leg of Lamb (above). Spicy Lamb Kebabs

Spicy Grilled Lamb

Fillets, or tenderloins as they are sometimes called, are delicate flavoured, fat-free portions of lamb that could also be used in this recipe.

PREPARATION TIME:
20 MINUTES +
30 MINUTES
MARINATING
COOKING TIME:
10 MINUTES
SERVES 6

6 lamb leg steaks

MARINADE
1 clove garlic, crushed
1 teaspoon grated fresh ginger (see note)
1 tablespoon lemon juice
1 tablespoon water
1/2 cup chopped coriander leaves
1 small onion, roughly chopped
1/4 teaspoon ground pepper
1 teaspoon mild curry powder
1/2 teaspoon garam marsala
salt and pepper, to taste

1 Place the lamb steaks in a shallow dish.

2 To make the marinade: Combine all the ingredients in a blender or food processor until smooth and pour over the lamb. Allow to marinate for 30 minutes. (If a food processor or blender is unavailable, finely chop the coriander, grate the onion and combine the marinade ingredients in a small bowl.)

3 Cook over a medium high heat on a barbecue grill plate for 5 minutes each side or until rosy pink inside, brown outside. Cut into thick diagonal slices to serve.

Note: If you don't often use fresh ginger, peel and slice a small root, place in a clean jar and cover with dry sherry or green ginger wine. It will keep in the refrigerator for months. The sherry or wine can also be used in Asian-style dishes.

Spicy Grilled Lamb (above). Tandoori-style Lamb

Tandoori-style Lamb

A tandoor is an earthen oven using charcoal as a fire source.
This Mongol-initiated style of cooking is adaptable for poultry, meats, fish and even vegetable dishes.
Cook this dish on a kettle barbecue.

PREPARATION TIME: 10 MINUTES +
1 HOUR MARINATING
COOKING TIME: 12 MINUTES
SERVES 4

12 rib loin cutlets

MARINADE
1 clove garlic, crushed
1 teaspoon grated fresh ginger
1/2 teaspoon ground pepper
1 teaspoon ground turmeric
1 teaspoon ground sweet paprika
1 teaspoon garam masala
1/4 cup plain yoghurt

1 Trim the loin cutlets of any excess fat. Then score the edges of the meat to prevent the cutlets from curling when they are barbecued.
2 To make the marinade: Make a paste with all the other ingredients and coat the cutlets with marinade. Set aside for 1 hour.
3 Preheat the barbecue and cook on the oiled grill plate for 6 minutes on each side.

Spiced Lamb with Cucumber Salsa

The 'coolness' of the salsa complements the spiciness of the lamb perfectly. Try this combination cold, in crusty rolls.

PREPARATION TIME: 15 MINUTES + 2 HOURS MARINATING
COOKING TIME: 30–40 MINUTES
SERVES 6

1.5-kg leg of lamb, boned
2/3 cup plain yoghurt
1 medium onion, chopped
1 teaspoon grated ginger
1 teaspoon ground cumin
1 teaspoon ground coriander
1 teaspoon poppy seeds
1 teaspoon turmeric
1/2 teaspoon garam masala
1/4 teaspoon ground nutmeg

CUCUMBER SALSA

**1 thin-skinned cucumber, cut
  into 1-cm cubes**

**1 small tomato, cut into 1-cm
  cubes**

1 small red onion, thinly sliced

grated rind and juice of 1 lime

**1 tablespoon chopped fresh
  coriander**

**1 tablespoon chopped fresh
  basil**

1 teaspoon soft brown sugar

1   Trim the meat of excess fat and sinew. Flatten out the leg.

2   Combine the yoghurt, onion, ginger, cumin, coriander, poppy seeds, turmeric, garam masala and nutmeg in a food processor bowl or blender and process for 10 seconds or until smooth.

3   Place meat in a large dish. Spread the yoghurt mixture over the meat and turn the lamb until well coated. Store in the refrigerator, covered with plastic wrap, for 2 hours or overnight. Bring to room temperature before cooking.

4   Place the meat on a preheated lightly greased grill or flatplate. Cook for 30 minutes, turning once. Cook another 5 minutes for a medium result and another 10 minutes for well done. Serve sliced with Cucumber Salsa.

5   To make Cucumber Salsa: Combine the ingredients in a bowl; mix well.

Lamb Cutlets with Rosemary Marinade

This dish is ideal for a barbecue picnic.

**PREPARATION
TIME:**
15 MINUTES +
20 MINUTES
MARINATING
COOKING TIME:
6–8 MINUTES
SERVES 4

12 lamb cutlets

1/4 cup olive oil

**2 tablespoons chopped fresh
  rosemary**

**1 1/2 teaspoons cracked black
  pepper**

1 bunch fresh rosemary, extra

1   Prepare and heat the barbecue. Trim the cutlets of excess fat and sinew. Place cutlets in shallow, non-metal dish and brush with oil.

2   Scatter half the chopped rosemary and pepper on the meat and set aside for 20 minutes. Turn the meat over and brush with the remaining oil, scatter over remaining rosemary and pepper. Tie the extra bunch of rosemary to the handle of a wooden spoon.

3   Arrange the cutlets on a hot lightly greased grill. Cook 2–3 minutes each side. As the cutlets cook, bat them frequently with the rosemary spoon. This will release flavoursome oils into the cutlets. When the cutlets are almost done, remove the rosemary from the spoon and drop it on the fire where it will flare up briefly and infuse rosemary smoke into the cutlets.

Lamb with Mixed Mushrooms

PREPARATION TIME:
30 MINUTES
COOKING TIME:
20 MINUTES
SERVES 4

750 g lamb loin
50 g butter
1 red onion, chopped
4 spring onions, cut into short lengths
1–2 cloves garlic, crushed
350 g mixed mushrooms, thickly sliced
3 tablespoons sherry
1/3 cup chopped fresh parsley

1 Lightly coat the lamb with some olive oil, then sprinkle liberally with freshly ground black pepper. Cover and refrigerate until ready to use.

2 Preheat a lightly oiled chargrill pan. Add the lamb and cook over high heat for about 4 minutes each side, taking care not to overcook. The lamb should be cooked through, but still slightly pink inside. Allow to rest for a few minutes before slicing into strips.

3 Meanwhile, wipe the chargrill pan clean and melt the butter on the hot plate. Add the onion, spring onion and garlic and cook for 2–3 minutes, or until softened but not browned. Add the mushrooms and cook over moderate heat, tossing frequently, for about 5 minutes, or until tender and golden brown. Pour in the sherry and sprinkle the parsley over the top. Arrange the lamb strips on warm plates and serve with the mixed mushrooms.

Lamb Pita

PREPARATION TIME:
20 MINUTES +
15 MINUTES
MARINATING
COOKING TIME:
5 MINUTES
SERVES 4

400 g lamb leg steaks
2 teaspoons finely grated lemon rind
3 teaspoons finely chopped fresh oregano
2 cloves garlic, finely chopped
2 tablespoons olive oil
1 red onion, thinly sliced
4 small pita breads
1/2 cup hummus
1/2 cup plain yoghurt
1 small Lebanese cucumber, thinly sliced
1 small red chilli, seeds removed, finely chopped
snow pea sprouts

1 Trim the lamb of excess fat and cut into thin strips. In a bowl, combine the lemon rind, oregano, garlic, olive oil and some freshly ground pepper. Add the lamb and refrigerate for 15 minutes.

2 Preheat a lightly oiled chargrill pan or barbecue flatplate until extremely hot. Cook the lamb and onion for 2–3 minutes, turning to brown the meat quickly and soften the onion. Remove and keep warm. Place the pita breads on the hotplate and warm both sides.

3 Spread each round of bread with a little of the hummus and yoghurt. Add the barbecued lamb and onions and scatter with the cucumber, chilli and a few snow pea sprouts. Serve immediately.

Lamb with Salsa Verde and Polenta

PREPARATION TIME: 40 MINUTES +
20 MINUTES SETTING
COOKING TIME: 35 MINUTES
SERVES 4

SALSA VERDE
1 cup fresh parsley, lower
  stalks removed
1 cup fresh basil leaves
1 cup fresh mint leaves
1/2 cup fresh dill
2 tablespoons capers
1–2 cloves garlic
1 tablespoon caster sugar
1 teaspoon grated lemon rind
1 tablespoon lemon juice
1 slice white bread
2–3 anchovy fillets
1/3 cup olive oil

POLENTA WEDGES
2 1/4 cups chicken stock
1 cup polenta (cornmeal)
50 g butter
1/2 cup cream
extra melted butter, for
  brushing

12 lamb cutlets, trimmed

1   To make the Salsa Verde:
Place the parsley, basil, mint, dill,
capers, garlic, sugar, lemon rind
and juice, bread and drained
anchovies in a food processor and
finely chop. With the motor
running, gradually add the oil and
blend the mixture until smooth.
2   To make the Polenta Wedges:
Heat the stock in a large pan
until boiling. Gradually add the
polenta, stirring continuously
over low heat for 20 minutes until
the polenta leaves the side of the
pan. Stir in the butter and cream
and season with salt and ground
pepper. Grease a deep 23 cm round
cake tin, spoon in the polenta and
smooth the surface. Set in the
refrigerator for 20 minutes.
3   Turn the polenta out of the tin,
cut into wedges and brush all over
with the melted butter. Lightly oil
a preheated chargrill pan or
barbecue grill or flatplate and cook
for 2–3 minutes each side, or until
brown. Remove and keep warm.
4   Place the lamb on the hot
plate and brown for about
2 minutes each side, or until
cooked through but still just pink
inside. Serve with the Salsa Verde
and Polenta Wedges.

Lamb Fillet with Eggplant, Tomato and Pesto

PREPARATION TIME:
30 MINUTES
COOKING TIME:
25 MINUTES
SERVES 4

PESTO
2 cups fresh basil leaves
2 cloves garlic, crushed
1/3 cup pine nuts
3/4 cup olive oil
3/4 cup grated Parmesan

1 medium eggplant
4 egg tomatoes, halved
6 lamb fillets
60 g goats cheese

1 To make the Pesto: Place the basil leaves, garlic and pine nuts in a food processor and finely chop. With the motor running slowly, gradually pour in the olive oil. Add the Parmesan and process the mixture briefly.

2 Cut the eggplant into thick slices and brush with some olive oil. Preheat a chargrill pan or barbecue grill or flatplate and cook the eggplant, brushing with a little more oil, for 3–4 minutes each side, or until golden brown and softened. Remove and keep warm. Add the tomatoes and cook, brushing with olive oil, until soft. Remove and keep warm.

3 Sprinkle each lamb fillet liberally with freshly ground black pepper. Wipe clean the preheated chargrill pan or barbecue grill or flatplate and lightly oil. Cook the lamb for 3–4 minutes, turning to brown on all sides, until the lamb is cooked through but still pink inside. Cut the fillets into diagonal slices and arrange on four plates. Arrange the tomato on top of the eggplant and top with a little pesto. Crumble the goats cheese over the top and serve with the lamb.

Note: Instead of using basil to make the pesto, you could use fresh coriander or mint, or a mixture of them both. If you prefer a milder taste, use ricotta or feta rather than goats cheese.

Moroccan Lamb with Pistachio Couscous

PREPARATION TIME: 40 MINUTES +
2 HOURS MARINATING
COOKING TIME: 15–20 MINUTES
SERVES 4

MOROCCAN MARINADE
3 tablespoons olive oil
1 tablespoon lemon juice
2 teaspoons honey
1–2 cloves garlic, crushed
1 teaspoon ground cumin
1/2 teaspoon ground turmeric
1/2 teaspoon ground cinnamon
1/4 teaspoon cayenne pepper

8–10 small lamb fillets
pinch of saffron
1 1/2 cups chicken stock
1 1/4 cups couscous
1 tablespoon olive oil
1 red onion, chopped
**1 red chilli, seeded and
  chopped**
2 cloves garlic, crushed
1/2 cup currants
100 g shelled pistachios
grated rind of 1 lemon
grated rind of 1 orange
1/4 cup chopped fresh mint

1 To make the Moroccan Marinade: Mix together all the ingredients in a bowl, pour over the lamb fillets to coat and cover and refrigerate for 2 hours.

2 Add the saffron powder or threads to the hot stock and pour over the couscous in a bowl. Set aside for 10 minutes, then stir to break up any lumps.

3 Heat the oil in a frying pan, add the onion, chilli and garlic and cook for about 3 minutes. Add the currants and pistachios and continue to cook for a further 5 minutes. Mix in the lemon and orange rind and the mint. Stir the mixture through the couscous.

4 Preheat a lightly oiled chargrill pan or barbecue grill or flatplate and add the drained lamb. Cook, turning once, over high heat until browned all over. Then continue to cook for a further 2–3 minutes, turning frequently. Remove and slice the lamb on the diagonal. Serve with the couscous.

Lamb Chops with Citrus Pockets

PREPARATION TIME:
25 MINUTES
COOKING TIME:
15 MINUTES
SERVES 4

4 lamb chump chops, about 250 g each
2 tablespoons lemon juice

FILLING
3 spring onions, finely chopped
1 celery stick, finely chopped
1 tablespoon grated fresh ginger
3/4 cup fresh breadcrumbs
2 tablespoons orange juice
2 teaspoons finely grated orange rind
1 teaspoon finely chopped fresh rosemary

1   Cut a deep, long pocket into the side of each of the lamb chops through the skin and fat.

2   To make the Filling: Combine in a bowl the spring onion, celery, ginger, breadcrumbs, orange juice and rind and the rosemary. Spoon the mixture into the lamb pockets.

3   Preheat a lightly oiled chargrill pan or barbecue grill or flatplate and cook the chops over high heat, turning once, for 15 minutes, or until the lamb is cooked through but still pink in the centre. Drizzle with the lemon juice and serve with boiled potatoes and a salad.

Lamb Satays with Chilli Peanut Sauce

Why not let your guests cook their own satays.

PREPARATION TIME: 25 MINUTES + 1 HOUR MARINATING
COOKING TIME: 15 MINUTES
SERVES 4

600 g lamb fillets
2 cloves garlic, crushed
1/2 teaspoon ground black pepper
6 teaspoons finely chopped lemongrass
2 tablespoons soy sauce
2 teaspoons sugar
1/4 teaspoon ground turmeric

CHILLI PEANUT SAUCE
1 1/2 cups unsalted roasted peanuts
2 tablespoons vegetable oil
1 medium onion, roughly chopped
1 clove garlic, roughly chopped
1 tablespoon sambal oelek
1 tablespoon soft brown sugar
1 tablespoon kecap manis (sweet soy sauce) or soy sauce
1 teaspoon grated ginger
1 1/2 teaspoons ground coriander
1 cup coconut cream
1/4 teaspoon ground turmeric
salt and pepper, to taste

1   Trim the lamb of excess fat and sinew and cut into thin strips. Thread onto soaked wooden skewers, bunching the strips along three-quarters of the length. Place the satays in a shallow non-metal dish.

2   Combine the garlic, pepper, lemongrass, soy sauce, sugar and turmeric in a small bowl and mix well. Brush the marinade over the skewered meat and set aside for 1 hour. Prepare and heat the barbecue.

3   To make Chilli Peanut Sauce: Process the peanuts in a food processor bowl for 10 seconds or until coarsely ground. Heat the oil in a small pan. Add the onion and garlic and cook over a medium heat for 3–4 minutes or until translucent. Add the sambal oelek, sugar, kecap manis, ginger and coriander. Cook, stirring, for 2 minutes.

4   Add the coconut cream, turmeric and processed peanuts. Reduce the heat and cook for 3 minutes or until thickened; season with salt and pepper. Remove from the heat.

5   Place the mixture in a food processor bowl. Process for 20 seconds or until almost smooth. Spoon into individual serving dishes to cool.

6   Barbecue the satays on a hot lightly greased grill or flatplate for 2–3 minutes each side or until browned.

Lamb Chops with Pineapple Salsa

PREPARATION
TIME:
20 MINUTES
COOKING TIME:
10 MINUTES
SERVES 6

12 lamb loin chops
2 tablespoons oil
1 teaspoon cracked black
   pepper

PINEAPPLE SALSA
1/2 ripe pineapple (or 400 g
   drained canned pineapple)
1 large red onion
1 fresh red chilli
1 tablespoon cider or rice
   vinegar
1 teaspoon sugar
salt and black pepper, to taste
2 tablespoons chopped mint

1 Prepare and heat the barbecue. Trim the meat of excess fat and sinew. Brush with oil and season with pepper.

2 To make Pineapple Salsa: Peel the pineapple and remove the core and eyes. Cut into 1-cm cubes. Peel the onion and finely chop. Slit open the chilli, scrape out the seeds and chop the chilli flesh finely. Combine the pineapple, onion and chilli in a medium bowl and mix lightly. Add the vinegar, sugar, salt, pepper and mint; mix well.

3 Place the lamb chops on a lightly greased barbecue grill or flatplate. Cook for 2–3 minutes each side, turning once, until just tender. Serve with Pineapple Salsa, baked potatoes and a green salad.

Ginger-Orange Pork Steaks

PREPARATION TIME: 15 MINUTES +
3 HOURS MARINATING
COOKING TIME: 20 MINUTES
SERVES 6

**6 pork butterfly steaks (200 g
each)**
1 cup ginger wine
1/2 cup orange marmalade
2 tablespoons oil
1 tablespoon grated ginger

1   Trim the pork steaks of excess
fat and sinew and place in a
shallow non-metal dish.

2   Combine the wine, marmalade,
oil and ginger in a small jug and
mix well. Pour the marinade over
the meat. Store, covered with
plastic wrap, in the refrigerator for
several hours or overnight,
turning occasionally. Prepare and
heat the barbecue 1 hour before
cooking. Drain the pork steaks
and reserve the marinade.

3   Place the pork on a hot lightly
oiled barbecue grill or flatplate.
Cook for 5 minutes each side or
until tender, turning once.

4   While meat is cooking, place
the reserved marinade in a small
pan. Bring to the boil, reduce
heat and simmer for 5 minutes
until the marinade has reduced
and thickened slightly. Pour over
the pork steaks immediately.

Pork Loin Chops with Apple Chutney

Try the Apple Chutney served with a cheese platter. It also goes well with cold meats.

PREPARATION TIME:
20 MINUTES +
3 HOURS
MARINATING
COOKING TIME:
25 MINUTES
SERVES 6

6 pork loin chops
2/3 cup white wine
2 tablespoons oil
2 tablespoons honey
1 1/2 teaspoons ground cumin
2 cloves garlic, crushed

APPLE CHUTNEY
3 medium green apples
1/2 cup apple juice
1/2 cup fruit chutney
15 g butter

1   Trim the pork chops of excess fat and sinew and place in a shallow, non-metal dish.

2   Combine wine, oil, honey, cumin and garlic in a small jug and mix well. Pour the marinade over the chops. Store, covered with plastic wrap, in the refrigerator for several hours or overnight, turning occasionally. Prepare and heat the barbecue 1 hour before cooking.

3   Place the chops on a hot lightly oiled barbecue grill or flatplate. Cook for 8 minutes each side or until tender, turning once. Serve immediately with Apple Chutney.

4   To make Apple Chutney: Peel the apples and cut them into small cubes. Place them in a small pan and cover with apple juice. Bring to the boil, reduce heat and simmer, covered, for 7 minutes or until completely soft. Add the chutney and butter and stir to combine. Serve warm.

Pork Loin Chops with Apple Chutney (above). Ginger-Orange Pork Steaks

Skewered Ginger Pork

Ginger and pork are a great combination and this recipe brings the two together in a delightful dish.

PREPARATION TIME:
20 MINUTES +
1 HOUR
MARINATING
COOKING TIME:
10 MINUTES
SERVES 6

500 g pork fillets
2 tablespoons grated fresh ginger
1/2 teaspoon ground pepper
1 teaspoon oriental sesame oil
1 tablespoon lemon juice
1 small onion, grated
salt and pepper, to taste

1   Cube the pork, combine the remaining ingredients and marinate the pork for 1 hour.

2   Skewer the pork and barbecue on a flatplate for 5 minutes each side or until cooked to personal taste. Serve with a salad and hot bread rolls.

Note: Pork fillets are a delicate cut with little fat visible. If not easy to come by, choose another lean cut as a substitute.

Pork Ribs with a Chilli Watermelon Sauce

PREPARATION TIME:
20 MINUTES
COOKING TIME:
1 HOUR
10 MINUTES
SERVES 4

1 kg pork spareribs, with the rind and fat
3 tablespoons orange juice
200 g watermelon flesh, seeds removed
2 cloves garlic, finely chopped
2 fresh red or green chillies, chopped
3 tablespoons tomato paste
1 teaspoon soy sauce

1 Preheat the oven to moderately hot 200°C (400°F/Gas 6). Place the ribs on a rack over a baking dish and brush all over with the orange juice. Cook for 1 hour, turning once.

2 Lightly mash the watermelon with a fork and combine with the garlic, chilli, tomato paste and soy sauce. Preheat a lightly oiled chargrill pan or barbecue grill or flatplate and cook the ribs for about 7 minutes, basting with some of the watermelon sauce.

3 Serve the spareribs drizzled with the remaining watermelon sauce.

Note: Baking the meat before chargrilling produces more succulent spareribs.

Pork with Apple and Onion Wedges

PREPARATION TIME: 25 MINUTES
COOKING TIME: 15 MINUTES
SERVES 4

2 pork fillets, about 400 g each
12 pitted prunes
2 green apples, cored, unpeeled and cut into wedges
2 red onions, cut into wedges
50 g butter, melted
2 teaspoons caster sugar
1/2 cup cream
2 tablespoons brandy
1 tablespoon chopped fresh chives

1   Trim the pork of any excess fat and sinew and cut each fillet into 2 even-sized halves. Make a slit with a knife through the centre of the pork fillets and push 3 prunes into each one. Brush the pork fillets and the apple and onion wedges with the melted butter and sprinkle just the apple and onion with the caster sugar.

2   Lightly oil a deep-sided preheated chargrill pan or barbecue flatplate and brown the fillets evenly on each side. Add the apple and onion wedges (depending on the size of the pan or plate, it may be necessary to cook these in batches). Cook, turning frequently, for 5–7 minutes, or until the pork is cooked through and the apple and onion are softened. Remove the pork, apple and onion from the pan and keep warm.

3   Mix together the cream, brandy and chives in a bowl. If you are using a chargrill pan with deep sides, add the mixture to the pan over a high heat. Alternatively, pour into a pan on top of the stove or barbecue.

Simmer for about 3 minutes, or until slightly thickened and reduced. Season to taste with salt and freshly ground black pepper.

4   Slice the meat on the diagonal, arrange on warm plates and pour on the sauce. Add the apple and onion wedges and serve with a green salad.

Pork and Tomato Burgers

PREPARATION TIME:
20 MINUTES +
15 MINUTES
REFRIGERATION
COOKING TIME:
15 MINUTES
SERVES 4

350 g pork and veal mince

100 g sun-dried tomatoes, chopped

3 spring onions, finely chopped

2 tablespoons chopped fresh basil

1 red capsicum, seeded and sliced

1 tablespoon balsamic vinegar

1 Combine the pork and veal mince, sun-dried tomato, spring onion, basil and salt and pepper in a bowl. Knead for 2 minutes, or until the meat becomes a little sticky. Form into four patties and refrigerate for 15 minutes.

2 Mix the capsicum with a little olive oil. Cook on a preheated chargrill pan or barbecue flatplate, tossing well and drizzling with the balsamic vinegar until just softened. Remove and set aside.

3 Wipe the hot plate clean and reheat. Brush the patties with olive oil and cook for 4–5 minutes on each side, or until browned and cooked through. Serve with the chargrilled capsicum.

Honey Pork with Bok Choy

PREPARATION TIME:
25 MINUTES +
1 HOUR
MARINATING
COOKING TIME:
25 MINUTES
SERVES 4

MARINADE
2 tablespoons soy sauce
1 tablespoon oil
1 tablespoon kecap manis
1 tablespoon honey
1 tablespoon oyster sauce

2 pork fillets, about 400 g each
2 tablespoons oil
2 cloves garlic, crushed
2 teaspoons grated fresh ginger
200 g shiitake mushrooms, sliced
6 baby bok choy, halved
1/4 cup chicken stock
100 g instant noodles
1/3 cup fresh coriander leaves

1   To make the Marinade: Combine the ingredients and marinate the pork for 1 hour in the refrigerator. Drain, reserving the marinade.

2   Preheat a lightly oiled chargrill pan or barbecue grill or flatplate and brown the pork over high heat for 2 minutes. Continue to cook, turning occasionally, for about 5 minutes. Remove and keep warm.

3   Heat the oil in a frying pan over the stove or barbecue. Cook the garlic and ginger for 2 minutes, then add the mushroom and cook for 3 minutes. Add the bok choy, reserved marinade and stock. Simmer, stirring, for 5 minutes.

4   Cook the instant noodles according to the manufacturer's instructions. Drain and add to the vegetables. Slice the pork and place on top of the noodles and vegetables, and sprinkle with the coriander.

Piquant Meatloaf

PREPARATION TIME:
10 MINUTES
COOKING TIME:
1 HOUR
SERVES 6–8

1 kg pork and veal mince
3/4 cup bottled plum sauce
1 medium onion, grated
1/2 cup chopped coriander
  leaves
2 cloves garlic, crushed
salt and pepper, to taste
2 eggs, lightly beaten
1 cup fresh breadcrumbs

BASTING MIXTURE
2 teaspoons chicken stock
  powder
2 tablespoons hot water

1 Combine the pork and veal mince in a bowl with the remaining meatloaf ingredients.

2 Place the pork and veal mixture in a 21 x 14 x 7-cm lightly greased or non-stick loaf tin.

3 Preheat the barbecue and place the loaf tin on a rack over the flatplate. Cook with the hood down for 1 hour, basting the meatloaf every 15 minutes with combined chicken stock powder and hot water.

4 Serve sliced with a crisp green salad.

Note: Bottled plum sauce can be purchased from supermarkets and Asian stores. Use barbecue sauce as a substitute.

Sweet and Sour Pork Kebabs

Chilli garlic sauce is available from Asian food shops and some supermarkets.

PREPARATION TIME:
30 MINUTES +
3 HOURS
MARINATING
COOKING TIME:
20 MINUTES
SERVES 6

1 kg pork fillets
1 large red capsicum
1 large green capsicum
425 g can pineapple pieces
1 cup orange juice
1/4 cup white vinegar
2 tablespoons soft brown sugar
2 teaspoons chilli garlic sauce
2 teaspoons cornflour

1 Trim the pork of excess fat and sinew and cut meat into 2.5-cm cubes. Cut both capsicums into 2-cm squares. Drain pineapple and reserve juice.

Thread the meat, alternately with the capsicum and pineapple, onto soaked wooden skewers.

2 Combine the reserved pineapple juice with orange juice, vinegar, sugar and sauce. Place the kebabs in a shallow non-metal dish and pour half the juice mixture over. Refrigerate, covered with plastic wrap, for 3 hours or overnight, turning occasionally. Prepare and heat barbecue 1 hour before cooking.

3 To make Sweet and Sour Sauce: Place the remaining marinade in a small pan. Mix the cornflour with a tablespoon of the marinade in a small bowl until smooth; add to pan. Stir over a medium heat until the mixture boils and thickens; transfer to a small serving bowl. Cover surface with plastic wrap and leave to cool.

4 Place the kebabs on a hot lightly oiled barbecue grill or flatplate and cook for 15 minutes, turning occasionally, until tender. Serve kebabs with Sweet and Sour Sauce.

Pork and Veal Pita Burgers

PREPARATION TIME:
10 MINUTES
COOKING TIME:
8 MINUTES
SERVES 4–6

500 g pork and veal mince
1 large onion, grated
salt and pepper, to taste
1 teaspoon ground oregano
   leaves
1 clove garlic, crushed
1 teaspoon hot chilli sauce
1/3 cup fresh breadcrumbs

1 Combine all the ingredients, mix well and divide into six. Shape the portions into flat, round patties and place on an oiled hamburger frame.

2 Barbecue on a medium high heat on the grill plate for 4 minutes, turn over and cook further 4 minutes. Serve the burgers on pita bread with a mixed salad, sour cream and pickled sour cucumbers.

Note: Ensure you make all of the burgers the same size to allow for even cooking.

Stars and Stripes Barbecue Ribs

PREPARATION TIME:
30 MINUTES +
OVERNIGHT
MARINATING
COOKING TIME:
15 MINUTES
SERVES 6–8

1.5 kg American-style pork
   spare ribs

SAUCE
1 teaspoon dry mustard, or
   prepared English mustard
1 teaspoon ground sweet
   paprika
1/2 teaspoon ground oregano
1/2 teaspoon ground cumin
3 tablespoons peanut oil
2 cloves garlic, crushed
1 teaspoon Tabasco sauce
1 cup tomato sauce
2 tablespoons Worcestershire
   sauce
1/3 cup tomato paste
1/3 cup brown sugar
1 tablespoon brown vinegar

1 To make the sauce: Mix the mustard and dry spices with oil in a medium pan. Blend in the sauce and remaining ingredients. Cook, stirring, over a medium heat for 5 minutes until combined. Cool before refrigerating. Store half for later use in a clean glass jar.

2 Coat the ribs with the remaining sauce and marinate overnight. Cook on a medium hot

barbecue grill, turning frequently, until and well done.

Note: This marinade and the sauce are equally good with beef spare ribs. However, if using beef ribs they should be simmered until tender and drained before marinating and barbecuing.

Pork and Veal Pita Burgers (above). Stars and Stripes Barbecue Ribs

Honey Soy Sausages

PREPARATION TIME:	8–10 thick pork or beef sausages
15 MINUTES + OVERNIGHT MARINATING	3 cm piece fresh ginger
	1/3 cup honey
COOKING TIME:	1/3 cup soy sauce
5–6 MINUTES	1 clove garlic, crushed
SERVES 4–6	1 tablespoon sweet sherry
	2 sprigs fresh thyme

1 Place the sausages in a large bowl or shallow non-metal dish. Peel the ginger and grate it finely. Combine the honey, soy sauce, ginger, garlic, sherry and thyme in a jug; mix well.

2 Pour the marinade over the sausages. Cover and refrigerate overnight to allow the flavours to be absorbed.

3 Prepare and heat the barbecue 1 hour before cooking. Lightly grease the barbecue grill or flatplate. Cook the sausages 5–6 minutes, away from the hottest part of the fire, brushing occasionally with marinade. Turn the sausages frequently to prevent the marinade burning (it should form a thick, slightly sticky glaze around the sausages).

Pork Medallions with Olive Tapenade

Tapenade is ideal with meats such as pork which have a mild, subtle flavour.

PREPARATION TIME: 20 MINUTES
COOKING TIME: 10 MINUTES
SERVES 4

- 4 x 200-g pork butterfly medallions or 4 pork loin medallion steaks, about 150 g each
- 2 tablespoons olive oil
- 1 tablespoon lemon juice
- 1 tablespoon fresh thyme leaves
- 1/4 teaspoon ground black pepper

OLIVE TAPENADE
- 2 tablespoons olive oil
- 1/2 small onion, finely chopped
- 1 clove garlic, crushed
- 125 g pitted black olives, finely chopped
- 2 anchovies, finely chopped
- 1 small, ripe tomato, peeled, seeded and chopped
- 2 teaspoons balsamic vinegar
- 1 medium red chilli, finely chopped
- 1 tablespoon chopped fresh basil leaves

1 If using pork loin medallion steaks, shape into rounds by securing the thinner tail end to the medallion with toothpicks. Trim meat of excess fat and sinew.

2 Combine the oil, lemon juice, thyme and pepper and brush over the meat.

3 Place the meat on a lightly oiled flatplate or grill. Cook over a medium heat for 5 minutes on each side or until tender. Serve with Olive Tapenade.

4 To make Olive Tapenade: Heat the oil in a small pan, add the onion and garlic, and stir until the onion is tender. Add the olives, anchovies, tomato, vinegar, chilli and basil and stir 1 minute to combine. Serve hot or cold.

Orange and Ginger-glazed Ham

Leftover ham can be sliced and served with fried eggs, or with grilled tomatoes. Cubed ham is delicious in fried rice. The ham bone can be used for stock or as the basis of pea soup.

PREPARATION TIME:
25 MINUTES
COOKING TIME:
1 HOUR 30 MINUTES
SERVES 20

6-kg ham on the bone
1/4 cup orange juice
3/4 cup orange marmalade
1 tablespoon grated ginger
2 teaspoons mustard powder
2 tablespoons soft brown sugar
whole cloves (about 30)

1 Prepare a Weber (kettle) barbecue for indirect cooking at moderate heat (normal fire).

2 Remove the rind by running your thumb around the edge of the ham, under the rind. Begin pulling from the widest edge. When the rind has been removed to within 10 cm of the shank end, cut through the rind around the shank. Using a sharp knife, remove excess fat from the ham and discard. (Reserve the rind for crackling, if desired. Rub the rind with salt and barbecue for 40 minutes.)

3 Using a sharp knife score the top of the ham with deep diagonal cuts. Score diagonally the other way, forming a diamond pattern. Place the ham on the barbecue; put on the lid and cook for 45 minutes.

4 Place the juice, marmalade, ginger, mustard and sugar in a small pan. Stir over a medium heat until combined; set aside to cool.

5 Remove the lid from the barbecue and carefully press cloves into the top of the ham (approximately one clove per diamond); brush all over with the marmalade mixture.

6 Cover the barbecue and cook a further 45 minutes. Serve garnished with clove-studded orange slices. Ham can be served warm or cold.

Poultry

*t*here is a great range of poultry cuts to choose from these days, and all of them — chicken thigh and breast fillets, maryland, wings and drumsticks — are ideal for the barbecue. Many butchers, delicatessens and poultry shops sell their own marinated chicken pieces, which makes the busy barbecue chef's life even easier. Quail, too, are small and tender — ideal for barbecue cooking — allow at least one bird per person.

When buying chicken, appearances are important. The flesh of a fresh chicken should be moist, with no dry spots and the breasts should be plump. If blood or juices are visible in the bottom of plastic packaging, it may mean that the chicken has been in the display cabinet for longer than is ideal. If offered on special, cook the chicken the same day.

Keep uncooked chicken in the coldest part of the refrigerator and cook within two days of purchase. A whole chicken should be removed from its wrappings, washed, patted dry and jointed, depending on how it is to be cooked. Wrap the pieces again in clean plastic wrap or foil and store in the refrigerator. Make sure that a frozen chicken is allowed to thaw completely in the refrigerator (don't remove the wrapping; the skin may dry out and toughen). Poultry is highly susceptible to bacterial growth at room temperature, so never try speeding up the defrosting process by leaving the bird out on the kitchen bench, it may result in food poisoning.

Poultry lends itself wonderfully to marinating — the various flavours will permeate the flesh, and the acid content in ingredients like lemon juice, wine or vinegar will increase its tenderness. For thicker cuts like breast fillets or drumsticks, slash the flesh in several places to allow the flavours of the marinade to be better absorbed. Baste the meat with the marinade occasionally during cooking to prevent it drying out.

Mango Chicken

Buy mangoes that are firm to soft. They may be green, yellow, or bright orange with a rosy blush depending upon the variety.

PREPARATION TIME:
20 MINUTES
COOKING TIME:
30 MINUTES
SERVES 6

2 onions
2 tablespoons oil
1 clove garlic, crushed
6 chicken breast fillets
salt and pepper, to taste
3 medium nearly ripe mangoes
 or 425-g can mangoes
watercress, to garnish

GLAZE
1/2 cup reserved mango juice or
 purée from fresh mangoes
1 tablespoon honey
2 teaspoons chicken stock
 powder
1 clove garlic, crushed
1 teaspoon cornflour
cold water

1   Finely slice the onions. Heat the oil and cook onions and garlic over a low heat until golden brown. Remove from heat.

2   Place the chicken breasts skin side down onto a board or work surface. Flatten each fillet out to enclose filling. Season each with salt and pepper to taste. Place equal portions of the onion and garlic over the surface of the chicken breast fillets.

3   Drain the mango and reserve the juice for the glaze. If using fresh mangoes you must peel the fruit and cut close to the sides of the seed to get two full slices from each mango. Slice off the remaining flesh and purée in a blender.

4   Arrange the mango slices on the chicken breasts. Fold the chicken breast over to enclose the mango slices and onions. Secure with toothpicks or metal skewers.

5   To make the glaze: Combine the mango purée or juice, honey, chicken stock powder and garlic in a small pan, cook over low heat until thoroughly combined. Add cornflour mixed smoothly with a tablespoon of cold water to the glaze. Stir over a low heat until thickened.

6   Cook chicken on a lightly oiled barbecue flatplate over medium heat for 15 minutes. Turn and cook for a further 10 minutes or until the chicken is done. Brush with the glaze during the last few minutes of cooking. Serve with remaining sauce on a platter garnished with watercress.

Garlic and Ginger Chicken

PREPARATION TIME:
15 MINUTES +
30 MINUTES
MARINATING
COOKING TIME:
50 MINUTES
SERVES 6–8

1.4-kg chicken

MARINADE
1/4 cup lemon juice
1/4 cup olive oil
1 tablespoon grated fresh
 ginger
2 cloves garlic, crushed
2 teaspoons mild curry powder
salt and pepper, to taste

GARLIC SAUCE
2 cloves garlic, crushed
3/4 cup mayonnaise
1 teaspoon mild curry powder
1/2 teaspoon white pepper

1   Rinse the chicken, pat dry with absorbent paper. Place on a tray.

2   To make marinade: Combine all the ingredients in a bowl and pour over the chicken. Allow to marinate for 30 minutes or overnight in the refrigerator.

3   To make Garlic Sauce: Combine all the ingredients and store covered in the refrigerator until required.

4   Preheat the barbecue. Remove the chicken from the marinade and skewer onto rotisserie. Cook the chicken for approximately 50 minutes on the rotisserie. The chicken should be tender inside and crisp golden brown on the outside. Serve immediately with Garlic Sauce.

Mango Chicken (above). Garlic and Ginger Chicken

Saffron Chicken

Saffron is the world's most expensive spice and has a wonderful flavour. Buy it from a reputable dealer (such as a chefs' supplier) or look for a well-known brand name.

PREPARATION TIME:
15 MINUTES +
30 MINUTES
MARINATING

COOKING TIME:
25 MINUTES

SERVES 8

8 chicken breast fillets

MARINADE
1/4 teaspoon saffron powder (see note)
2 tablespoons hot water
1 tablespoon lime juice
1 teaspoon ground sweet paprika
1/2 teaspoon ground pepper
1 clove garlic, crushed
2 tablespoons olive oil
1 teaspoon onion powder
3 teaspoons chicken stock powder
1/4 cup sour cream
1 teaspoon cornflour
1/2 cup milk

1 Lightly score the chicken breast fillets, and pat dry with absorbent paper. Place in a shallow dish. Dissolve the saffron in the hot water and combine with the lime juice, paprika, pepper, garlic, olive oil and onion powder.

2 Pour over the chicken and turn to coat in the marinade. Allow the chicken to stand for 30 minutes.

3 Remove the chicken from the marinade and cook on a preheated flatplate over low heat for 8–10 minutes each side, or until the chicken is tender and golden, turning once during the cooking.

4 Place the remaining marinade in a small pan with the chicken stock powder and sour cream. Combine the cornflour and milk, stir into the sauce and heat until thickened. Season to taste with pepper. Serve this sauce with the chicken.

Note: If purchasing saffron strands (most brands are sold in strand form), lightly toast half a teaspoon of the strands in a dry pan, shaking the pan to prevent burning. Empty onto a small saucer and when cool and crisp, crush with the back of a spoon.

Marinated Chicken Satay

Chicken satay can also be served as an entrée course.

PREPARATION TIME:
15 MINUTES +
1 HOUR
MARINATING

COOKING TIME:
6 MINUTES

SERVES 6

500 g skinless chicken breast or thigh fillets

MARINADE AND SAUCE
1 large onion, grated
2 tablespoons lemon or lime juice
2 cloves garlic, crushed
2 teaspoons grated fresh ginger
2 teaspoons sambal oelek or crushed chillies
1/3 cup soy sauce
2 tablespoons brown sugar
1 tablespoon sesame oil
3/4 cup coconut milk
1/2 cup crunchy peanut butter
2 tablespoons toasted sesame seeds

1 Cut the chicken breasts into bite-sized squares. Combine the onion, lemon juice, garlic, ginger, sambal oelek, soy sauce, brown sugar and sesame oil. Pour over the prepared chicken and stir to coat all the pieces thoroughly. Allow to marinate for 1 hour in the refrigerator. Meanwhile, soak the bamboo skewers in cold water.

2 Remove the chicken pieces from the marinade and thread onto twelve soaked bamboo skewers, leaving a portion of the skewer free for handling. Barbecue over preheated grill for about 6 minutes, turning until they are browned. Brush with a little extra oil if necessary.

3 Pour the remaining marinade into a pan and place on the edge of the barbecue. Add the coconut milk and peanut butter, stir until the mixture boils and thickens. Serve satays on a platter, sprinkled with sesame seeds. Accompany with steamed rice and serve with satay sauce.

Saffron Chicken (above). Marinated Chicken Satay. Spicy Chicken Wings (right)

Spicy Chicken Wings

PREPARATION TIME:
10 MINUTES +
1 HOUR
MARINATING
COOKING TIME:
20–25 MINUTES
SERVES 6

12 chicken wings
6 teaspoons mild curry powder
2 cloves garlic, crushed
1 tablespoon oil
2 tablespoons lemon juice
1/2 teaspoon white pepper
1/4 cup water
1 tablespoon chicken stock powder

1 Remove the tips from the chicken wings, rinse and pat dry with absorbent paper. Score through the skin and flesh with a sharp knife.

2 Combine the remaining ingredients, mixing well.

3 Pour the marinade over the prepared wings. Mix to coat well.

4 Grill over a lightly oiled preheated barbecue on medium heat for 12 minutes, turn and continue cooking until tender and golden brown.

Barbecued Quail with Garlic and Sour Cream

These small birds make good eating, especially when well cooked over a barbecue.

PREPARATION TIME:
15 MINUTES +
30 MINUTES
MARINATING
COOKING TIME:
40 MINUTES
SERVES 6

12 quail

MARINADE
6 tablespoons olive oil
1/3 cup dry white wine
1/3 cup finely chopped spring onions
1/2 cup chopped fresh herbs
2 cloves garlic, crushed
6 whole heads of garlic

SOUR CREAM SAUCE
1 cup sour cream
2 tablespoons finely chopped spring onions
salt and white pepper, to taste
lime or lemon juice, to taste

1   Place the quail on a board breast-side down. Cut through the back with poultry shears to butterfly and discard backbone.

2   To make the marinade: Combine the olive oil, white wine, spring onions, fresh herbs and garlic. Pour over the quail and allow to marinate for 30 minutes.

3   Wrap the garlic heads in a double layer of industrial-strength foil.

4   Place the wrapped garlic directly into the coals — not flames — of the fire, or place on top of the grill. Cook for 30–40 minutes. This long, slow cooking mellows the flavour of the garlic.

5   Remove the quail from the marinade and barbecue on a lightly oiled grill for 12–15 minutes. Turn occasionally and brush with the marinade during cooking.

6   To make Sour Cream Sauce: Combine the sour cream and spring onions and season with salt, pepper, and juice to taste. Serve the barbecued quail with knobs of garlic and Sour Cream Sauce.

Chicken and Prawn Kebabs

This recipe is a less expensive version of the American combination of lobster and steak — 'Surf 'n' Turf', as it is known.

PREPARATION TIME:
25 MINUTES +
30 MINUTES
MARINATING
COOKING TIME:
20 MINUTES
SERVES 6

350 g chicken breast fillets
500 g large green prawns
425-g can apricot halves, in natural juice
440-g can pineapple rings
2 teaspoons grated fresh ginger
2 tablespoons olive oil
salt and white pepper, to taste
2 teaspoons cornflour
1 tablespoon water
1 teaspoon grated fresh ginger, extra
2 spring onions, finely sliced

1   Cut the chicken into large pieces. Peel and devein the prawns. Drain the apricot halves and pineapple slices, reserving the juice. Cut the pineapple slices into four. Thread the prepared chicken, prawns and fruit alternately onto soaked bamboo or metal skewers.

2   Combine 1 cup reserved pineapple juice with grated ginger, olive oil, salt and pepper. Pour the mixture over the kebabs and allow to marinate for 30 minutes.

3   Remove from the marinade and barbecue over a hot flatplate for 5 minutes each side or until the chicken is tender and prawns have turned pink. Meanwhile, heat the remaining marinade in a pan on the edge of the barbecue, thicken with combined cornflour and water, add the extra grated ginger and spring onions and allow to boil until the sauce thickens. Serve Chicken and Prawn Kebabs immediately.

Barbecued Quail with Garlic and Sour Cream (above). Chicken and Prawn Kebabs (right). Chicken Maryland

Chicken Maryland

Not the original Chicken Maryland (crumbed and deep fried), but much healthier.

PREPARATION TIME: 20 MINUTES +
30 MINUTES MARINATING
COOKING TIME: 30 MINUTES
SERVES 6

440-g can pineapple slices
6 chicken maryland pieces

MARINADE
2 tablespoons oil
1/2 cup tomato sauce
1 tablespoon malt vinegar
1 tablespoon barbecue sauce
1 tablespoon brown sugar
1/4 cup reserved pineapple juice
1 clove garlic, crushed
salt and pepper, to taste

1   Drain the pineapple slices and reserve the juice.

2   To make the marinade: Combine the oil, tomato sauce, vinegar, barbecue sauce, sugar, pineapple juice, garlic, salt and pepper in a small pan over a low heat. Brush the marinade over the surface of the chicken and allow to marinate for 30 minutes, or longer in the refrigerator if a strong flavour is required.

3   Remove the chicken and cook over preheated lightly oiled barbecue flatplate for 30–35 minutes or until tender and the juices run clear. Turn often and brush with remaining marinade towards the end of cooking. Cook the pineapple rings along with the chicken during the last 5 minutes, brushing with the marinade.

89

Oriental Chicken Kebabs

A delicious meal served with a salad and crisp French bread.

PREPARATION TIME: 30 MINUTES + 30 MINUTES MARINATING
COOKING TIME: 10 MINUTES
SERVES 4

1 tablespoon light soy sauce
1 tablespoon white wine
2 teaspoons whole grain mustard
2 teaspoons snipped chives
1 teaspoon oil
1 clove garlic, crushed
1 teaspoon grated ginger
4 chicken breast fillets, cut into chunks
bamboo skewers, soaked in water
12 button mushrooms
12 cherry tomatoes
1 onion, cut into eighths
1 green capsicum, seeded and cubed
3 canned, unsweetened pineapple rings, quartered

1   Combine the soy sauce, wine, mustard, chives, oil, garlic and ginger in a glass or ceramic bowl. Add the chicken. Marinate for 30 minutes, turning the chicken frequently.

2   Thread the chicken onto skewers, alternating the meat with the mushrooms, tomatoes, onion, capsicum and pineapple.

3   Cook on a preheated lightly greased barbecue grill or flatplate for 5–10 minutes, turning frequently and basting occasionally.

Kashmiri Chicken Roast

This larger chicken is best cooked on a kettle rotisserie barbecue.

PREPARATION TIME: 20 MINUTES + 30 MINUTES MARINATING
COOKING TIME 1 HOUR 10 MINUTES
SERVES 4–6

1.4-kg chicken

MARINADE
1/4 teaspoon ground saffron
2 tablespoons hot water
2 teaspoons ground fenugreek leaves
2 cloves garlic, crushed
1 teaspoon grated fresh ginger
1/2 teaspoon chilli powder
2 teaspoons garam masala
1/2 teaspoon turmeric
1/2 teaspoon ground pepper
3 tablespoons blanched almonds or 1/4 cup ground almonds
1/2 cup chopped fresh coriander
1 tablespoon ghee or unsalted butter
1/2 cup warm water

1 Remove the skin from the chicken and lightly score the flesh criss-cross fashion.

2 To make the marinade: Dissolve the saffron in hot water and combine with the remaining ingredients. Use the marinade to coat the entire chicken, both inside and out. Place onto a rotisserie bar.

3 Heat the kettle barbecue to high, arrange the skewered chicken in place and roast for 20 minutes.

4 Lower the heat to medium and cook a further 30 minutes. Baste the chicken with the remaining marinade. Raise the heat and cook a final 10 minutes. Stand covered for 10 minutes before carving. Serve with salad and flat bread, chapatis or naan.

Chicken with Orange and Mustard Glaze

PREPARATION TIME:
15 MINUTES
COOKING TIME:
15 MINUTES
SERVES 8

8 chicken breast halves on the bone

salt and pepper, to taste

SAUCE
1/2 cup chicken stock
3/4 cup marmalade
1 tablespoon seeded mustard
1 tablespoon French mustard

1 Trim the chicken breasts and pat dry with absorbent paper. Season lightly with salt and pepper on both sides.

2 To make the sauce: Place all ingredients in a small pan and place on the barbecue flatplate to heat through.

3 Cook the chicken breasts over a hot, oiled flatplate for 10–15 minutes, brushing with a little sauce from time to time during the last 5 minutes of cooking.

4 Serve the remaining sauce with the cooked chicken.

Indonesian Chicken

PREPARATION TIME:
20 MINUTES +
1 HOUR
MARINATING
COOKING TIME:
45 MINUTES
SERVES 6–8

1.4-kg chicken

MARINADE
2 cloves garlic, crushed
1 medium onion, chopped
1 teaspoon chopped fresh ginger
3 red chillies, chopped
1 teaspoon turmeric
salt and pepper, to taste
1 teaspoon grated lemon rind
1 teaspoon ground coriander
1/2 cup coconut milk
4 lime leaves
1 tablespoon brown sugar
2 tablespoons white vinegar
1 1/2 cups coconut milk, extra
1 cup water

1 Split the chicken in half, through the breastbone and down the back and remove the backbone.

2 To make the marinade: Blend the garlic, onion, ginger, chillies, turmeric, salt, pepper, lemon rind, coriander and coconut milk. Marinate the chicken with the mixture for 1 hour and remove.

3 In a wok, heat the remaining marinade, lime leaves, brown sugar, vinegar, coconut milk and water. Cook for 2–3 minutes. Add the marinated chicken

and simmer for 15 minutes, basting while cooking. Turn over and cook another 15 minutes.

4 Remove the chicken from the wok. Place on a barbecue and cook until browned and firm to the touch.

5 Serve the remaining marinade as a sauce. Sprinkle with chopped coriander.

Chicken with Orange and Mustard Glaze (above). Indonesian Chicken

Southern-style Drumsticks

PREPARATION TIME: 15 MINUTES + 4 HOURS MARINATING **COOKING TIME:** 25 MINUTES SERVES 4	**8 drumsticks** **1/2 cup buttermilk** **2 cloves garlic, crushed** **1 teaspoon ground cumin** **1/4 teaspoon cayenne pepper** **1/4 teaspoon salt** **1/4 teaspoon black pepper** **2 cobs of corn, halved** **20 g butter** **4 drops Tabasco sauce**

1 Trim the chicken of excess fat and sinew.

2 Place the drumsticks in a shallow glass or ceramic dish. Combine the buttermilk, garlic, cumin, cayenne pepper, salt and black pepper and pour over the chicken. Cover with plastic wrap and refrigerate for 4 hours, turning occasionally. Drain the chicken.

3 Place drumsticks on a lightly oiled grill or flatplate. Grill on a medium heat for 25 minutes, turning occasionally, until the chicken is tender and cooked through. Serve immediately, with cooked corn cobs.

4 Cook the corn in a large pan of boiling water for 10 minutes. Drain and place on individual pieces of aluminium foil. Melt the butter; add Tabasco and brush liberally onto the corn. Wrap in foil and place on the barbecue for 10 minutes, turning occasionally.

Thai Thigh Fillets

PREPARATION TIME:
15 MINUTES +
1 HOUR
MARINATING
COOKING TIME:
12 MINUTES
SERVES 6

500 g skinless chicken thigh fillets

MARINADE
3 tablespoons pepper coriander paste (see note)
1 clove garlic, crushed
1/2 teaspoon turmeric
1/2 teaspoon chilli powder or to taste
1 tablespoon water
2 teaspoons chicken stock powder
1 tablespoon peanut oil

1 Cut each thigh in half, lightly score criss-cross and set aside.

2 To make the marinade: Combine all the ingredients, mix well and marinate chicken for 1 hour or longer in the refrigerator.

3 Heat the barbecue flatplate and place the chicken pieces on the flatplate, grilling them 6 minutes each side, or until done to your liking. Serve with salad.

Note: Pepper Coriander Paste: Pound, in a mortar and pestle, 3 tablespoons chopped fresh coriander, 2 cloves garlic and 1 teaspoon whole black peppercorns.

Opposite: Garlic Chicken (left). Chicken Koftas

Garlic Chicken

PREPARATION TIME:
10 MINUTES +
1 HOUR
MARINATING

COOKING TIME:
5–10 MINUTES

SERVES 8

8 chicken breast fillets
1/3 cup olive oil
6 cloves garlic, crushed
salt and pepper, to taste

1   Trim all visible fat from fillets; dry and score the smooth surface. In a baking dish, combine the oil, garlic and seasonings. Add fillets and spoon over the garlic oil. Cover and refrigerate overnight, or allow to marinate at room temperature for 1 hour.
2   Heat the barbecue grill plate and cook chicken over a medium heat until firm to the touch.

Chicken Koftas

PREPARATION TIME:
20 MINUTES

COOKING TIME:
8 MINUTES

SERVES 8

500 g minced chicken
1/4 teaspoon black pepper
1 tablespoon chopped fresh coriander
1 egg, lightly beaten
1 clove garlic, crushed
1 teaspoon salt
1 cup cornflake crumbs
2 teaspoons chilli sauce

1   Mix all ingredients together and form into eight long koftas on flat metal or bamboo skewers.
2   Place on a rack over heated barbecue. Cover and cook 8 minutes, turning frequently to avoid charring. Cook to golden brown and serve between hot split torpedo rolls with salad and a rich tomato sauce (see page 237).

Chicken in a Thyme Cream Sauce

PREPARATION TIME:
15 MINUTES
COOKING TIME:
10 MINUTES
SERVES 4

4 chicken breast fillets, about 200 g each

3 tablespoons plain flour

2 tablespoons olive oil

3 teaspoons chopped fresh lemon thyme

2 teaspoons dry sherry

1/3 cup cream

1 Trim the chicken fillets of any excess fat and sinew and toss in the flour.

2 Brush a preheated deep-sided chargrill pan with the olive oil. Cook the chicken fillets for about 5 minutes on each side, or until golden brown, then sprinkle with the lemon thyme. Turn the fillets over, brush with the sherry and pour over about half the cream. Cook for another 2–3 minutes before turning the fillets over again and drizzling with the remaining cream. Season to taste with salt and pepper and serve.

Chicken and Kidney Kebabs

PREPARATION TIME:
15 MINUTES +
20 MINUTES
MARINATING
COOKING TIME:
5–10 MINUTES
SERVES 4

200 g lamb kidneys
3 cloves garlic, finely chopped
2 bay leaves, torn into small pieces
3 tablespoons olive oil
300 g chicken breast fillets
150 g double smoked ham
2 small onions
2 tablespoons dry sherry

1   Place 8 bamboo skewers in water to soak. Trim the kidneys of any sinew or fat and cut into bite-sized pieces. Combine the garlic, bay leaves and olive oil. Add the kidneys, cover and marinate in the refrigerator for about 20 minutes.

2   Cut the chicken and ham into bite-sized pieces and the onions into small wedges.

3   Drain the kidneys and reserve the marinade. Thread the pieces of onion, kidney, chicken and ham alternately onto the bamboo skewers.

4   Lightly oil a preheated chargrill pan or barbecue grill or flatplate and cook the kebabs for about 5–10 minutes, brushing lightly with the reserved marinade and sherry as they cook and turning them regularly. When golden brown, remove from the hotplate and serve with rice or mashed potatoes.

Note: If you prefer, chicken livers may be used in place of the lamb kidneys.

Chicken with Couscous and Sweet Potato

PREPARATION TIME: 45 MINUTES
COOKING TIME: 55 MINUTES
SERVES 4

4 chicken breast fillets
2 cloves garlic, crushed
2 teaspoons olive oil
350 g sweet potatoes, peeled
 and cut into cubes
1 red onion, cut into wedges
1 small red capsicum, seeded
 and sliced
1 1/4 cups couscous
1 1/2 cups chicken stock
 or water
310 g can chickpeas, drained
 and rinsed
3 spring onions, finely
 chopped
2 tablespoons chopped
 fresh mint

HARISSA DRESSING
1/3 cup olive oil
2 tablespoons lime juice
2 teaspoons harissa
1 clove garlic, crushed

1 Trim the chicken of any excess fat and sinew and brush with the combined garlic and oil. Cover and refrigerate. Preheat the oven to moderately hot 190°C (375°F/Gas 5). Spread the sweet potato, onion and capsicum in a single layer in a baking dish and brush with a little olive oil. Bake for 45 minutes, stirring occasionally. Remove from the oven and keep warm.

2 To make the Harissa Dressing: Combine the dressing ingredients in a jar and shake well.

3 Place the couscous in a large bowl, boil the stock or water and then pour over. Allow to stand for 5 minutes, then stir in the chickpeas, spring onion and mint. Pour over half the dressing and stir until the couscous is an even colour.

4 Preheat a lightly oiled chargrill pan or barbecue grill or flatplate. Add the chicken and cook for 4–5 minutes each side, or until tender.

5 Cut each fillet into slices. Pile the couscous onto plates, top with the sweet potato mixture and drizzle with the remaining dressing. Arrange the chicken slices on top. Season to taste with salt and cracked pepper.

Mirin and Sake Chicken

PREPARATION TIME:
10 MINUTES +
15 MINUTES
MARINATING
COOKING TIME:
20 MINUTES
SERVES 4

4 large chicken breast fillets
2 tablespoons mirin
2 tablespoons sake
1 tablespoon oil
5 cm piece of fresh ginger, very finely sliced
3 teaspoons soy sauce

1   Trim the chicken of excess fat and sinew and place in a non-metallic dish. Combine the mirin, sake and oil and pour over the chicken. Refrigerate for 15 minutes, then drain, reserving the marinade.

2   Preheat a lightly oiled chargrill pan or barbecue grill or flatplate. Add the chicken and cook for about 5 minutes each side, or until golden brown and tender. Remove and keep warm. If you are using a chargrill pan with deep sides, add the ginger slices and cook until softened, pouring over the remaining marinade and boiling the mixture for about 7 minutes. Alternatively, cook the ginger in a pan on the stove top or barbecue.

3   Drizzle the soy sauce over the chicken and top with the ginger. Serve immediately.

Chicken Burger with Tarragon Mayonnaise

**PREPARATION
TIME:**
25 MINUTES
COOKING TIME:
20 MINUTES
SERVES 6

1 kg chicken mince
1 small onion, finely chopped
2 teaspoons lemon rind
2 tablespoons sour cream
1 cup fresh breadcrumbs
6 onion bread rolls

TARRAGON MAYONNAISE
1 egg yolk
1 tablespoon tarragon vinegar
1/2 teaspoon French mustard
1 cup olive oil
**salt and white pepper,
  to taste**

1 Prepare and heat the barbecue.

2 Place the chicken mince in a mixing bowl. Add the onion, rind, sour cream and breadcrumbs. Using your hands, mix until thoroughly combined. Divide the mixture into six equal portions and shape into 1.5-cm thick patties.

3 Place the patties on a hot lightly oiled barbecue grill or flatplate. Cook for 7 minutes each side, turning once. Serve on an onion roll with salad fillings and Tarragon Mayonnaise.

4 To make Tarragon Mayonnaise: Place egg yolk, half the vinegar and the mustard in a small mixing bowl. Whisk together for 1 minute until light and creamy. Add the oil about 1 teaspoon at a time, whisking constantly until the mixture thickens. Increase the flow of oil to a thin stream and continue whisking until all the oil has been incorporated. Stir in the remaining vinegar and salt and white pepper.

Chicken Breast with Flaming Sauce

PREPARATION TIME:
15 MINUTES

COOKING TIME:
12 MINUTES
SERVES 4

4 chicken breast fillets
chives, for garnish

SAUCE
3 medium-sized tomatoes, very ripe
2 teaspoons olive oil
1 small onion, chopped roughly
1 clove garlic, crushed
1 tablespoon paprika
1/2 teaspoon dried thyme
1 large red capsicum, seeded and sliced

1   Pour boiling water over the tomatoes, leave for 1 minute then plunge them into cold water. Remove skins and dice roughly.

2   Heat oil and cook the onion, covered, for 2–3 minutes. Add the garlic, paprika and thyme and cook a further 1 minute. Add the capsicum and tomatoes and cook for 10 minutes or until soft. Purée the mixture until smooth.

3   While the sauce is cooking, place the chicken on a preheated lightly greased barbecue grill. Cook for 6–8 minutes or until the chicken is just cooked, turning once. Serve the chicken breasts on top of the sauce and garnish each serve with a couple of whole chives.

Chicken Teriyaki

Serve these kebabs with steamed rice or Japanese-style egg noodles and stir-fried vegetables.

PREPARATION TIME:	**750 g chicken tenderloins**
20 MINUTES +	**1/4 cup soy sauce**
2 HOURS	**2 tablespoons mirin (optional)**
MARINATING	**2 tablespoons sherry**
COOKING TIME:	**2 tablespoons soft brown sugar**
6 MINUTES	**2 teaspoons grated fresh ginger**
MAKES 12	**2 tablespoons oil**

1   Trim the chicken of excess fat and sinew. Soak twelve bamboo skewers in water to prevent burning.
2   Place the chicken in a shallow glass or ceramic dish. Combine the soy sauce, mirin, sherry, brown sugar and ginger. Stir to dissolve the sugar, then pour over the chicken. Cover and refrigerate for up to 2 hours, turning occasionally. Drain and cut the tenderloins in half.
3   Thread the chicken onto skewers.
4   Brush the kebabs with oil and place on a lightly oiled grill or flatplate. Cook over medium high heat 6 minutes or until tender, turning and brushing with oil occasionally.

Cranberry Wings

These make a great entrée or snack to nibble on.

PREPARATION TIME:	**1.5 kg chicken wings**
20 MINUTES +	**freshly ground black pepper**
2 HOURS	**3/4 cup orange marmalade**
MARINATING	**1/2 cup bottled cranberry sauce**
COOKING TIME:	**1/2 cup spicy red barbecue**
30 MINUTES	**sauce**
SERVES 6	**1/3 cup white vinegar**

1   In a glass or ceramic container, combine the chicken wings, pepper, marmalade, cranberry sauce, barbecue sauce and vinegar. Stir to coat the chicken wings in the sauce mixture. Refrigerate, covered, for about 2 hours or leave overnight.
2   Barbecue the wings on a preheated lightly greased flatplate, turning them occasionally, for 15–20 minutes. Continue cooking, basting wings with the sauce mixture until cooked through and well glazed, about 10 minutes more.

Tarragon Lemon Chicken

Mix any selection of your favourite herbs and spices with the butter and use for basting. This chicken dish is delicious served hot or cold.

PREPARATION TIME:	**90 g unsalted butter**
20 MINUTES	**2 tablespoons finely chopped chives**
COOKING TIME:	**1 tablespoon finely chopped fresh coriander**
20 MINUTES	**1 tablespoon lemon juice**
SERVES 4	**1/2 teaspoon dried tarragon leaves**
	1/4 teaspoon paprika
	8 chicken thigh fillets
	freshly ground pepper

1   Place the butter in a small pan over a low heat, stirring until melted, and add the chives, coriander, lemon juice, tarragon and paprika.
2   Sprinkle the chicken with pepper. Barbecue over a medium low flame on a preheated lightly greased barbecue flatplate until tender and golden, turning and basting frequently with the butter mixture for about 15–20 minutes. Serve chicken with a seasonal salad and potatoes.

Chicken Teriyaki (above). Tarragon Lemon Chicken. Cranberry Wings

Honey Soy Chicken Drumsticks

Add a little chilli sauce for those who prefer it hotter. This is best cooked on a kettle barbecue.

PREPARATION TIME:
15 MINUTES +
1 HOUR
MARINATING
COOKING TIME:
25–30 MINUTES
SERVES 6

1/3 cup soy sauce
2 cloves garlic, crushed
1 small onion, grated
1/2 teaspoon white pepper
1 tablespoon honey
1/4 cup green ginger wine
12 chicken drumsticks

1 Combine the soy sauce, garlic, onion, pepper, honey and green ginger wine in a small pan, stir over a low heat until the honey softens and the ingredients are thoroughly mixed.

2 Remove the skin from the drumsticks and score through the flesh at 2-cm intervals. Pour the marinade over the prepared chicken and allow to marinate for 1 hour.

3 Remove the drumsticks from the marinade and barbecue over a preheated, oiled flatplate with the hood down for 20–25 minutes, turning occasionally until the chicken is tender and the juices are clear. Brush two or three times with the remaining marinade towards the end of cooking. Serve with salad.

Note: If using an open barbecue, allow extra time for cooking.

Lemon Honey Chicken

This recipe is best suited to a kettle barbecue. Try the cooked garlic cloves spread on crusty toast with a little olive oil, salt and pepper.

PREPARATION TIME:
10 MINUTES
COOKING TIME:
1 HOUR 30 MINUTES
SERVES 4–6

1.8-kg chicken
salt
1/2 teaspoon cracked pepper
1 whole bulb garlic
small bunch of fresh lemon thyme
1 teaspoon salt, extra
1 1/2 teaspoons grated lemon rind
1 teaspoon honey
2 tablespoons olive oil
20 g butter, melted

1 Light barbecue using 2-kg bag of heat beads and about eight firelighters. Allow 40 minutes for coals to be fully alight. Coals should be arranged either side of the grill, not directly underneath.

2 Remove giblets and any large fat deposits from chicken. Wipe chicken and pat dry with absorbent paper. Season cavity with salt and pepper, to taste.

3 Using a sharp knife, cut off the top of the garlic bulb. Push the whole bulb of garlic, unpeeled, and the bunch of lemon thyme into the cavity. Close the cavity with several toothpicks or a skewer.

4 Rub the skin with combined salt, rind, honey, oil and butter. Place on the barbecue over drip tray. Cook for 1 hour, brushing occasionally with oil mixture to keep the skin moist. Test if chicken is done by inserting a skewer into the thigh. If the juice runs clear the chicken is cooked.

5 Stand chicken away from the heat for 5–6 minutes before carving. Carefully separate garlic cloves and serve with the chicken.

Bacon-wrapped Chicken Parcels

PREPARATION TIME: 10 MINUTES
COOKING TIME: 10 MINUTES
SERVES 3

6 chicken breast fillets
2 tablespoons olive oil
2 tablespoons lime juice
1/4 teaspoon ground coriander
salt and freshly ground black
**   pepper, to taste**
1/3 cup fruit chutney
1/4 cup chopped pecan nuts
6 rashers bacon

1   Trim the chicken of excess fat and sinew and remove skin. Place the oil, juice, coriander, salt and pepper in a small bowl and mix well.

2   Using a sharp knife, cut a pocket in the thickest section of each fillet.

3   Combine the chutney and nuts in a small bowl. Spoon 1 tablespoon of chutney mixture into each chicken breast pocket.

4   Turn the tapered end of the fillets to the underside. Wrap a bacon rasher firmly around each fillet to enclose the filling. Secure bacon with a toothpick.

5   Place chicken parcels onto a lightly oiled grill or flatplate. Cook over a medium heat for 5 minutes each side or until well browned and cooked through, turning once.

6   Brush parcels with the lime juice mixture several times during cooking. Pour any leftover mixture over the cooked chicken just before serving.

Chicken Parcels with Honey Mustard Glaze

PREPARATION TIME:
35 MINUTES
COOKING TIME:
20–25 MINUTES
SERVES 6–8

8 chicken thigh fillets
16 pitted prunes
8 spring onions, halved
2 tablespoons flaked almonds
4 rashers rindless bacon, halved lengthways

HONEY MUSTARD GLAZE
1 tablespoon brown sugar
1 tablespoon Dijon mustard
1 tablespoon honey
15 g butter, melted
freshly ground black pepper

1 Open out each thigh fillet and place 2 prunes, 2 pieces of spring onion and a few flaked almonds on each one.
2 Roll up the fillets, wrap a piece of bacon around each one and secure with toothpicks.
3 Barbecue on a preheated lightly greased barbecue flatplate or grill until cooked, about 20 minutes. Baste frequently with glaze.
4 To prepare Honey Mustard Glaze: Blend all ingredients together in a small bowl.

Smoked Chicken Fillets

This is a dish just made for a Weber (or kettle) barbecue. Serve it with chilli noodles.

PREPARATION TIME:
5 MINUTES
COOKING TIME:
25 MINUTES
SERVES 4

4 chicken breast fillets
1 tablespoon olive oil
seasoned pepper, to taste
hickory or mesquite chips, for smoking

1 Prepare the Weber (kettle) barbecue for indirect cooking at moderate heat (normal fire). Trim the chicken of excess fat and sinew.
2 Brush the chicken with oil and sprinkle over the seasoned pepper.
3 Spoon a pile of smoking chips (about 25) over the coals in each charcoal rail.
4 Cover the barbecue and cook the chicken for 15 minutes. Test with a sharp knife. If the juices do not run clear, cook another 5–10 minutes until cooked.

Note: Chicken is best smoked just before serving.

Chicken Burger with Tangy Garlic Mayonnaise

PREPARATION TIME:
20 MINUTES +
3 HOURS MARINATING
COOKING TIME: 15 MINUTES
SERVES 4

4 chicken breast fillets
1/2 cup lime juice
1 tablespoon sweet chilli
   sauce
4 bacon rashers
4 hamburger buns
4 lettuce leaves
1 large tomato, sliced

GARLIC MAYONNAISE
2 egg yolks
2 cloves garlic, crushed
1 tablespoon Dijon mustard
1 tablespoon lemon juice
1/2 cup olive oil

1   Place the chicken in a shallow, non-metal dish and prick the chicken breasts with a skewer several times.

2   Combine the lime juice and chilli sauce in a jug. Pour over the chicken and cover. Marinate for 3 hours or overnight.

3   Prepare and light the barbecue 1 hour before cooking. Remove and discard the rind from the bacon, cut the bacon in half crossways.

4   Place the chicken and bacon on a hot lightly greased barbecue grill or flatplate. Cook the bacon 5 minutes or until crisp. Cook the chicken another 5–10 minutes until well browned and cooked through, turning once.

5   Cut the hamburger buns in half and toast each side until lightly browned. Top the bases with lettuce, tomato, chicken and bacon. Top with Garlic Mayonnaise and finish with the remaining bun top.

6   To make Garlic Mayonnaise: Place the egg yolks, garlic, mustard and lemon juice in a food processor bowl or blender. Process until smooth. With the motor constantly running, add the oil in a thin, steady stream. Process until the mayonnaise reaches a thick consistency. Refrigerate, covered, until required.

Chicken with Orange-Chive Butter

PREPARATION TIME:
20 MINUTES +
2 HOURS
MARINATING

COOKING TIME:
20 MINUTES
SERVES 4

8 chicken thighs
1/2 cup orange juice
1 teaspoon ground black pepper
2 teaspoons sesame oil

ORANGE-CHIVE BUTTER
100 g butter
1 teaspoon finely grated orange rind
1 tablespoon finely chopped chives
1 tablespoon orange marmalade
salt, to taste

1 Trim the chicken meat of excess fat and sinew.
2 Place the chicken in a shallow glass or ceramic dish.
3 Combine juice, pepper and oil in a small jug and pour over chicken. Cover with plastic wrap and refrigerate for 2 hours, turning occasionally. Drain chicken and reserve marinade. Place chicken on a preheated lightly greased barbecue grill or flatplate and cook for 10 minutes each side, brushing occasionally with reserved marinade. Serve immediately with slices of Orange-Chive Butter.
4 To make Orange-Chive Butter: Allow the butter to soften slightly at room temperature. Place in a small mixing bowl and beat with a wooden spoon for 1 minute until creamy. Add the remaining ingredients and mix until well combined.
5 Place the butter on a sheet of plastic wrap and form into a log shape. Roll up tightly and refrigerate until required. Serve sliced.

Chicken Kebabs with Curry Mayonnaise

Serve these kebabs with rice and fried pappadums, or wrapped in sheets of Lebanese bread.

PREPARATION TIME: 25 MINUTES + 30 MINUTES MARINATING
COOKING TIME: 10 MINUTES
SERVES 4

600 g chicken breast fillets
4 large spring onions
1 small red capsicum
1 small green capsicum
1/4 cup olive oil
1 teaspoon freshly ground black pepper
1/2 teaspoon ground turmeric
1 1/2 teaspoons ground coriander

CURRY MAYONNAISE
3/4 cup whole egg mayonnaise
1 tablespoon hot curry powder
1/4 cup sour cream
1 tablespoon sweet fruit or mango chutney, mashed
1/4 cup finely chopped, peeled cucumber
1/2 teaspoon toasted cumin seeds
1 tablespoon finely chopped fresh mint
1 teaspoon finely chopped fresh mint, extra

1   Prepare and heat the barbecue. Trim chicken of excess fat and sinew. Cut chicken into 3-cm cubes.
2   Trim the spring onions, cut white stems and the thicker parts of green stems into 3-cm lengths; discard tops. Cut the red and green capsicum into 3-cm squares.
3   Thread the chicken, spring onions and red and green capsicum onto skewers, using at least two pieces of each. Arrange the kebabs, side by side, in a shallow, non-metal dish. Combine the oil, pepper, turmeric and coriander in a jug. Pour over the kebabs and set aside for 30 minutes at room temperature.
4   To make Curry Mayonnaise: Combine the mayonnaise, curry powder, sour cream, chutney, cucumber, cumin seeds and mint in a bowl and mix well. Spoon into a dish or jug for serving. Sprinkle mayonnaise with extra chopped mint.
5   Place kebabs on a hot lightly oiled barbecue grill or flatplate. Cook for 2–3 minutes each side or until cooked through and tender. Serve Curry Mayonnaise separately.

1   Secure skin of drumsticks to joint with toothpicks.
2   Make three deep cuts into the thickest section of the drumstick.
3   Combine the curry paste, lime rind and juice, coconut cream, honey and salt in a large bowl. Add the chicken and mix to coat well. Store, covered, in refrigerator 3 hours or overnight, stirring occasionally. Drain; reserve the marinade.
4   Place drumsticks on a preheated lightly greased barbecue grill or flatplate. Cook for 8 minutes each side or until cooked through, brushing occasionally with reserved marinade. Discard the toothpicks.
5   Combine the coconut and extra lime rind, sprinkle over the chicken. Serve hot.

Curry, Coconut and Lime Drumsticks

A deliciously different way to serve a barbecue favourite. Serve as an entrée, or try them with jasmine rice.

PREPARATION TIME:	8 chicken drumsticks
10 MINUTES + 3 HOURS MARINATING	6 teaspoons curry paste
	1 teaspoon grated lime rind
	2 tablespoons lime juice
COOKING TIME:	2/3 cup coconut cream
16 MINUTES	3 teaspoons honey
SERVES 4	salt, to taste
	2 tablespoons desiccated coconut
	3 teaspoons grated lime rind, extra

Chilli Chicken with Salsa

Salsa can be made a day ahead and stored in the refrigerator. Serve it at room temperature.

PREPARATION TIME:
10 MINUTES +
3 HOURS
MARINATING
COOKING TIME:
10 MINUTES
SERVES 4

8 chicken thigh cutlets
1/2 cup lemon juice
1/2 teaspoon bottled crushed chilli
2 tablespoons oil
2 teaspoons sesame oil
2 tablespoons soy sauce
2 tablespoons honey
1 clove garlic, crushed
2 spring onions, chopped
2 tablespoons finely chopped fresh coriander
salt, to taste

SALSA
1 small green cucumber, chopped
1 small red onion, finely chopped
1 medium tomato, chopped
2 tablespoons olive oil
1 tablespoon white wine vinegar
1/4 teaspoon caster sugar
1/4 cup fresh coriander leaves

1 Trim the chicken of excess fat and sinew.
2 Combine the juice, chilli, oils, soy sauce, honey, garlic, spring onions, coriander and salt in a large bowl and mix well.
3 Add the chicken and stir to combine. Cover with plastic wrap. Refrigerate for 3 hours or overnight, stirring occasionally.
4 Drain chicken and reserve the marinade. Place chicken on lightly oiled grill or flatplate. Cook over medium heat for 5 minutes each side or until tender and cooked through. Brush with the reserved marinade in the last minutes of cooking. Serve hot with Salsa.
5 To make Salsa: Combine all ingredients in a bowl and mix well.

Tandoori Chicken on Skewers

Drumsticks can also be marinated in tandoori mixture. Cook whole, as directed, turning often.

PREPARATION TIME:
15 MINUTES +
3 HOURS
MARINATING
COOKING TIME:
8 MINUTES
MAKES ABOUT 16

6 single chicken breast fillets
2 teaspoons turmeric
1 teaspoon sweet paprika
1 teaspoon garam masala
1/2 teaspoon ground cardamom
1 teaspoon ground coriander
1 small onion, grated
1 clove garlic, crushed
2 teaspoons lemon juice
2 teaspoons sugar
salt, to taste
1 cup plain yoghurt
red food colouring (optional)

1 Soak bamboo skewers for several hours in water. Trim the chicken of excess fat and sinew.
2 Combine the turmeric, paprika, garam masala, cardamom, coriander, onion, garlic, lemon juice, sugar, salt and yoghurt in a large mixing bowl and mix until well combined, stirring in a few drops of red food colouring if desired.
3 Cut chicken fillets into long strips, 2 cm wide. Add to the marinade and mix until chicken is well coated. Store, covered with plastic wrap, in the refrigerator for 3 hours or overnight, stirring occasionally. Drain and reserve marinade.
4 Thread the chicken onto skewers. Place skewers on lightly greased grill or flatplate. Cook over medium high heat 8 minutes or until tender and well browned, turning often and brushing with reserved marinade several times during cooking.

Tandoori Chicken on Skewers (above). Chilli Chicken with Salsa

Honey-glazed Chicken Breasts

For a distinctive taste to this dish, use honeys with a strong, dark flavour, such as leatherwood, lavender or rosemary.

PREPARATION TIME: 6 MINUTES + 20 MINUTES MARINATING
COOKING TIME: 10 MINUTES
SERVES 6

6 chicken breast fillets
50 g butter, softened
1/4 cup honey
1/4 cup barbecue sauce
2 teaspoons seeded mustard

1 Trim the chicken of excess fat and sinew and remove the skin.
2 Use a sharp knife to make three or four diagonal slashes across one side of each chicken breast. Prepare and heat barbecue.
3 Combine the butter, honey, barbecue sauce and mustard in a small bowl. Spread half of the marinade thickly over the slashed side of the chicken and cover. Set the remaining marinade aside. Stand the chicken at room temperature for 20 minutes.
4 Place the chicken breasts, slashed-side up, on a hot lightly greased grill or flatplate. Cook for 2–3 minutes each side or until tender. Brush with the reserved marinade several times during cooking. Serve hot with buttered ribbon noodles.

Chicken Fajitas

Tomato salsa is available from supermarkets.

PREPARATION TIME:
35 MINUTES +
3 HOURS
MARINATING
COOKING TIME:
10 MINUTES
SERVES 4

4 chicken breast fillets
2 tablespoons olive oil
1/4 cup lime juice
2 cloves garlic, crushed
1 teaspoon ground cumin
1/4 cup chopped fresh coriander leaves
8 flour tortillas
1 tablespoon olive oil, extra
2 medium onions, sliced
2 medium green capsicums, cut into thin strips
1 cup grated cheddar cheese
1 large avocado, sliced
1 cup bottled tomato salsa

1 Trim the chicken of fat and sinew and cut it into thin strips. Place in a shallow non-metal dish.

2 Combine the oil, juice, garlic, cumin and coriander in a jug and mix well. Pour over the chicken. Store, covered, in the refrigerator for several hours or overnight. Prepare and heat barbecue 1 hour before cooking.

3 Wrap the tortillas in foil and place on a cool part of the barbecue grill for 10 minutes to warm through. Heat the oil on a flatplate. Cook the onion and capsicum for 5 minutes or until soft. Push over to a cooler part of the plate to keep warm.

4 Place the chicken and marinade on the plate and cook 5 minutes until just tender. Transfer the chicken, vegetables and wrapped tortillas to a serving platter. Make up individual fajitas by placing chicken, cooked onion and capsicum, grated cheese and avocado over flat tortillas. Top with salsa. Roll up to enclose filling.

Chicken Cutlets with Corn Relish

PREPARATION TIME: 20 MINUTES
COOKING TIME: 25 MINUTES
SERVES 4

8 chicken thigh cutlets, with skin on
1 tablespoon olive oil
1 small clove garlic, crushed
1/4 teaspoon ground turmeric
1/2 teaspoon salt

CORN RELISH
1 cup frozen or canned corn kernels
1 tablespoon olive oil
1 red chilli, seeded and chopped

1 small green capsicum, finely chopped
1 medium onion, finely chopped
1/3 cup white vinegar
1/4 cup sugar
1 teaspoon seeded mustard
1/2 cup water
3 teaspoons cornflour
1 teaspoon paprika
1 teaspoon finely chopped fresh coriander leaves
1 tablespoon olive oil, extra

1   Prepare and heat the barbecue. Trim the chicken of excess fat and sinew.

2   Prick the skin of the cutlets with the point of a knife. Place the cutlets in a large frying pan of boiling water. Reduce heat and simmer for 5 minutes. Remove from pan and drain. Cool. Combine the olive oil, garlic, turmeric and salt and rub over the skin side of the cutlets. Set aside.

3   To make Corn Relish: Cook corn in a pan of boiling water for 2–3 minutes or until tender; drain. (If using canned corn, drain, but do not cook.) Heat oil in a medium pan. Add the chilli, capsicum and onion. Cook over a medium heat until tender. Add the corn, vinegar, sugar and mustard, and cook, stirring, a further 5 minutes. Add blended water and cornflour. Bring to the boil, reduce heat and stir until thickened. Stir in the paprika, coriander and remaining extra oil. Remove from heat; cool.

4   Place the cutlets, skin-side up, on a hot lightly greased barbecue grill or flatplate. Cook for 2 minutes; turn and cook skin-side down for 4 minutes. Continue cooking another 5–10 minutes, turning frequently, until the chicken is well browned and cooked through. Serve with Corn Relish.

1   Prepare and heat the Weber (kettle) barbecue for indirect cooking. Place the drip tray underneath top grill.

2   Remove giblets and any large deposits of fat from the chicken. Wipe and pat dry chicken with absorbent paper.

3   Pour boiling water over couscous and set aside for 15 minutes for couscous to swell and soften. Soak the dates and apricots in lime juice; set aside.

4   Heat the oil and butter in pan, add onion and garlic; cook 3–4 minutes until translucent. Remove from heat and add the couscous and soaked dried fruit, salt, pepper, coriander and parsley. Mix well. Spoon the stuffing into the chicken cavity and close with toothpicks or a skewer. Tie the legs together with string.

5   Rub chicken skin all over with combined salt, pepper, cumin and extra oil. Place the chicken in the centre of a large piece of greased foil. Gather the edges of the foil and wrap them securely.

6   Place the parcel on a barbecue grill over the drip tray. Cover the barbecue and cook for 50 minutes. Open the foil, crimping the edges to form a tray to retain most of the cooking liquids. Cook a further 20 minutes or until tender and golden. Remove from heat and stand 5–6 minutes before carving.

Middle Eastern Baked Chicken

PREPARATION TIME:
30 MINUTES
COOKING TIME:
1 HOUR 15 MINUTES
SERVES 6

1.6-kg chicken
1/2 cup boiling water
1/2 cup instant couscous
4 pitted dates, chopped
4 dried apricots, chopped
1 tablespoon lime juice
1 tablespoon olive oil
20 g butter
1 medium onion, chopped
1–2 cloves garlic, chopped
1 teaspoon salt
1/4 teaspoon cracked black pepper
1 teaspoon ground coriander
2 tablespoons chopped parsley
salt and pepper, extra
1 teaspoon ground cumin
1 tablespoon olive oil, extra

Buffalo Chicken Wings with Ranch Dressing

A taste of the Wild West in your own backyard.

PREPARATION TIME: 25 MINUTES + 3 HOURS MARINATING
COOKING TIME: 10 MINUTES
SERVES 4

8 large chicken wings
2 teaspoons black pepper
2 teaspoons garlic salt
2 teaspoons onion powder
olive oil, for deep frying
1/2 cup tomato sauce
2 tablespoons Worcestershire
  sauce
20 g butter, melted
2 teaspoons sugar
Tabasco sauce, to taste

RANCH DRESSING
1/2 cup whole egg mayonnaise
1/2 cup sour cream
2 tablespoons lemon juice
2 tablespoons chopped chives
salt and white pepper, to taste

1 Wash the wings thoroughly and pat dry with absorbent paper. Cut the tips off each wing and discard. Bend each wing back to snap the joint and cut through to create two pieces.

2 Combine the pepper, garlic salt and onion powder. Using your fingers, rub mixture into each piece.

3 Heat oil to moderately hot in a deep heavy-based pan. Cook the chicken pieces in batches for 2 minutes. Remove with tongs or slotted spoon and drain on absorbent paper.

4 Transfer the chicken to a non-metal bowl or shallow dish. Combine the sauces, butter, sugar and Tabasco and pour over the chicken and stir to coat. Refrigerate, covered, for several hours or overnight. Prepare and heat the barbecue 1 hour before cooking.

5 Place the chicken on a hot lightly oiled barbecue grill or flatplate. Cook for 5 minutes, turning and brushing with marinade. Serve with Ranch Dressing.

6 To make Ranch Dressing: Combine the mayonnaise, cream, juice, chives, salt and pepper in a bowl and mix well.

Thai Chicken Cutlets

PREPARATION TIME: 20 MINUTES +
1 HOUR MARINATING
COOKING TIME: 20 MINUTES
SERVES 4–6

12 chicken thigh fillets
6 cloves garlic
1 teaspoon black peppercorns
3 coriander roots and stems,
 roughly chopped
1/4 teaspoon salt

CHILLI GARLIC DIP
4–5 dried red chillies
2 large cloves garlic, chopped
1/4 cup sugar
1/3 cup cider or rice vinegar
pinch salt
1/4 cup boiling water

1 Prepare and heat the barbecue. Trim the chicken of excess fat and sinew.

2 Place the garlic, peppercorns, coriander and salt in a food processor bowl. Process for 20–30 seconds or until the mixture forms a smooth paste. Place the chicken in a shallow non-metal dish. Spread with the garlic mixture. Stand the chicken at room temperature for 1 hour.

3 To make Chilli Garlic Dip: Soak the chillies in hot water for 20 minutes. Drain and chop finely. Place in a mortar with the garlic and sugar. Grind to a smooth paste. Place mixture in a small pan. Add the vinegar, salt and water. Bring to boil, reduce heat and simmer for 2–3 minutes. Allow to cool.

4 Barbecue the chicken on hot greased grill or flatplate 5–10 minutes each side, turning once. Serve with Chilli Garlic Dip.

119

Citrus Chicken Drumsticks

This is a refreshing, tangy dish.

PREPARATION TIME:
20 MINUTES +
3 HOURS
MARINATING
COOKING TIME:
20 MINUTES
SERVES 4

8 chicken drumsticks
1/3 cup orange juice
1/3 cup lemon juice
1 teaspoon grated orange rind
1 teaspoon grated lemon rind
1 teaspoon sesame oil
1 tablespoon olive oil
1 spring onion, finely chopped

1 Wash the drumsticks and pat dry with absorbent paper. Trim any excess fat and score the thickest part of chicken with a knife. Place in a shallow non-metal dish.

2 Combine the juices, rinds, oils and spring onion in a jug and pour over the chicken. Store, covered with plastic wrap, in the refrigerator for several hours or overnight, turning occasionally. Drain the chicken and reserve the marinade. Prepare and heat the barbecue 1 hour before cooking.

3 Cook the drumsticks on a hot lightly oiled barbecue grill or flatplate for 15–20 minutes or until tender. Brush occasionally with the reserved marinade. Serve immediately.

Tandoori Weber Chicken

Tandoori chicken requires a slow heat. Do not place chicken on the barbecue while the fire is still very hot.

PREPARATION TIME:
15 MINUTES +
4 HOURS
MARINATING
COOKING TIME:
1 HOUR
SERVES 4

4 chicken marylands (drumstick and thigh), skin removed
1 teaspoon salt
2 cloves garlic, crushed
1 tablespoon lemon juice
1 cup plain yoghurt
1 1/2 teaspoons garam masala
1/2 teaspoon ground black pepper
1/2 teaspoon ground turmeric
2–3 drops red food colouring
20–30 mesquite or hickory chips, for smoking
olive oil, for basting

1 Place the marylands in a non-metal dish; rub them with salt and garlic.

2 Combine the lemon juice, yoghurt, garam masala, pepper and turmeric in a jug. Add food colouring to make the marinade a bright orange-red colour. Pour over the chicken, and coat evenly with the back of a spoon. Cover and set aside for 4 hours, turning the chicken every hour and redistributing the marinade. During the last hour of marinating, heat and prepare Weber (kettle) barbecue for indirect cooking.

3 When the barbecue coals are covered with fine white ash, add mesquite or hickory chips to coals. Cover the barbecue and leave until the smoke is well established (about 5 minutes).

4 Brush the barbecue grill with oil. Arrange the marylands on the grill and put the lid on the barbecue. Smoke-cook for 45 minutes–1 hour or until the chicken is well crisped. Brush chicken with oil several times during cooking. Serve with side salad and onion rings.

Citrus Chicken Drumsticks (above). Tandoori Weber Chicken

Spiced Chicken

PREPARATION TIME:
20 MINUTES +
1 HOUR
MARINATING
COOKING TIME:
10 MINUTES
SERVES 6

1/4 teaspoon black pepper
1 tablespoon chopped fresh coriander
1 clove garlic, crushed
1 teaspoon grated fresh ginger
2 teaspoons curry powder
1/4 teaspoon citric acid
1/4 cup water
2 teaspoons chicken stock powder
1 tablespoon peanut oil
1/4 teaspoon salt
1 teaspoon garam masala
500 g skinless chicken thigh fillets

1 Mix together the pepper, coriander, garlic, ginger, curry powder, citric acid, water, chicken stock powder, peanut oil, salt and garam masala.

2 Lightly score the chicken, in criss-cross fashion. Place the chicken fillets in the marinade and marinate for about 1 hour or refrigerate overnight.

3 Preheat the barbecue and cook the chicken for 10 minutes over medium heat turning once, until the chicken is done. Eat with steamed rice or flat bread and a salad.

Seafood

*t*here are numerous delicious ways to barbecue seafood. Depending on the variety and size, it may be wrapped in foil and char-grilled, cooked in a fish basket, marinated and tossed on the barbecue or skewered as kebabs. Remember, though, that seafood should not be marinated for longer than an hour, otherwise the flesh may become 'powdery'. If the marinade is acidic, for example, if it is based on lemon juice or wine, marinate the seafood for no longer than half an hour.

When barbecuing fish on an electric or gas barbecue, a medium high heat is required. Always remember that cooking times are approximate, so use your judgement. Be careful to avoid burning fish. Overcooking shellfish will cause it to shrink and toughen. If you are cooking over an open charcoal grill, cook over glowing coals, not over flames, and grease the barbecue plate before cooking, so that the seafood doesn't stick.

No matter the type of seafood you're after, one rule always applies: buy from a reputable fishmonger. If it's busy all the time, it's a good indication that the stock is turning over regularly. Stay away from the store which has strong fishy odours, as opposed to a fresh, seaside fragrance. When purchasing whole fish, look for bright and bulging eyes. The flesh should be firm and gills bright pink. Ask the fish shop to gut and scale the fish you have selected.

Purchasing fillets can be a little tricky. Often shops fillet fish left over from the previous day. Look for fillets which are shiny and firm with a good shape and not discoloured. If you're not happy with the fillets on display, ask them to fillet the fish you choose. The head and bones can be used for stock, which can be frozen.

Shellfish should have no discolouration around the joint and be firmly closed. Shells should be lustrous and not broken in any way. They should smell of the sea.

Seafood Kebabs

Serve these delicious Seafood Kebabs with a variety of salads and crusty bread.

PREPARATION TIME:
15 MINUTES +
15 MINUTES MARINATING

COOKING TIME:
7 MINUTES

SERVES 6–8

750 g firm white fish fillets
18 large green prawns
18 scallops
1 red capsicum
1 green capsicum
1 yellow capsicum

MARINADE
3 tablespoons olive oil
3 tablespoons lemon juice
2 teaspoons chopped fresh dill
1/2 teaspoon salt
1/2 teaspoon white pepper
lemon wedges, to serve

1 Remove skin from the fillets if necessary. Cut into 3-cm square pieces. Peel and devein the prawns. Cut the red, green and yellow capsicum into pieces the same size as the fish. Place prepared ingredients in a bowl.

2 To make the marinade: Combine all the ingredients. Pour over the fish and turn to coat. Allow to marinate for 15 minutes.

3 Thread the ingredients alternately onto soaked bamboo skewers or metal skewers.

4 Cook kebabs on a preheated oiled flatplate until fish turns white and prawns are pink and opaque. Serve immediately with lemon wedges and a tartare sauce.

Note: Soaking the bamboo skewers is a must when barbecuing. The longer they soak, the less they'll burn. Wrap foil around the exposed end to prevent scorching. If using metal skewers it may be necessary to reduce the cooking time slightly. To make a quick Tartare Sauce: Add ¼ cup chopped gherkins, 1 tablespoon chopped capers, 2 tablespoons chopped red capsicum and 2 tablespoons chopped parsley to 1½ cups mayonnaise; mix well. Serve with hot or cold seafoods.

Seafood Kebabs (above). Tandoori Prawns

Tandoori Prawns

Although this recipe is not cooked in a tandoor oven, you will be more than happy with the result.

PREPARATION TIME:
20 MINUTES +
15 MINUTES MARINATING

COOKING TIME:
5 MINUTES

SERVES 6 AS ENTREE, 3–4 AS MAIN MEAL

24 large green prawns
1/2 cup plain yoghurt
1/3 cup finely chopped fresh coriander leaves
2 tablespoons finely chopped mint leaves
salt, to taste
1 tablespoon chopped fresh ginger
2 cloves garlic, crushed
1 teaspoon chilli powder
1 teaspoon turmeric
1 teaspoon ground coriander
1 teaspoon garam masala
few drops bright red food colouring (optional)
2 lemons, cut into wedges, to serve

1 Shell and devein the prawns, leaving only the tail on. Rinse and pat dry.

2 Combine yoghurt with fresh coriander, mint and salt. Pour over the prawns and leave for 5 minutes.

3 Mix together the remaining ingredients and use to marinate the prawns for 10 minutes.

4 Thread the prawns onto metal skewers and cook on elevated charcoal grill for about 5 minutes. Turn the skewers so the prawns cook evenly. Prawns are ready when they start to curl and turn opaque. Serve with lemon wedges.

Note: Complement this dish with a tomato onion sambal. Finely chop one medium tomato that has been peeled and seeded, combine with one small finely chopped white or purple onion. Add some lime or lemon juice to moisten. Or try the following cool Cucumber and Yoghurt Sauce: Peel a large cucumber, cut in half and scoop out the seeds. Finely chop cucumber flesh, sprinkle with a little salt and stand for 5–6 minutes. Drain off the accumulated liquid. Add cucumber to ½ cup plain yoghurt and two teaspoons chopped mint.

Blackened Fish Fillets

For the best results when barbecuing, choose firm white fish fillets which are an even thickness of about 1 cm.

PREPARATION TIME:
10 MINUTES + 30 MINUTES MARINATING
COOKING TIME:
5 MINUTES
SERVES 4

4 medium firm white fish fillets

SEASONING MIXTURE
2 tablespoons ground black pepper
3 teaspoons garlic powder
3 teaspoons onion powder
1 tablespoon dried thyme
1 teaspoon salt
3 teaspoons hot chilli powder
1 tablespoon plain flour
2 teaspoons ground dried oregano
Tabasco sauce to taste
1/4 cup olive oil or ghee

1   Pat fish fillets dry with absorbent paper. To make the seasoning mixture: Combine all ingredients and use to coat fish. Allow to stand for 30 minutes.

2   Heat flatplate of open barbecue. Spread the surface with olive oil or ghee.

3   Cook fillets approximately 4–5 minutes each side, turning only once.

Barbecued Lobster

This is probably one of the most expensive recipes in the book but one of the most enjoyable.

PREPARATION TIME:
20 MINUTES
COOKING TIME:
5 MINUTES
SERVES 6–8

6 small green lobster tails
3 tablespoons olive oil
salt, to taste
3 tablespoons lemon juice
1 tablespoon chopped fresh dill
ground pepper, to taste
lemon wedges, to serve

1   Cut the lobster tails in half lengthwise and slit the underside of the tails with the point of a sharp knife to allow access to the flesh. Combine the olive oil, salt, lemon juice, dill and pepper to taste.

2   Brush the marinade onto the lobster flesh. (Retain the shell to protect the delicate flesh from intense heat.)

3   Barbecue the lobster on a preheated and oiled flatplate. First turn the cut side down to seal, just for a few seconds. Then use tongs to turn the pieces over and cook covered for 5 minutes or until the shells turn pink. Serve lobster with lemon wedges, a lemony mayonnaise and a tossed green salad.

Chilli Scallop and Prawn Kebabs

If you are not too sure about your chilli tolerance, reduce the chilli bean sauce.

PREPARATION TIME:
20 MINUTES + 10 MINUTES MARINATING
COOKING TIME:
8 MINUTES
SERVES 6–8

1 clove garlic, crushed
1 tablespoon grated fresh ginger
2 teaspoons sesame oil
1 tablespoon oriental chilli bean sauce (see note)
1 tablespoon soy sauce
2 teaspoons tomato paste
1 tablespoon sugar
1 tablespoon lemon juice
1 kg large green prawns
250 g scallops

1   Combine the crushed garlic, ginger, sesame oil, chilli bean sauce, soy sauce, tomato paste, sugar and lemon juice.

2   Peel prawns and devein, leaving tails on. Clean the scallops. Add prawns and scallops to the marinade. Cover and marinate for 10–15 minutes.

3   Skewer prawns and scallops on flat metal skewers.

4   Cook on a preheated lightly oiled barbecue flatplate or grill plate for 4 minutes each side. Baste with the remaining marinade during cooking. Serve with rice.

Note: Chilli bean sauce is an oil-based soya bean, garlic and extra hot chilli paste. Use with caution. Available from Chinese and Asian food outlets.

Barbecued Lobster (above). Blackened Fish Fillets (right). Chilli Scallop and Prawn Kebabs

Moroccan Fish with Fresh Tomato Sauce

This type of tomato sauce, called 'Salsa', makes a very good quick sauce for grilled or fried fish.

PREPARATION TIME: 30 MINUTES + 3 HOURS STANDING
COOKING TIME: 5–10 MINUTES
SERVES 6

750 g white fish fillets, skinned
1 medium red onion, peeled and finely chopped
1 clove garlic, crushed
2 tablespoons chopped fresh coriander
1/3 cup chopped flat-leaved parsley
1/2 teaspoon ground sweet paprika
1/4 teaspoon chilli powder
1/3 cup olive oil
2 tablespoons lemon juice

TOMATO SAUCE
4 large, red, ripe tomatoes, peeled, seeded and chopped
2 small red chillies, cut in half, seeded and finely sliced
4 spring onions, including some green, finely sliced
1/2 bunch fresh coriander, chopped finely
1/2 cup olive oil, extra virgin
ground pepper
lemon or lime juice (optional)
1 red onion, finely chopped (optional)

1 Cut fish across grain into 2-cm squares. Combine onion, garlic, coriander, parsley, paprika, chilli powder, olive oil and lemon juice and spoon over fish cubes. Mix well and leave to marinate for at least 2 hours or overnight.
2 Place fish on metal skewers and barbecue, turning frequently, until lightly browned on all sides.

3 To make Tomato Sauce: Combine tomatoes, chillies, spring onions and coriander in a bowl, add olive oil and pepper to taste.
4 Add lemon or lime juice and chopped onion if using.
5 Allow the Tomato Sauce to stand for at least an hour in the refrigerator before serving with fish.

Barbecued Scallops

Serve with steamed rice and accompany with a little chilli sauce if desired.

PREPARATION TIME:
15 MINUTES +
15 MINUTES
MARINATING
COOKING TIME:
5 MINUTES
SERVES 4–6

500 g scallops
2 tablespoons olive oil
1 clove garlic, crushed
2 spring onions, finely shredded
salt and pepper, to taste

1 Rinse the scallops, removing any visible veins or dirt. Mix together the remaining ingredients and stir in the scallops. Marinate for 15 minutes in the refrigerator.

2 Cook over a moderately hot flatplate, or at the edge of the barbecue where the heat is not too fierce, until they turn white. Do not overcook or they will toughen.

Note: Scallops require a short cooking time. They can easily become tough and rubbery with excess cooking so wait until your guests are ready before you cook them. If you are using scallops which have been frozen, allow them to defrost completely in the refrigerator and drain well before marinating.

Citrus Fish with Avocado Salsa

PREPARATION TIME:
20 MINUTES
COOKING TIME:
10 MINUTES
SERVES 4

3 teaspoons finely grated orange rind

3 teaspoons finely grated lemon rind

1 tablespoon lime juice

2 tablespoons olive oil

4 firm white fish cutlets, about 185 g each

AVOCADO SALSA

1 1/2 teaspoons ground cumin

1 large avocado, finely chopped

1 red onion, very finely chopped

1 small red chilli, seeds removed and finely chopped

2 teaspoons lemon juice

2 teaspoons olive oil

1   Combine the orange and lemon rind, lime juice and olive oil and season with freshly ground black pepper. Pour over the fish and set aside to marinate for about 5 minutes.

2   Lightly oil a preheated chargrill pan or barbecue grill or flatplate and cook the fish for 3–5 minutes on each side, or until just tender.

3   To make the Avocado Salsa: Dry-fry the cumin in the chargrill pan or a frying pan for about 40 seconds, shaking the pan. Mix together the cumin with the avocado, onion, chilli, lemon juice and olive oil in a bowl. Serve the fish steaks with the Avocado Salsa and steamed baby potatoes.

King Prawns with Noodles and Coconut Dressing

PREPARATION TIME:
30 MINUTES +
20 MINUTES
MARINATING
COOKING TIME:
12 MINUTES
SERVES 4

24 raw king prawns
1 cup coconut milk
1 tablespoon grated fresh ginger
1 tablespoon sweet chilli sauce
1–2 red chillies, finely chopped
1/4 cup chopped fresh basil
150 g dried soba noodles
fresh basil leaves, to garnish

1 Peel and devein the prawns, leaving the tails intact. Combine the coconut milk, ginger, sweet chilli sauce, red chilli and basil in a bowl. Pour the marinade over the prawns and refrigerate for 20 minutes, then drain the prawns and reserve the marinade.

2 Place the prawns in a single layer on a lightly oiled and preheated chargrill pan or barbecue grill or flatplate and cook for 2–3 minutes, turning once, until cooked through. It may be necessary to cook the prawns in batches. Set aside on a warm plate.

3 If you are using a chargrill pan with deep sides, reduce the heat then pour in the reserved coconut mixture. Alternatively, use a pan to heat the sauce on the stove or barbecue. Bring to the boil briefly, just enough to heat the mixture through. Do not overheat or the coconut milk will become oily.

4 Meanwhile, cook the soba noodles in a large pan of boiling, salted water, following the manufacturer's instructions. Then add a cup of cold water and drain. Divide the noodles and prawns among four warm plates and spoon over the sauce. Garnish with the basil leaves.

Sardines with Capers and Baby Garlic Potatoes

PREPARATION TIME:
20 MINUTES +
15 MINUTES
MARINATING
COOKING TIME:
12 MINUTES
SERVES 4

24 sardine fillets
3 tablespoons olive oil
2 tablespoons lime juice
2 cloves garlic, crushed
1/2 teaspoon dried oregano leaves
1 tablespoon baby capers
fresh oregano sprigs
2 limes, quartered

BABY GARLIC POTATOES
2 x 410 g cans baby potatoes or cooked baby new potatoes
30 g butter
2 cloves garlic, crushed

1 Lay the sardines in a single layer in a non-metallic dish. Combine the olive oil, lime juice, garlic and oregano leaves in a jug. Pour the marinade over the sardines and refrigerate for 15 minutes. Do not marinate them for any longer or they start to 'cook' and will break up when heated. Drain the sardines, reserving the marinade.

2 To make the Baby Garlic Potatoes: Dry the potatoes well with paper towels. Melt the butter in a heavy-based frying pan and add the garlic and potatoes. Shake and turn the potatoes over high heat for about 3–4 minutes, or until lightly golden. Drain on paper towels and keep warm.

3 Lightly brush a preheated chargrill pan or barbecue grill or flatplate with olive oil. Add the sardines in a single layer (it may be necessary to cook them in batches) and cook for about 2 minutes, turning once. Brush several times with the reserved marinade while cooking and take care not to overcook the sardines or they may fall apart.

4 Place the sardines on a warm plate and top with the baby capers, oregano sprigs and some freshly ground black pepper. Serve with the lime wedges and a few of the Baby Garlic Potatoes.

Scallops with Sesame Bok Choy

PREPARATION TIME:
10 MINUTES +
15 MINUTES
MARINATING
COOKING TIME:
8 MINUTES
SERVES 4

24 large scallops with corals
2 tablespoons light soy sauce
1 tablespoon fish sauce
1 tablespoon honey
1 tablespoon kecap manis
grated rind and juice of 1 lime
2 teaspoons grated fresh
   ginger
1 lime, cut into wedges,
   to garnish

SESAME BOK CHOY
1 tablespoon sesame oil
1 tablespoon sesame seeds
1 clove garlic, crushed
8 baby bok choy, halved
   lengthways

1   Rinse the scallops, remove the dark vein and dry with paper towels. Combine the soy and fish sauce, honey, kecap manis, lime rind and juice and ginger. Pour over the scallops, cover and refrigerate for about 15 minutes. Drain and reserve the marinade.

2   To make the Sesame Bok Choy: Pour the oil onto a preheated chargrill pan or barbecue flatplate and add the sesame seeds and garlic. Cook, stirring, for 1 minute, or until the seeds are golden. Arrange the bok choy in a single layer on the hot plate and pour over the reserved marinade. Cook for 3–4 minutes, turning once, until tender. Remove and keep warm.

3   Wipe clean the hot plate, brush with some oil and reheat. Add the scallops and cook, turning, for about 2 minutes, or until they become opaque.

4   Place the scallops on top of the Sesame Bok Choy and serve with the lime wedges.

133

Swordfish Kebabs with Roast Potatoes

PREPARATION TIME:
40 MINUTES

COOKING TIME:
1 HOUR

SERVES 4

600 g potatoes, cut in half
2 cloves garlic, crushed
1 red onion, cut into 8 wedges
1 red capsicum, cut into cubes
2 zucchini, cut into pieces
1 kg swordfish, cut into cubes
bay leaves, torn in half
1 tablespoon lemon juice

1   Preheat the oven to moderately hot 190°C (375°F/Gas 5). Brush the potatoes with olive oil and place cut-side-up in a baking dish. Bake for 40 minutes, or until crisp.

2   Preheat a lightly oiled chargrill pan or barbecue flatplate. Add the garlic, onion and capsicum and cook, stirring, for 5 minutes. Toss in the zucchini and cook for a further 5 minutes, or until the vegetables are tender. Remove from the heat and season to taste.

3   Thread the swordfish cubes onto 8 metal skewers, interspersed with the bay leaves. Lightly coat with olive oil and the lemon juice.

4   Reheat and lightly oil the hot plate and cook the kebabs for about 4 minutes, turning frequently. Arrange the vegetables on four warm plates, top with the kebabs and serve the potatoes on the side.

Garlic Calamari with Parmesan

PREPARATION TIME:
30 MINUTES + 10 MINUTES MARINATING

COOKING TIME:
5 MINUTES

SERVES 2–4

350 g fresh calamari tubes, cleaned

4 cloves garlic, chopped

2 tablespoons olive oil

2 tablespoons finely chopped fresh parsley

1 large tomato, peeled, seeded and finely chopped

1/4 cup grated Parmesan

1 Cut the calamari tubes in half lengthways, wash and pat dry. Lay them flat, with the soft, fleshy side facing upwards, and cut into rectangular pieces, about 6 x 2.5 cm. Finely honeycomb by scoring the fleshy side with diagonal strips, one way and then the other, to create a diamond pattern.

2 Mix the garlic, oil, half the parsley, salt and pepper in a bowl. Add the calamari and refrigerate for at least 10 minutes.

3 Heat a lightly oiled chargrill pan or barbecue flatplate until very hot. Cook the calamari in 2 batches, tossing regularly, until they turn white. Add the chopped tomato and toss through to just heat.

4 Arrange the calamari on a plate and scatter over the Parmesan and remaining parsley.

Tuna Steaks with Tapenade

PREPARATION TIME:
15 MINUTES +
10 MINUTES
MARINATING
COOKING TIME:
6 MINUTES
SERVES 4

2 tablespoons tapenade (olive paste)
2 tablespoons olive oil
2 cloves garlic, finely chopped
2 teaspoons finely grated lemon rind
4 tuna steaks
chopped spring onion, to garnish

1 Combine the olive paste, oil, garlic, lemon rind and some black pepper. Spread over both sides of the tuna and refrigerate for 10 minutes.

2 Place the tuna on a lightly oiled and preheated chargrill pan or barbecue grill or flatplate and cook, turning once, for about 3 minutes each side. When cooked, the steak should still be pink in the centre. Sprinkle with the spring onion.

Prawns with Mango Salsa

PREPARATION
TIME:
25 MINUTES +
1 HOUR
MARINATING
COOKING TIME:
10 MINUTES
SERVES 4–6

1 kg raw prawns
1/3 cup lemon juice
1/3 cup olive oil
1/4 cup chopped fresh dill
450 g mango (fresh or
   canned), cubed
1 onion, finely diced
1 red chilli, seeded and
   finely chopped
1 tablespoon grated lemon
   rind
150 g rocket leaves

1   Peel and devein the raw prawns, keeping the tails intact.

2   Combine the lemon juice, olive oil, dill and a teaspoon of salt in a bowl, add the prawns and toss well. Cover and refrigerate for 1 hour.

3   Preheat a deep-sided chargrill pan until very hot. Drain the prawns, reserving the marinade, and cook for 3 minutes, or until they change colour. Remove the prawns. Add the reserved marinade to the pan, boil for 5 minutes and mix in to the prawns. Cool the mixture slightly.

4   In a bowl, combine the mango, onion, chilli, lemon rind and some salt and pepper. Add the prawns to the salsa and serve on a bed of rocket.

Salmon with Gremolata and Griddle Cakes

PREPARATION TIME:
25 MINUTES
COOKING TIME:
20 MINUTES
SERVES 4

GREMOLATA
1/3 cup finely chopped fresh parsley
grated rind of 1 lemon
grated rind of 1 orange
2 cloves garlic, crushed

POTATO GRIDDLE CAKES
250 g potatoes
250 g sweet potatoes, peeled
1/3 cup chopped fresh chives
2 tablespoons plain flour
1 egg, lightly beaten
4 salmon fillets, about 200 g each
2–3 teaspoons baby capers, drained

1 To make the Gremolata: Combine the parsley, lemon and orange rind and garlic.

2 To make the Potato Griddle Cakes: Coarsely grate the peeled potatoes and sweet potatoes and squeeze handfuls of the mixture to remove any excess moisture. Mix with the chives, flour, egg and salt and pepper. Preheat a barbecue flatplate and drizzle with some olive oil. Use a heaped tablespoon of the mixture to make each patty. Add this to the hot plate and flatten slightly. You may need to cook the patties in two batches. Cook, turning once, for about 5 minutes, or until golden.

3 Drizzle some oil over the hot plate and add the salmon steaks. Cook for 2–3 minutes each side, or until just tender.

4 Place the steaks on warmed plates and top with the Gremolata and the capers. Serve immediately with the Potato Griddle Cakes.

Scallops with Green Peppercorns

PREPARATION TIME:
20 MINUTES +
20 MINUTES
MARINATING
COOKING TIME:
5 MINUTES
SERVES 4

1/4 cup olive oil
2 teaspoons green peppercorns, chopped
2 teaspoons finely grated lime rind
1 teaspoon finely grated fresh ginger
500 g scallops with corals, deveined
salad leaves
strips of pickled ginger

1 Combine the oil, peppercorns, rind and fresh ginger. Add the scallops and refrigerate for 20 minutes.

2 Heat a chargrill pan or barbecue flatplate until very hot. Cook the scallops in batches, stirring gently, for about 2 minutes, or until they become lightly golden brown.

3 Place the scallops on the salad leaves and top with the ginger strips.

Tuna Steaks with Rosemary Potatoes

PREPARATION TIME:
20 MINUTES
COOKING TIME:
40 MINUTES
SERVES 4

ROSEMARY POTATOES
600 g new potatoes, unpeeled
30 g butter
3 tablespoons olive oil
2 cloves garlic, crushed
1 tablespoon chopped fresh rosemary

4 thick tuna steaks, about 200 g each
rind and juice of 1 lemon or lime
1 tablespoon finely chopped fresh parsley

1 To make the Rosemary Potatoes: Wash the potatoes, pat dry with paper towels and cut into halves.

2 Heat the butter and olive oil on a chargrill pan or barbecue grill or flatplate, add the potatoes and season with freshly ground black pepper. Cook over medium heat, tossing regularly to ensure that the potatoes are evenly coloured, for about 30 minutes, or until they are tender, crisp and golden.

3 Stir in the garlic, rosemary and some salt and toss to coat for a few minutes. Remove and keep warm.

4 Add the tuna steaks to the hot plate and cook for 3–4 minutes each side. When cooked, the tuna steaks should still be pink inside. Sprinkle with the lemon or lime rind and juice and the parsley. Serve at once with the Rosemary Potatoes.

Note: You can use another kind of fish to replace the tuna. Try swordfish, salmon or blue-eye cod.

King Prawns with Dill Mayonnaise

PREPARATION
TIME:
40 MINUTES +
2 HOURS
MARINATING
COOKING TIME:
10–15 MINUTES
SERVES 4

MARINADE
1/2 cup olive oil
1/3 cup lemon juice
**2 tablespoons wholegrain
  mustard**
2 tablespoons honey
**2 tablespoons chopped
  fresh dill**
16–20 raw king prawns

DILL MAYONNAISE
3/4 cup whole egg mayonnaise
**2 tablespoons chopped
  fresh dill**
1 1/2 tablespoons lemon juice
1 gherkin, finely chopped
1 teaspoon chopped capers
1 clove garlic, crushed

1 To make the Marinade: Combine the olive oil, lemon juice, mustard, honey and dill in a bowl, pour over the unpeeled prawns and coat well. Cover and refrigerate for at least 2 hours, turning occasionally.
2 To make the Dill Mayonnaise: In a small bowl, whisk together the mayonnaise, dill, lemon juice, gherkin, capers and garlic. Cover and refrigerate.
3 Lightly oil a preheated chargrill pan or barbecue grill or flatplate. Add the drained prawns and cook in batches over high heat for 4 minutes, turning frequently until pink and cooked through. Serve with the Dill Mayonnaise.

Minty Barbecued Fish Cakes

PREPARATION TIME: 15 MINUTES
COOKING TIME: 10 MINUTES
SERVES 6

500 g firm white fish fillets
1 medium brown onion,
**   chopped**
3 macadamia nuts or 6 cashew
**   nuts**
1 teaspoon chilli powder
1/2 teaspoon turmeric
1 tablespoon finely chopped
**   fresh lemongrass**
1 teaspoon finely chopped
**   Vietnamese mint (optional)**
1/2 teaspoon ground black
**   pepper**
salt, to taste
1 tablespoon sugar
1/2 cup thick coconut milk
1 tablespoon ground roasted
**   dried coriander**
pieces of banana leaf or
**   baking paper, 16 cm square**

1   Remove any small bones from the fish fillets. Cut into large pieces, about 3 cm square. Combine in a food processor with the remaining ingredients except for the banana leaves, until smooth. Alternatively, finely chop the fish with a cleaver to make a paste and mix in the remaining ingredients.

2   Soften the banana leaves in boiling water for 1–2 minutes. Dry with absorbent paper. Place 2 tablespoons of the fish mixture onto a piece of banana leaf and fold into a packet. Fasten with a toothpick. Repeat with the

remaining filling. If banana leaves are unavailable use squares of baking paper, then wrap the paper in foil the same size.

3 Place fish parcels on a preheated barbecue flatplate. Cook for 5 minutes each side or until fish is cooked.

Note: Vietnamese mint may also be added to main course dishes or soups.

Chilli Crab

Peanut oil is unrefined and has quite a strong peanutty fragrance and flavour. You can simply use a wok on your conventional hotplate if you don't have a wok attachment.

PREPARATION TIME:
20 MINUTES
COOKING TIME:
15 MINUTES
SERVES 2–4 AS
AN ENTREE

3 medium-sized cooked crabs
1/3 cup peanut oil
3 cloves garlic, crushed
2 fresh red chillies, finely chopped
1 teaspoon grated fresh ginger
1 tablespoon chilli paste or sambal oelek
1/3 cup tomato sauce
2 tablespoons sugar
1 tablespoon soy sauce
1 teaspoon oriental sesame oil

1 Using a cleaver or a heavy-bladed sharp knife, cut the crabs in half. Wash the crabs under cold water, remove fibrous tissues and stomach bag.

2 Heat the wok, add the oil and swirl to heat. Stir-fry crab halves for 5 minutes and remove to a dish.

3 Reduce heat and stir-fry the garlic, chillies and ginger for 3 minutes, then add chilli paste, tomato sauce, sugar, soy sauce and sesame oil. Mix well and bring to the boil.

4 Return the crabs to the wok, stir well and simmer for 5 minutes, adding a little water or stock if the dish is in danger of drying out. Serve immediately.

Minty Barbecued Fish Cakes (left). Chilli Crab

Thai Fish Cakes

In Bangkok they serve these spicy morsels as an entrée. Double the quantities for a main dish.

PREPARATION TIME:
30 MINUTES
COOKING TIME:
8 MINUTES
SERVES 6

10 spinach leaves
250 g bream fillets
1 tablespoon fish sauce
1/4 cup finely chopped spring onions
1 tablespoon finely chopped fresh coriander leaves, roots and stems
2 teaspoons grated lime rind
1 clove garlic, crushed
1 teaspoon chilli sauce
1/4 teaspoon ground pepper
1/4 cup thick coconut milk
1 egg

1   Blanch the spinach leaves in boiling water for 10 seconds and cool them in iced water.
2   Remove skin, any stray bones and cut fish fillets into pieces. Combine in a food processor with the remaining ingredients until the mixture is smooth. Divide the fish mixture between six spinach leaves, placing two leaves together if they are small. Roll the spinach over to enclose the fish filling. Wrap each parcel in foil.
3   Place on a preheated barbecue flatplate and cook for 4 minutes each side, turning once. Serve immediately and let each person remove the foil from their portion.

Note: The use of the roots of coriander herb in this recipe is not a mistake. It lends a stronger flavour to the dish and is used in most Thai recipes.

Mexican Fish Cakes in Corn Husks

If cooking corn without the husks, wrap in foil or place on the coolest part of the barbecue.

PREPARATION TIME:
30 MINUTES +
10 MINUTES
STANDING
COOKING TIME:
20 MINUTES
SERVES 4

4 corn cobs, complete with husks
450 g firm white fish fillets, diced
2 cloves garlic, crushed
2 teaspoons Mexican chilli powder (see note)
1/3 cup finely chopped fresh coriander
1 tablespoon chopped canned jalapeño chillies
1 egg, beaten
1/2 teaspoon ground black pepper
1 tablespoon lemon juice
2 tablespoons chopped spring onions
1 teaspoon ground cumin
foil squares, for wrapping

1   Remove only four husks from each corn cob and set aside. Turn back the remaining husks (being careful not to detach them) and remove the thread-like cornsilk. Pull the husks back into position to enclose the corn. Soak the cobs in cold water for 10–15 minutes.

2   Process fish in a processor until just smooth, combine with remaining ingredients. Divide into eight equal portions.

3   Wrap each portion in two of the reserved corn husks taken from the corn cobs. Then wrap parcels in squares of foil.

4   Start grilling the corn on the barbecue for 20 minutes, turning them once or twice.

5   Place wrapped fish cakes on medium hot flatplate during last 8 minutes and both should be ready at the same time.

Note: Mexican chilli powder is available in all supermarket spice ranges. It contains a mixture of paprika, chillies, cumin and oregano.

Prawns with Lemon and Garlic

Sea salt is available from good kitchen shops and leading food outlets.

PREPARATION TIME:	
20 MINUTES + 10 MINUTES MARINATING	**1 kg large green prawns**
	1/4 cup olive oil
	1 tablespoon lemon juice
	2 cloves garlic, crushed
	2 spring onions, finely chopped
COOKING TIME:	**1/2 teaspoon sea salt**
5 MINUTES	**ground black pepper, to taste**
SERVES 4–6	**lemon quarters, to serve**

1   Shell and devein prawns. Mix remaining ingredients in a glass or ceramic bowl and stir in prawns. Allow to marinate for 10 minutes.

2   On a flatplate over full heat toss prawns until they start to curl up and become opaque. Serve with lemon quarters and crusty white bread.

Prawn Burgers

A delicious burger variation to serve for special occasions.

PREPARATION TIME: 15 MINUTES
COOKING TIME: 4 MINUTES
SERVES 6

- 500 g large green prawns, shelled and deveined
- 1 egg, lightly beaten
- 1 tablespoon dry sherry
- 1 teaspoon grated fresh ginger
- 1 clove garlic, crushed
- 2 tablespoons cornflour
- 3 tablespoons finely chopped spring onions
- 2 tablespoons finely chopped water chestnuts
- 1/2 cup cornflake crumbs
- salt, to taste
- 3 tablespoons oil

SAUCE
- 2 teaspoons Worcestershire sauce
- 1 tablespoon white wine vinegar
- 2 tablespoons water
- 2 teaspoons sugar
- 1 teaspoon grated fresh ginger
- Tabasco sauce, to taste
- lime wedges, to serve
- 6 hamburger buns, to serve

Barbecued Spiced Fish (above). Prawn Burgers

1 Finely chop the prawns and combine with egg, sherry, ginger, garlic, cornflour, spring onions, water chestnuts and cornflake crumbs. Mix well. Season to taste.

2 To make the sauce: Combine ingredients in a small bowl.

3 Heat the barbecue flatplate to medium-hot and spread with oil. Divide prawn mixture evenly into six portions and cook in egg rings brushed with oil. Cook for 2 minutes on each side or until set and firm. Do not overcook. Serve Prawn Burgers with combined sauce ingredients, lime wedges and hamburger buns.

Note: Serve with a crisp salad.

Barbecued Spiced Fish

PREPARATION TIME:	4 large, firm white fish fillets
15 MINUTES	60 g butter, melted
COOKING TIME:	
20 MINUTES	**DRY MARINADE**
SERVES 4	1/2 teaspoon salt
	2 teaspoons ground sweet paprika
	1/2 teaspoon white pepper
	1/2 teaspoon ground cayenne
	1/4 teaspoon ground dried oregano
	1/4 teaspoon dried basil
	1/4 teaspoon dried thyme
	1 teaspoon garlic powder
	1 teaspoon onion powder

1 Dry fish fillets with absorbent paper and brush with melted butter, set aside.

2 To make the dry marinade: Combine all the dry spices and sprinkle over the buttered fish fillets.

3 Cook fillets on a lightly greased flatplate for 8–10 minutes, turning once during the cooking time.

Note: You may find it easier to make a double quantity of this dry marinade and store the remaining mixture for later use. Store in a covered airtight jar in the freezer for best results. It adds flavour to seafood, poultry and beef.

Coriander Chilli Prawns

It's a nice idea to offer fingerbowls to everyone with this dish.

PREPARATION TIME:	48 medium green king prawns
20 MINUTES +	1/3 cup finely chopped fresh coriander
1 HOUR MARINATING	2 tablespoons oil
COOKING TIME:	1/4 cup soy sauce
10 MINUTES	1/4 cup sweet chilli sauce
SERVES 8	1 tablespoon sweet soy sauce
	2 tablespoons plum sauce
	zest of 2 limes
	1/4 cup lime juice

1 Using a sharp knife, cut down the back of each prawn and remove the vein, leaving the shell intact. Discard any prawns with broken shells.

2 Combine remaining ingredients in large mixing bowl, stir until well combined. Add prawns, mix well. Cover with plastic wrap, refrigerate 1 hour. Drain and reserve marinade.

3 Place prawns on lightly oiled flatplate. Cook for 5–10 minutes or until the prawns are pink and crisp. Baste with marinade while cooking.

Firecracker Prawns

These prawns certainly have some fire, but if you really like them spicy, adjust the cayenne pepper according to your taste.

PREPARATION TIME: 15 MINUTES
COOKING TIME: 8 MINUTES
SERVES 6

1 kg large green prawns
2 tablespoons olive oil

DRY SPICE MIXTURE
2 teaspoons black pepper
1/2 teaspoon salt
1 teaspoon onion powder
1 teaspoon dried chilli flakes
1 teaspoon ground sweet paprika
1/2 teaspoon cayenne pepper
1 teaspoon ground dried oregano
1 teaspoon thyme
1 teaspoon garlic powder

1   Peel the prawns, leaving tails on. Skewer six prawns on eight metal skewers. Brush with olive oil.

2   To make the dry spice mixture: Combine ingredients and sprinkle over the prawns on both sides. Grill over a hot barbecue flatplate or grill plate for 4 minutes each side or until prawns are pink and tender. Serve with Garlic Herb Hollandaise (see page 237).

Firecracker Prawns (left). Herb-stuffed Bream

Herb-stuffed Bream

Make sure you do not overcook the fish, which would cause the flesh to toughen and dry. When ready, the flesh should be tender and white.

PREPARATION TIME:
15 MINUTES
COOKING TIME:
20 MINUTES
SERVES 4

1 large bream, gutted and scaled

FILLING
1 cup fresh breadcrumbs
2 tablespoons chopped fresh parsley
1 tablespoon chopped fresh thyme
1 lemon
1/2 teaspoon salt
1/2 teaspoon white pepper
15 g butter, melted
2 tablespoons olive oil
lemon wedges, to serve

1 Clean the inside cavity of the fish with absorbent paper dipped in coarse salt. Score both sides of the fish at 2-cm intervals with a sharp knife.

2 To make the filling: Place breadcrumbs, parsley and thyme in a small bowl. Finely grate the rind of the lemon, squeeze and strain juice. Add to the breadcrumbs with salt, pepper and melted butter; mix well.

3 Fill the fish cavity with the prepared filling and secure with small metal skewers. Brush the outside with a little olive oil.

4 Place the fish in a fish frame or grill plate and barbecue over a lightly oiled flatplate for 15–20 minutes, turning once, or until cooked. Serve with wedges of lemon.

Note: A fisheroo or fish frame is obtained from barbecue or camping accessory outlets. Fish can also be cooked in a well greased foil parcel of double thickness. Thyme can be used fresh or dried, it is a herb that improves with drying.

Dill Fish with Lemon Sauce

PREPARATION TIME:
10 MINUTES +
3 HOURS
MARINATING

COOKING TIME:
10 MINUTES
SERVES 4

4 boneless white fish fillets (perch or whiting)
6 teaspoons lemon pepper
1–2 tablespoons chopped fresh dill
1/3 cup lemon juice

LEMON SAUCE
2 tablespoons lemon juice
1/2 cup cream
40 g butter, chopped
2 tablespoons chopped fresh chives

1 Rinse the fish under cold water.

2 Sprinkle pepper all over fillets and place in a shallow non-metal dish. Combine dill and lemon juice. Pour over the fish, cover and refrigerate several hours. Prepare and heat the barbecue 1 hour before cooking.

3 Cook the fish on a hot lightly greased barbecue flatplate for 2–3 minutes each side or until the flesh flakes back easily with a fork. Serve with Lemon Butter Sauce, barbecued citrus slices and a green salad.

4 To make Lemon Sauce: Simmer the lemon juice in a small pan until reduced by half. Add cream and stir until mixed through. Whisk in the butter a little at a time until all the butter has melted; stir in the chives.

Thai Marinated Fish

PREPARATION TIME:
10 MINUTES +
3 HOURS
MARINATING
COOKING TIME:
15 MINUTES
SERVES 4

1 medium-sized white-fleshed
   fish, cleaned and scaled
3/4 cup fresh coriander leaves
2 cloves garlic, crushed
1 tablespoon soy sauce
1 tablespoon fish sauce
1 tablespoon sweet chilli sauce
2 teaspoons sesame oil
3 spring onions, finely chopped
2 teaspoons grated fresh ginger
1 tablespoon lime juice
1 teaspoon soft brown sugar

1 Place the fish in a large, shallow non-metal dish.

2 Fill the fish cavity with coriander leaves.

3 Combine garlic, soy, fish and chilli sauces, oil, spring onions, ginger, juice and sugar in jug; mix well. Pour marinade over the fish. Cover and refrigerate for 2–3 hours. Prepare and heat the barbecue 1 hour before cooking.

4 Cook fish on a hot lightly greased flatplate for about 15 minutes, taking care not to burn the skin of the fish. (Move the fish away from the flame and dampen the fire if the fish begins to stick to plate.) Brush it frequently with marinade until flesh flakes back easily with a fork, and has turned opaque.

Barbecued Seafood

PREPARATION TIME:
20 MINUTES +
1 HOUR
MARINATING
TIME
COOKING TIME:
5 MINUTES
SERVES 4

8 baby octopus
1/2 cup red wine
1 tablespoon olive oil
2 cloves garlic, crushed
2 tablespoons chopped parsley
12 green king prawns
8 scallops
freshly ground pepper

1   Remove heads and beaks of octopus and cut tentacles in halves.

2   Combine wine, oil, garlic and parsley and marinate octopus for an hour or more in refrigerator.

3   Have barbecue flatplate very hot. Remove octopus from marinade, dry on paper towels and cook for 4–5 minutes.

4   Add prawns and cook for 3–4 minutes. Add scallops and cook for 1–2 minutes (they toughen if overcooked). Serve seafood immediately with freshly ground pepper.

Salmon Cutlets with Fruit Salsa

PREPARATION TIME:
20 MINUTES +
3 HOURS MARINATING
COOKING TIME: 10 MINUTES
SERVES 4

4 **salmon cutlets**
6 **teaspoons seasoned pepper**
2 **tablespoons lemon juice**
1/2 **cup lime juice**
1 **tablespoon chopped fresh thyme**

FRUIT SALSA
1/2 **small pawpaw, peeled**
1/4 **small pineapple, peeled**
3 **spring onions, chopped**
1 **tablespoon chopped fresh coriander**
2 **tablespoons lime juice**
3 **teaspoons caster sugar**
salt, to taste

1   Sprinkle salmon cutlets all over with seasoned pepper.
2   Place salmon cutlets in shallow non-metal dish. Combine lemon juice, lime juice and thyme in small jug. Pour over salmon cutlets. Cover and refrigerate several hours.
3   Place salmon on hot lightly greased barbecue grill or flatplate; brush with any remaining marinade. Cook 5–10 minutes each side, turning once, until outside is lightly browned and flesh is just cooked on the inside. Serve with Fruit Salsa.
4   To make Fruit Salsa: Chop pawpaw and pineapple into 1-cm cubes. Combine in medium bowl with spring onions, coriander, lime juice, caster sugar and salt.

Barbecued Salmon with Cucumber Vinaigrette

PREPARATION TIME:
30 MINUTES +
SEVERAL HOURS
REFRIGERATION
COOKING TIME:
40–50 MINUTES
SERVES 12

3.5 kg whole Atlantic salmon
1 large tomato, thickly sliced
1 lemon, thinly sliced
60 g butter, melted
1 clove garlic, crushed
salt, pepper

CUCUMBER VINAIGRETTE
1/2 cup olive oil
2 tablespoons lime juice
1 tablespoon honey
1 clove garlic, crushed
1/2 teaspoon ground coriander
1 tomato, seeded, chopped
1 large Lebanese cucumber,
   chopped

This recipe is best suited to a Weber barbecue. As an alternative, buy salmon cutlets, place a slice of tomato and a slice of lemon on each and wrap well in foil. Cook them on the barbecue for 10–15 minutes.

1   Light the barbecue using a 2-kg bag of heat beads and about eight firelighters. Allow 25–30 minutes for the coals to be fully alight. Coals should be arranged either side of the grill, not directly underneath. Rinse and pat dry salmon, inside and out. Trim fins and tail with scissors. Place salmon on a sheet of oiled foil large enough to enclose the whole fish. Arrange tomato and lemon slices inside the fish cavity.

2   Combine butter, garlic, salt and pepper in small bowl. Brush liberally over fish. Pour any remaining mixture inside cavity. Wrap the salmon firmly in foil. Wrap in foil a second time to keep the fish together.

3   Curl the fish to a size to fit the barbecue and tie with string at regular intervals to retain its shape. (You may wish to make string handles for easier lifting once cooked.)

4   Sit the fish, gut-side down, on the centre of the barbecue grill with drip tray underneath; cover with lid, leaving vents open throughout cooking. Cook for 40 minutes. Remove from the coals. Stand covered 10 minutes. Transfer to serving platter. Gently peel back skin to expose cooked flesh; discard skin. Accompany with Cucumber Vinaigrette.

5   To make Cucumber Vinaigrette: Combine all ingredients in small bowl. Refrigerate several hours or overnight if possible.

Whole Fish with Lemon Herb Butter

Although this recipe is ideal for a kettle barbecue, it can also be cooked on a flatplate with double-thickness foil.

PREPARATION TIME:	**2 kg whole white-fleshed fish**
15 MINUTES	**1 small lemon, sliced**
COOKING TIME:	**HERB BUTTER**
1 HOUR	**80 g butter, softened**
SERVES 4	**1 tablespoon chopped parsley**
	3 teaspoons thyme leaves
	1 tablespoon chopped chives
	2 teaspoons grated lemon rind

1   Prepare the Weber (kettle) barbecue for indirect cooking at moderate heat (normal fire).

2   Wash and scale the fish and pat it dry with absorbent paper. Place fish on a large sheet of oiled aluminium foil.

3   To make Herb Butter: Blend the butter, herbs and lemon rind in a small bowl and beat until smooth. Spread half of the butter mixture inside the cavity of the fish. Transfer the remaining butter mixture to a serving bowl.

4   Lay lemon slices over the fish, enclose fish in foil and place on the barbecue grill. Cover, cook for 1 hour or until the flesh flakes back easily with a fork. Serve with extra Herb Butter.

Sweet and Sour Fish Kebabs

PREPARATION TIME: 20 MINUTES +
3 HOURS MARINATING
COOKING TIME: 10 MINUTES
MAKES 12 SKEWERS

750 g boneless white fish
   fillets (hake or cod)
225 g can pineapple pieces
1 large red capsicum
3 teaspoons soy sauce
6 teaspoons soft brown sugar
2 tablespoons white vinegar
2 tablespoons tomato sauce
salt, to taste

1   Soak wooden skewers in water for several hours.

2   Cut the fish into 2.5-cm cubes. Drain the pineapple, reserving 2 tablespoons of liquid. Cut the capsicum into 2.5-cm pieces. Thread the capsicum, fish and pineapple alternatively onto skewers.

3   Place the kebabs in a shallow non-metal dish. Combine the soy sauce, reserved pineapple juice, sugar, vinegar, tomato sauce and salt in a small bowl and mix well. Pour the marinade over the kebabs. Cover; refrigerate for 2–3 hours. Prepare and heat the barbecue 1 hour before cooking.

4   Barbecue kebabs on a hot lightly greased flatplate, brushing frequently with marinade, 2–3 minutes each side or until just cooked through. Serve immediately with cooked noodles and a dressed green salad.

Cajun Calamari

PREPARATION TIME:
15 MINUTES +
3 HOURS
MARINATING
COOKING TIME:
5 MINUTES
SERVES 4

600 g large calamari (or squid) hoods
1/4 cup lemon juice
2 cloves garlic, crushed
2 teaspoons tomato paste
1 teaspoon garam masala
2 teaspoons ground coriander
2 teaspoons paprika
2 teaspoons seasoned pepper
2 teaspoons caster sugar
1 tablespoon grated fresh ginger
1 tablespoon olive oil
1/4 teaspoon ground nutmeg
pinch chilli powder

1   Wash calamari thoroughly, removing any membrane. Pat dry with absorbent paper.
2   Using a sharp knife, cut through one side of each hood, open out to give a large, flat piece of flesh. With inside facing up, score flesh diagonally, in a criss-cross pattern, taking care not to cut all the way through. Against the grain of those cuts, slice flesh into long strips about 2 cm thick.
3   Combine juice, garlic, tomato paste, spices, sugar, ginger, oil, nutmeg and chilli in bowl; mix well. Add calamari strips; stir to combine. Cover and refrigerate several hours or overnight. Prepare and heat barbecue 1 hour before cooking.
4   Cook calamari and marinade on hot lightly greased barbecue flatplate 5 minutes or until flesh curls and turns white. Remove from the heat and serve immediately.

Steamed Fish and Vegetable Parcels

PREPARATION TIME:
15 MINUTES
COOKING TIME:
10 MINUTES
SERVES 4

4 bream fillets
2 tablespoons horseradish cream
1 small tomato, finely chopped
130-g can corn kernels, drained
2/3 cup grated cheddar cheese
1 celery stick, finely chopped
1/2 red capsicum, finely chopped
3 spring onions, chopped
1 1/2 teaspoons dried mixed herbs
salt and pepper, to taste

1 Prepare and heat the barbecue.
2 Grease four large sheets of foil, each double thickness.
3 Place a piece of fish in the centre of each piece of foil. Spread each fish fillet with a quarter of the horseradish cream.
4 Top each fillet with tomato, corn, cheese, celery, capsicum and spring onions. Sprinkle with herbs, salt and pepper. Bring the foil edges together, enclosing the fish in a neat parcel.
5 Cook parcels, fish-side down, on a hot barbecue grill or flatplate for 5–10 minutes, without turning, until the fish is cooked through. (Check the fish after 5 minutes; cooked fish flakes easily and the flesh turns opaque.) Serve fish and vegetables immediately.

Barbecued Tuna with Onions

PREPARATION TIME:
10 MINUTES + 3 HOURS MARINATING
COOKING TIME:
10 MINUTES
SERVES 4

4 fresh tuna steaks
4 small onions
1 1/2 cups red wine
1/4 cup soft brown sugar
salt and pepper, to taste

Steamed Fish and Vegetable Parcels (above). Barbecued Tuna with Onions

1 Place the tuna in a shallow non-metal dish.
2 Cut the onions in half and slice them finely. Sprinkle them over the fish. Combine the wine, sugar, salt and pepper in a jug and mix well.
3 Pour the marinade over the fish. Cover and refrigerate for 2–3 hours. Prepare and heat the barbecue 1 hour before cooking.
4 Drain fish and onion, reserving marinade.
5 Cook the tuna steaks and onions on a hot lightly greased barbecue flatplate for 8–10 minutes or until lightly browned and *just* cooked through. Pour the marinade over the tuna and onions a little at a time during cooking.

Creole-style Barbecued Shrimps

PREPARATION TIME:
30 MINUTES
COOKING TIME:
8 MINUTES
SERVES 4

500 g large raw prawns (jumbo shrimps)
3 tablespoons melted butter
1 teaspoon ground black pepper
1 1/2 teaspoons coarsely cracked black pepper
2 tablespoons Creole Seasoning
2 tablespoons Worcestershire sauce
1 teaspoon crushed garlic
2 tablespoons dry sherry
1/2 cup cream

CREOLE SEASONING
2 tablespoons paprika
1 1/2 tablespoons salt
1 tablespoon onion powder
1 tablespoon garlic powder
2 teaspoons ground black pepper
1 teaspoon cayenne pepper
1 teaspoon ground dried thyme
1 teaspoon ground dried oregano

1 To make Creole Seasoning: Combine all the ingredients thoroughly and store in an airtight container.
2 Remove only the hard portion of the shell covering the prawn head. Split the shell down the curve of the back with kitchen scissors, but do not

remove it. Lift out the sandy vein. Rinse and dry the prawns and put them into a bowl.

3 Make a marinade with all the other ingredients except the cream, pour it over the prawns and mix well. Leave for at least 10 minutes, or cover and refrigerate until ready to cook and serve.

4 Transfer the prawns to a preheated lightly greased barbecue flatplate or grill, reserving the marinade. Cook the prawns for 5–8 minutes or until they turn pink.

5 Heat the marinade in a small saucepan, add the cream and stir until the sauce bubbles. Pour over the prawns. Serve with crusty bread. This is finger food, so supply bowls of warm water with a wedge of lemon for freshening up afterwards.

Honeyed Prawn and Scallop Skewers

PREPARATION TIME:	500 g medium green prawns
15 MINUTES +	250 g fresh scallops with corals intact
3 HOURS MARINATING	1/4 cup honey
COOKING TIME:	2 tablespoons soy sauce
5 MINUTES	1/4 cup bottled barbecue sauce
MAKES	2 tablespoons sweet sherry
8 SKEWERS	

1 Soak eight wooden skewers in water.

2 Remove heads from prawns. Peel and devein prawns, keeping tails intact. Clean scallops, removing brown vein.

3 Thread prawns and scallops alternatively onto eight skewers (about three of each per skewer). Place in base of shallow non-metal dish. Combine honey, sauces and sherry in jug and pour over skewers. Cover and refrigerate several hours or overnight. Prepare and heat barbecue 1 hour before cooking.

4 Cook skewers on a hot lightly greased barbecue flatplate for 5 minutes or until cooked through. Brush frequently with marinade while cooking.

Fish Patties

PREPARATION TIME:	750 g white fish fillets, cut into cubes
25 MINUTES	1 cup stale white breadcrumbs
COOKING TIME:	3 spring onions, chopped
10 MINUTES	1/4 cup lemon juice
MAKES	2 teaspoons seasoned pepper
8–10 PATTIES	1 tablespoon chopped fresh dill
	2 tablespoons chopped fresh parsley
	3/4 cup grated cheddar cheese
	1 egg
	1/2 cup plain flour, for dusting

HERBED MAYONNAISE

1/2 cup mayonnaise

1 tablespoon chopped fresh parsley

1 tablespoon chopped fresh chives

2 teaspoons chopped capers

1 Prepare and heat barbecue. Place fish in food processor bowl. Process for 20–30 seconds until smooth.

2 Place minced fish in large bowl. Add breadcrumbs, spring onions, juice, pepper, herbs, cheese and egg. Mix well. Divide into eight to ten portions. Shape into round patties. Place on tray and refrigerate 15 minutes or until firm.

3 Toss patties in flour, shake off excess. Cook on a hot lightly greased barbecue flatplate 2–3 minutes each side until browned and cooked through. Serve with Herbed Mayonnaise and a green salad.

4 To make Herbed Mayonnaise: Combine mayonnaise, herbs and capers in a small bowl.

Honeyed Prawn and Scallop Skewers (above). Fish Patties

Seafood and Vegetable Parcels

These tasty parcels are almost a meal on their own. Serve them with steamed rice or tossed salad.

PREPARATION TIME: 15 MINUTES
COOKING TIME: 15 MINUTES
SERVES 4

- 4 small bream fillets
- 12 large green prawns, shelled and deveined
- 8 scallops
- 1 red capsicum, cut into strips
- 2 small carrots, cut into strips
- 2 small zucchini, cut into strips

MARINADE
- 1/2 cup chopped fresh coriander
- 2 tablespoons finely chopped spring onions
- 1/2 teaspoon grated fresh ginger
- 2 tablespoons white wine
- 1 tablespoon olive oil
- 1 teaspoon lemon pepper
- 2 tablespoons water
- 2 teaspoons chicken stock powder

1 Prepare four sheets of double foil about 30 cm square. Top each square of foil with a piece of baking paper about the same size. Place a fish fillet on each square. Place three prawns and two cleaned scallops on each fish fillet.

2 Blanch the vegetables for 1 minute in boiling water. Drain and divide evenly between the parcels.

3 To make the marinade: Combine all the ingredients and spoon over the seafood and vegetables. Bring the paper over the top of the seafood and fold tightly to make an enclosed parcel. Wrap the foil over the paper to enclose and strengthen the parcel. Place on a baking tray.

4 Cook on a preheated moderately hot barbecue plate for approximately 15 minutes.

Note: Be careful not to overcook, as the seafood will become tough very quickly.

Chilli Garlic Prawns

PREPARATION TIME:	1 kg large green prawns
15 MINUTES	
COOKING TIME:	**CHILLI–GARLIC OIL**
3 MINUTES	2/3 cup olive oil
SERVES 6	90 g butter, melted
	4 cloves garlic, crushed
	2 teaspoons finely chopped red chillies
	1/2 teaspoon ground black pepper
	salt, to taste

1 Peel and devein the prawns, slit them through the back to butterfly. Heat six cast-iron pots on a preheated barbecue flatplate.

2 To make Chilli–Garlic Oil: Combine the remaining ingredients and heat until bubbling hot in a heavy frying pan. Add the prawns and toss until they are coated with the mixture.

3 Divide the garlic mixture between the pots and cook until the prawns curl and turn pink, about 2 or 3 minutes.

4 Serve immediately with crusty bread.

Seafood and Vegetable Parcels (left). Chilli Garlic Prawns

Chargrilled Baby Octopus

PREPARATION TIME:	1 kg baby octopus
15 MINUTES +	3/4 cup red wine
3 HOURS	2 tablespoons balsamic vinegar
MARINATING	2 tablespoons soy sauce
COOKING TIME:	2 tablespoons hoisin sauce
5 MINUTES	1 clove garlic, crushed
SERVES 4	

1 Wash octopus thoroughly and wipe dry with absorbent paper.

2 Use a small sharp knife to slit open the head; remove the gut. Grasp the body firmly and push the beak out with your index finger. Remove and discard beak. If octopus are large, cut tentacles in half.

3 Place octopus in a large bowl. Combine wine, vinegar, sauces and garlic in a jug; pour over octopus and stir to coat completely. Cover and refrigerate several hours or overnight. Prepare and heat barbecue 1 hour before cooking.

4 Drain octopus; reserve marinade. Cook octopus on a hot, lightly greased flatplate 3–5 minutes until octopus flesh turns white. Pour over the reserved marinade while cooking. Serve warm or cold.

Vegetables, salads and breads

f ortunately we have a fantastic variety of salad greens and vegetables to choose from nowadays, and the salads and vegetable dishes in this chapter reflect this. Many of the vegetable recipes in this chapter can be cooked on the barbecue as you are cooking other dishes. During autumn when salad ingredients are less abundant try some of the following vegetable recipes to complement your barbecue menu. Many of the recipes are meals in their own right — there is plenty to choose here for the vegetarian — barbecues aren't just for carnivores!

Always be sure to buy good quality salad ingredients and store them in the refrigerator as soon as possible. Wash them well and allow to dry before storing them in large airtight containers if you have them. Otherwise, use plastic bags and close them securely.

Serve salads with a selection of dressings, making use of some of the wonderful flavoured vinegars and oils available. Salads should serve as a complement or contrast to the meal and are also an excellent source of vitamins and minerals. Make use of fresh herbs from the garden to add fragrance and flavour to your vegetable and salad dishes.

Breads are also an essential addition to any barbecue, whether as an appetiser or to accompany the main meal. They are easy to prepare and some, like damper, herb or garlic bread, can be cooked directly on the barbecue. If you don't have time to make any of the recipes here, buy a selection of rolls and loaves and serve them with an assortment of flavoured butters that can be prepared in advance and frozen.

Chargrilled Potatoes with Pistachio Salsa

PREPARATION TIME:
25 MINUTES
COOKING TIME:
20 MINUTES
SERVES 4

PISTACHIO SALSA
2 ripe tomatoes, chopped
2 cloves garlic, finely chopped
1 small red chilli, finely chopped
150 g pistachio nuts, toasted and roughly chopped
2 tablespoons chopped fresh parsley
1 tablespoon chopped fresh mint
1 teaspoon finely grated lemon rind

500 g potatoes
3 tablespoons plain flour
2 tablespoons olive oil
sour cream, to serve

1   To make the Pistachio Salsa: Combine the tomatoes with the garlic, chilli, nuts, herbs, lemon rind and salt and pepper.

2   Peel the potatoes and cut into large wedges. Place in a pan and cover with water, bring to the boil and cook for 5 minutes. Transfer to a colander and rinse under running water to stop the cooking. Pat the wedges dry with paper towels.

3   Sprinkle the flour over the potatoes in a bowl and toss to lightly coat. Place the potato wedges in a single layer on a lightly oiled preheated chargrill pan or barbecue grill or flatplate. Cook for 5–10 minutes, or until golden brown and tender, drizzling with the olive oil and turning the potatoes regularly while cooking. Serve the potato wedges with the Pistachio Salsa and a bowl of sour cream.

Warm Marinated Mushroom Salad

PREPARATION TIME:
25 MINUTES +
20 MINUTES
MARINATING
COOKING TIME:
5 MINUTES
SERVES 4

750 g mixed mushrooms
(such as baby button, oyster,
Swiss brown, shiitake and
enoki)
2 cloves garlic, finely
chopped
1/2 teaspoon green
peppercorns, crushed
3 tablespoons olive oil
3 tablespoons orange juice
250 g salad leaves,
watercress or baby spinach
leaves
1 teaspoon finely grated
orange rind

1 Trim the mushroom stems and wipe the mushrooms with a damp paper towel. Cut any large mushrooms in half. Mix together the garlic, peppercorns, olive oil and orange juice. Pour over the mushrooms and marinate for about 20 minutes.

2 Arrange the salad leaves in a serving dish.

3 Drain the mushrooms, reserving the marinade. Lightly oil a preheated chargrill pan or barbecue grill or flatplate and cook the flat and button mushrooms for about 2 minutes. Add the softer mushrooms and cook for 1 minute, or until they just soften.

4 Scatter the mushrooms over the salad leaves and drizzle with the marinade. Sprinkle with orange rind and season well with salt and pepper.

Antipasto Polenta Cakes

PREPARATION TIME:
15 MINUTES +
2 HOURS
REFRIGERATION
COOKING TIME:
35 MINUTES
SERVES 6

3/4 cup polenta (cornmeal)
100 g Cheddar, grated
50 g mozzarella, grated
2 tablespoons chopped fresh parsley
2 teaspoons chopped fresh thyme
1 teaspoon finely chopped fresh rosemary
3 tablespoons plain flour
3 tablespoons olive oil
300 g marinated antipasto vegetables

1 Bring 3 cups water to the boil. Gradually add the polenta and stir constantly over medium heat until the mixture comes back to the boil and thickens. Reduce the heat to low and cook, stirring, for about 20 minutes, until the polenta comes away from the side of the pan. Stir in the Cheddar and mozzarella, parsley, thyme and rosemary.

2 Lightly brush a 28 x 18 cm tin with oil, line the base with baking paper, spoon in the polenta and smooth the surface. Chill for about 2 hours, or until set.

3 Turn out the solid polenta block and cut out 6 rounds using a 7 cm scone cutter. Coat lightly with the flour.

4 Brush a preheated chargrill pan or barbecue grill or flatplate with a little of the olive oil. Cook the polenta cakes, drizzling with the remaining oil, for about 4 minutes on each side, or until they are golden brown. Be careful when handling so the cakes do not break up. Serve with the antipasto vegetables.

Chargrilled Asparagus

PREPARATION TIME:
5 MINUTES
COOKING TIME:
3 MINUTES
SERVES 4

500 g asparagus
50 g Parmesan

DRESSING
2 cloves garlic, crushed
2 tablespoons balsamic vinegar
2 tablespoons olive oil

1 Break off any woody ends from the asparagus. Brush with some olive oil and cook on a preheated chargrill pan or barbecue grill or flatplate for about 3 minutes, or until the asparagus is bright green and tender.

2 Using a vegetable peeler, make shavings from the Parmesan.

3 To make the Dressing: Whisk together the garlic, vinegar and olive oil in a bowl.

4 Pour the dressing over the warm asparagus, and top with the Parmesan shavings and lots of freshly ground black pepper.

Barbecue Vegetable Platter

PREPARATION TIME: 25 MINUTES
COOKING TIME: 1 HOUR
SERVES 8

HERB VINAIGRETTE
1/2 cup olive oil
2 tablespoons balsamic
    vinegar
2 cloves garlic, crushed
2 tablespoons fresh lime juice
1/3 cup chopped fresh mint,
    basil and coriander,
    combined

4 potatoes, unpeeled and
    halved
400 g pumpkin, unpeeled and
    cut into large pieces
300 g sweet potatoes,
    unpeeled and cut into large
    pieces
4 slender eggplants, halved
2 red onions, cut into wedges
1 yellow capsicum, seeded
    and quartered
1 red capsicum, seeded and
    quartered
1 green capsicum, seeded
    and quartered
8 large flat mushrooms,
    stems trimmed

BASIL MAYONNAISE
4 egg yolks
2 teaspoons mustard
1/4 cup fresh lemon juice
1 2/3 cups olive oil
1/3 cup fresh basil leaves

1   To make the Herb Vinaigrette: Whisk together the ingredients.

2   Preheat the barbecue to high. Brush the potato, pumpkin and sweet potato with the vinaigrette and wrap in foil and cook on the barbecue for 40–50 minutes, or until tender but not so soft they fall apart.

3   Brush the eggplant, onion, capsicum and mushrooms with the vinaigrette. Place on the barbecue or chargrill pan for 10 minutes, or until golden.

4   To make the Basil Mayonnaise: Place the egg yolks, mustard and lemon juice in a food processor and process for 1 minute, or until the mixture is pale and creamy. Slowly add the oil while the motor is running. When it is thick, add the basil, salt and pepper and process for 20 seconds.

5   Serve the vegetables drizzled with the remaining vinaigrette and accompanied by the Basil Mayonnaise.

Chargrilled Haloumi Cheese

PREPARATION TIME:
20 MINUTES
COOKING TIME:
10 MINUTES
SERVES 4

200 g haloumi cheese, cut into thick slices

2 tablespoons plain flour

2 teaspoons chopped fresh oregano

2 teaspoons chopped fresh sage or parsley

1 tablespoon chopped fresh chives

1 red capsicum, seeded and cut into thick strips

4 egg (Roma) tomatoes, halved

1 zucchini, cut into thick strips

1 teaspoon caster sugar

1 Coat the cheese slices lightly in the flour. Heat a chargrill pan or barbecue flatplate until moderately hot and add a little olive oil. Cook the cheese for about 3 minutes each side, or until golden brown all over, sprinkling on the chopped herbs. Remove, cover and keep warm.

2 Wipe clean the hot plate and lightly brush with some olive oil. Add the capsicum, tomato and zucchini pieces. Sprinkle on the sugar and cook, turning frequently, for 5 minutes, or until softened.

3 Place the vegetables on a plate, top with the cheese and serve with toasted French bread or focaccia.

Note: Haloumi cheese can be bought from good delicatessens or some supermarkets.

Lentil and Chickpea Burger with Coriander Garlic Cream

Coriander Garlic Cream is delicious with chicken or fish burgers.

PREPARATION TIME: 30 MINUTES
COOKING TIME: 20 MINUTES
MAKES
10 BURGERS

1 cup red lentils
1 tablespoon oil
2 onions, sliced
1 tablespoon tandoori mix
   powder
425-g can chickpeas,
   drained
1 tablespoon grated fresh
   ginger
1 egg
1/4 cup chopped fresh
   parsley
2 tablespoons chopped fresh
   coriander
2 1/4 cups stale
   breadcrumbs
flour, for dusting

CORIANDER GARLIC CREAM
1/2 cup sour cream
1/2 cup cream
1 clove garlic, crushed
2 tablespoons chopped fresh
   coriander
2 tablespoons chopped fresh
   parsley

1 Prepare and heat the barbecue.

2 Bring a large pan of water to the boil. Add the lentils to boiling water and simmer uncovered for 8 minutes or until tender. Drain well.

3 Heat oil in pan and cook the onions until tender. Add the tandoori mix; stir until fragrant; cool the mixture slightly.

4 Place the chickpeas, half the lentils, ginger, egg and onion mixture in a food processor bowl. Process for 20 seconds or until smooth. Transfer to a bowl. Stir in the remaining lentils, parsley, coriander and breadcrumbs and combine well.

5 Divide the mixture into ten portions. Shape the portions into round patties using your hands. (If the mixture is too soft, refrigerate for 15 minutes or until firm.) Toss the patties in flour. Shake off excess.

6 Place the patties on a hot lightly greased barbecue grill or flatplate. Cook for 3–4 minutes each side or until browned, turning once. Serve with Coriander Garlic Cream.

7 To make Coriander Garlic Cream: Combine the sour cream, cream, garlic and herbs in a bowl and mix well.

Spiced Sweet Potatoes

PREPARATION TIME:	500 g orange sweet potatoes
20 MINUTES	1/4 cup demerara sugar
COOKING TIME:	3/4 teaspoon mixed spice
25 MINUTES	30 g butter, chopped
SERVES 4–6	1/3 cup orange juice

1 Prepare the Weber (kettle) barbecue for indirect cooking at moderate heat (normal fire). Peel the sweet potatoes and cut into thick slices.

2 Arrange the slices in layers in a shallow greased tray. Sprinkle over the combined sugar and mixed spice and dot with butter. Sprinkle over the orange juice.

3 Cover the tray with foil, place on the top grill of the barbecue, replace the lid and cook for 20 minutes. Remove the foil and test with a sharp knife; cook for a few more minutes, if necessary. Sprinkle over a little more orange juice if the potatoes begin to dry out.

Golden Nugget Vegetable Slice

Prepare these stuffed pumpkins up to the final stages of cooking, set aside and finish the cooking just prior to serving.

PREPARATION TIME:
10 MINUTES
COOKING TIME:
10 MINUTES
SERVES 6–8

2 golden nugget pumpkins

FILLING
4 spring onions, chopped
10 green beans, chopped
1/2 red capsicum, chopped
1 small seedless cucumber, halved and chopped
1 clove garlic, crushed
3 teaspoons beef stock powder
1 teaspoon turmeric
1/2 teaspoon ground pepper
1/2 cup pecan pieces
1/2 cup fresh breadcrumbs
2 teaspoons Worcestershire sauce
3 tablespoons olive oil

1 Remove the tops from the nugget pumpkins and remove the seeds with a spoon and discard. Cover with plastic wrap and microwave on High (100%) for 3 minutes. Or blanch pumpkin in boiling water until barely tender, drain and cool under running water. Allow to stand while you prepare the filling.
2 Blend the spring onions, beans, capsicum and cucumber until finely chopped in a food processor. Add the remaining ingredients and mix well. Spoon the mixture into the nugget pumpkins.
3 Barbecue over a high heat for 10 minutes.
4 Cut each pumpkin into three slices or into quarters to serve.

Note: If preferred, substitute twelve medium mushroom caps for the pumpkins. Cook directly on the barbecue for 4–5 minutes. Serve immediately. Pumpkins can also be cooked in a moderate oven 180°C for about 15–20 minutes or until tender. Larger zucchini may also be used for this recipe. Slice in half lengthwise and remove the centre with a small teaspoon. Place the stuffing inside the hollow and barbecue over a low heat for 8 minutes.

Barbecued Vegetable Kebabs

For extra flavour, serve with Herb Butter (see page 239).

PREPARATION TIME:
20 MINUTES
COOKING TIME:
15 MINUTES
SERVES 6

6 small onions
12 button mushrooms
2 small zucchini
1 red capsicum
12 large cherry tomatoes

MARINADE
1/2 cup olive oil
2 tablespoons lemon juice
1 teaspoon lemon pepper
2 teaspoons chopped fresh thyme
or 1/2 teaspoon dried thyme

1 Peel the onions and blanch in boiling water for 5 minutes or until barely tender. Drain, cool in iced water and set aside.
2 Trim the mushrooms, slice the zucchini and cut the capsicum into large pieces. Thread all the vegetables and tomatoes alternately onto skewers and place in a shallow dish.
3 To make the marinade: Combine all the ingredients and pour over the vegetables. Allow to marinate for 30 minutes, turning occasionally.
4 Cook the kebabs on a preheated barbecue for 8 minutes or until vegetables are tender, turning after 4 minutes and basting from time to time with the remaining marinade.

Note: When buying cherry tomatoes for kebabs, choose them hard and firm so they will stay on the skewers when barbecued. Use any fresh seasonal vegetables for this recipe. When purchasing vegetables, always select items free from blemishes and decay. Vegetables that have been grown locally and purchased in season are less costly than those imported when they otherwise would not be available.

Golden Nugget Vegetable Slice (above). Barbecued Vegetable Kebabs. Damper (page 207)

Barbecued Mushrooms

Any type of mushroom can be used in this recipe. Larger types such as flat or field mushrooms will take longer to cook than button or cup.

PREPARATION TIME: 10 MINUTES
COOKING TIME: 5 MINUTES
SERVES 6

6 large mushrooms
50 g butter, melted
2 cloves garlic, crushed
**2 tablespoons finely chopped
  fresh chives**
**1 tablespoon fresh thyme
  leaves**
**1/2 cup shredded parmesan
  cheese**

1 Prepare and heat the barbecue. Carefully peel the skin from the mushroom caps. Remove the stalks.
2 Combine the butter and garlic in a small bowl. Brush tops of mushrooms with garlic butter, place top-side down on hot barbecue flatplate and cook over the hottest part of the fire for 2 minutes or until the tops have browned. Turn the mushrooms over. Brush the upturned bases with garlic butter and cook for 2 minutes.
3 Sprinkle the bases with combined chives and thyme, then cheese and cook a further 3 minutes, until the cheese begins to melt. Serve immediately.

Barbecued Mushrooms (above). Chinese Vegetable Stir-fry

Chinese Vegetable Stir-fry

PREPARATION TIME:
20 MINUTES

COOKING TIME:
6 MINUTES

SERVES 4–6

1 medium red capsicum
100 g oyster mushrooms
425-g can baby corn
500 g Chinese cabbage
1 tablespoon olive oil
250 g fresh bean sprouts
5 spring onions, cut into 3-cm pieces
2 cloves garlic, crushed
1 tablespoon olive oil
2 teaspoons sesame oil
2 tablespoons teriyaki marinade
1/2 teaspoon sugar
sweet chilli sauce, to taste

1 Prepare and heat the barbecue. Cut the capsicum in half and remove the seeds and membrane. Cut into thin strips.

2 Slice the mushrooms in half. Cut any large baby corn in half. Cut the cabbage into thick slices, then crosswise into squares.

3 Brush the barbecue flatplate with oil. Stir-fry the capsicum, mushrooms, corn, cabbage, sprouts, spring onions and garlic for 4 minutes, tossing and stirring to prevent burning or sticking.

4 Pour over the combined olive oil, sesame oil, teriyaki marinade and sugar and stir thoroughly to coat. Cook for 1 minute longer. Serve immediately. Drizzle with sweet chilli sauce.

Marinated Grilled Vegetables

PREPARATION TIME:
30 MINUTES +
1 HOUR
MARINATING

COOKING TIME:
5 MINUTES

SERVES 6

3 small slender eggplants
2 small red capsicums
3 medium zucchini
6 medium mushrooms

MARINADE
1/4 cup olive oil
1/4 cup lemon juice
1/4 cup shredded basil leaves
1 clove garlic, crushed

1 Cut the eggplants into diagonal slices. Place on a tray in a single layer; sprinkle with salt and let them stand for 15 minutes. Rinse thoroughly and pat dry with absorbent paper.

2 Trim the capsicums, removing the seeds and membrane and cut into long, wide pieces. Cut the zucchini into diagonal slices. Trim each mushroom stalk so that it is level with the cap. Place all the vegetables in a large, shallow non-metal dish.

3 To make marinade: Place the oil, juice, basil and garlic in a small screw-top jar. Shake vigorously to combine. Pour over the vegetables and combine well. Store, covered with plastic wrap, in the refrigerator for 1 hour, stirring occasionally. Prepare and heat the barbecue.

4 Place the vegetables on a hot, lightly greased barbecue grill or flatplate. Cook each vegetable piece over the hottest part of the fire for 2 minutes each side. Transfer to a serving dish once browned. Brush the vegetables frequently with any remaining marinade while cooking.

Corn on the Cob with Tomato Relish

PREPARATION TIME:
15 MINUTES
COOKING TIME:
1 HOUR
SERVES 6

TOMATO RELISH
400-g can peeled tomatoes
2/3 cup white vinegar
1/2 cup white sugar
1 clove garlic, finely chopped
2 spring onions, finely chopped
4 sun-dried tomatoes, finely chopped
1 small fresh red chilli, finely chopped
1/2 teaspoon salt
1/2 teaspoon cracked black pepper

6 large cobs fresh corn
1–2 tablespoons olive or vegetable oil
60 g butter, to serve
salt to taste

1 To make Tomato Relish: Roughly chop the tomatoes or process them briefly in a food processor bowl.

2 Combine the vinegar and sugar in a medium pan. Stir over a medium heat until the sugar dissolves. Bring to the boil. Reduce the heat and simmer for 2 minutes.

3 Add the tomatoes, garlic, spring onions, sun-dried tomatoes and chilli. Bring to the boil, reduce heat and simmer for 35 minutes, stirring frequently. Add salt and pepper and continue to cook until the relish has thickened. Remove from the heat and allow to cool.

4 Prepare and heat the barbecue. Brush the corn with oil and cook on the hot lightly greased barbecue grill for 5 minutes each side, until the corn is soft and flecked with brown in places. Using tongs, lift the corn onto the flatplate and moisten each with a square of butter. Sprinkle with salt. Serve at once with Tomato Relish.

Baked Vegetables

If barbecuing a chicken or leg of lamb, cook the vegetables simultaneously, timing them to be ready with the meat.

PREPARATION
TIME:
20 MINUTES
COOKING TIME:
1 HOUR 15
MINUTES
SERVES 6

6 medium potatoes
60 g butter, melted
1/4 teaspoon paprika
750 g pumpkin
6 small onions
150 g green beans
150 g broccoli
20 g butter, chopped, extra

1   Prepare the Weber (kettle) barbecue for indirect cooking at moderate heat (normal fire). Peel the potatoes and cut in half.

2   Using a small, sharp knife, make deep, fine cuts into the potato, taking care not to cut all the way through. Take two large sheets of aluminium foil, fold them in half and brush liberally with some melted butter. Place the potatoes unscored-side down on the foil and fold up the edges of foil to create a tray. Brush potatoes generously with melted butter and sprinkle with paprika.

3   Cut the pumpkin into three wedges and cut each wedge in half. Peel the onions and trim the bases slightly, so they will sit flat on the grill. Brush the pumpkin and onions with melted butter. Place the tray of potatoes, pumpkin pieces and onions on the barbecue grill. Put the lid on the barbecue and cook for 1 hour.

4   Top and tail the beans; cut the broccoli into florets. Place them on a sheet of foil brushed with melted butter. Dot with extra butter and enclose completely in foil. Add the 'parcel' to the other vegetables on the grill and cook a further 15 minutes. (See photograph page 50.)

Red Potato Salad

PREPARATION
TIME:
20 MINUTES
COOKING TIME:
10 MINUTES
SERVES 8

1.25 kg red potatoes
1 medium red onion
2 teaspoons oil
3 rashers bacon, finely chopped
3/4 cup whole egg mayonnaise
3/4 cup plain yoghurt
3 spring onions, finely chopped

1   Scrub the potatoes thoroughly and cut into 3-cm pieces. Cook potatoes in a large pan of boiling water for 5 minutes or until just tender. Drain and cool completely.

2   Cut the onion in half and slice finely. Heat the oil in a frying pan. Cook the bacon for 5 minutes or until well browned and crisp. Drain on absorbent paper.

3   Place potatoes, bacon and onion in a large mixing bowl. Combine the mayonnaise, yoghurt and spring onions in a small mixing bowl and pour over the potato mixture.

4   Fold through gently, taking care not to break up the potatoes. Transfer to a large serving bowl and serve at room temperature.

Beetroot with Mustard Cream Dressing

PREPARATION TIME: 10 MINUTES
COOKING TIME: APPROXIMATELY 1 HOUR 15 MINUTES
SERVES 6–8

2 rashers bacon, finely chopped
1 bunch fresh beetroot

MUSTARD CREAM DRESSING
250 g sour cream
3 teaspoons horseradish cream
3 teaspoons grainy mustard
1/2 teaspoon hot mustard powder (optional)
salt and pepper, to taste
3–4 fresh chives

1   Cook the bacon in a frying pan for 5–10 minutes until crisp. Drain on absorbent paper and set aside.

2   Trim the beetroot by removing the stems and leaves. Place in a pan and cover with cold water. Bring to the boil, reduce the heat and simmer gently for 1 hour or until the beetroot are tender.

3   Drain the beetroot and set aside until cool. Peel and cut them into wedges. (Leave any small beetroot whole.) Arrange in a serving bowl.

4   To make Mustard Cream Dressing: Combine the sour cream, horseradish and mustard and beat until smooth. Add the hot mustard and season with salt and pepper. Pour the dressing over the beetroot and top with fried bacon and snipped chives.

Rosemary Sautéed Potatoes

PREPARATION TIME:
10 MINUTES
COOKING TIME:
25 MINUTES
SERVES 6

4–5 large potatoes (about 1.5 kg)
1/3 cup olive oil
1 tablespoon chopped fresh rosemary
1 clove garlic, crushed
salt and black pepper, to taste

1   Peel the potatoes and cut them into 2-cm cubes. Rinse the potatoes in cold water, drain well and dry thoroughly on a clean tea towel.

2   Heat the oil in a large heavy-based frying pan. Add the potatoes and cook slowly, shaking the pan occasionally, for 20 minutes or until tender. Turn the potatoes frequently to prevent sticking. Partially cover the pan halfway through the cooking. The steam will help to cook the potatoes through.

3   Add the rosemary and garlic, with salt and pepper to taste, in the last few minutes of cooking. Increase the heat to crisp the potatoes, if required.

Stuffed Pumpkins with Cheesy Sauce

These stuffed pumpkins are a meal in one. Make them in advance and set aside. Do the final stages of cooking when ready to serve. Two medium butternut pumpkins can be used.

PREPARATION TIME:
35 MINUTES
COOKING TIME:
35 MINUTES
SERVES 8

8 golden nugget pumpkins
3 small carrots, peeled
3 small zucchini
100 g mushrooms
1 large potato, peeled
100 g green beans
3 tablespoons olive oil
2 onions, finely chopped
1 clove garlic, crushed

SAUCE
30 g butter
1/4 cup plain flour
3/4 cup cream
3/4 cup milk
1 cup grated cheddar cheese
2 tablespoons chopped chives
salt and pepper, to taste

1 Remove the tops from the pumpkins and scoop out the seeds with a spoon. Place the pumpkins and tops in a large baking tray with 3 tablespoons water. Cover with foil and bake in a hot oven 200°C for 20 minutes or until tender. Allow to cool.

2 Slice the carrots, zucchini and mushrooms and dice the potato. Top and tail the beans and cut into bite-sized pieces.

3 Heat the olive oil in a large pan and cook the onion and garlic until soft and golden. Add the carrots and potatoes. Stir to coat with the butter, cover and cook the vegetables over a low heat for 5 minutes. Add the remaining vegetables and cook covered, until tender, adding a little water from time to time to prevent them catching.

Marinated Barbecued Mushrooms (left). Stuffed Pumpkins with Cheesy Sauce

4 To make the sauce: In a separate pan, melt the butter and add the flour. Stir over a moderate heat for 1–2 minutes. Remove the pan from the heat and add the cream and milk. Continue to cook, stirring until the sauce simmers and thickens. Add half the grated cheese, chives, salt and pepper to taste.

5 Add the sauce to the vegetables and mix well. Spoon the prepared vegetables into the pumpkin cases. Sprinkle with a little extra cheese and replace the tops. Place into a baking tray, with a little water to prevent them burning. Cover with foil and set aside.

6 Place onto a preheated barbecue grill and cook for 10–15 minutes or until the cheese melts and pumpkins are heated through. Serve immediately.

Marinated Barbecued Mushrooms

For best results use white button mushrooms, fully closed; the firmer, the better.

PREPARATION TIME: 10 MINUTES **COOKING TIME:** 2–5 MINUTES SERVES 4–6	**500 g firm button mushrooms** **1/4 cup olive oil** **1 clove garlic, crushed** **2 tablespoons lime juice** **salt and pepper, to taste**

1 Wipe any dirt from the mushrooms with damp absorbent paper. Trim the ends off the stems and discard. Slice the mushrooms, not too thinly.

2 In a bowl, combine the oil, garlic, lime juice, salt and pepper. Toss the sliced mushrooms in this dressing and allow to stand for about half an hour before cooking.

3 Cook the mushrooms over a high heat on the barbecue flatplate. Toss the mushroom slices constantly until starting to brown. Serve as a side dish to meat or chicken.

Ratatouille

A flavoursome combination of vegetables. Make it in advance and warm in a large pan on the edge of the barbecue. This is also a perfect vegetarian meal for four people when served with crusty bread rolls.

PREPARATION
TIME:
25 MINUTES
COOKING TIME:
40 MINUTES
SERVES
8 AS AN
ACCOMPANIMENT

2 large eggplants
4 medium zucchini
2 red capsicums
425-g can peeled tomatoes
2 large potatoes
1/3 cup olive oil
2 large onions, chopped
2 large cloves garlic, crushed
1 teaspoon dried basil
1/4 cup chopped fresh
   coriander
2 teaspoons garlic pepper
   seasoning

1   Wash the eggplants, zucchini and capsicums. Cut the eggplant into large pieces and thickly slice zucchini. Remove the seeds from the capsicums and cut them into large pieces. Drain the tomatoes, reserving the liquid, and roughly chop. Peel the potatoes and cut into large cubes.

2   Heat the olive oil in a large pan or wok and cook the onions and garlic until the onions are tender. Add the prepared eggplants, zucchini and capsicums. Cook for 1–2 minutes. Add the tomatoes and reserved juice with the potatoes, basil, coriander and garlic pepper seasoning. Cover and cook, adding a little water to prevent sticking if necessary, for 30 minutes or until the vegetables are tender.

3   Serve hot immediately or warm on the edge of the barbecue, stirring occasionally until heated.

Note: If you enjoy a more fiery dish, try adding 2 teaspoons of sambal oelek with the peeled tomatoes. Sambal oelek is a prepared chilli relish of Indonesian origin, containing chilli, garlic and salt. It is used as a flavour enhancer, making the dish hotter and more appetising. Sambal oelek is available from most supermarkets and Asian food stores.

Broccoli and Cauliflower with Sesame Soy Dressing

If your barbecue set-up does not include a wok, this can easily be prepared back in the kitchen. Simply steam the broccoli and cauliflower over a little boiling water or microwave until tender. Prepare the sauce in a small pan and spoon over the vegetables when ready to serve.

PREPARATION
TIME:
10 MINUTES
COOKING TIME:
4 MINUTES
SERVES 6

4 cups water
4 cups broccoli florets
4 cups cauliflower florets

SAUCE
3 tablespoons dry sherry
2 tablespoons water
3 tablespoons dark soy sauce
   (see note)
2 teaspoons grated fresh green
   ginger
2 teaspoons sugar
1/2 cup toasted sesame seeds,
   crushed
2 teaspoons cornflour
3 tablespoons water

1   Bring water to the boil in a wok or large pan. Drop in the broccoli and cauliflower and boil, covered, for 4 minutes. Drain; place on a serving dish.

2   To make the sauce: Place the sherry, water, soy sauce, ginger, sugar and crushed sesame seeds in the wok. Bring to a boil. Meanwhile, combine the cornflour and water, and add to the simmering mixture. Stir until thickened and pour over the broccoli and cauliflower. Serve with barbecued fish.

Note: Dark soy sauce is less salty and more caramelised than the lighter styles of soy sauces available.

Ratatouille (above). Broccoli and Cauliflower with Sesame Soy Dressing

Hot Mushrooms and Tomato

When making foil parcels for the barbecue, use a double thickness of foil.

PREPARATION TIME:
10 MINUTES
COOKING TIME:
10 MINUTES
SERVES 6

375 g button mushrooms
3 tomatoes, finely diced
6 spring onions, finely chopped
2 teaspoons herb pepper seasoning
60 g butter
Tabasco sauce, to taste

1 Wipe the mushrooms and place evenly into the base of six small foil pie plates. Alternatively, prepare six squares of heavy-duty or industrial-strength foil.
2 Put the diced tomatoes and chopped spring onions into the pie plates or on the foil squares. Sprinkle each parcel with herb pepper seasoning to taste. Dot the tops of each parcel with a little butter and Tabasco sauce. Cover the foil plates with foil or enclose the ingredients in the prepared foil squares.
3 Place on the outer edge of a preheated barbecue grill and cook for 10 minutes or until heated through. Serve immediately as a side dish to meat and poultry.

Spicy Mint Potatoes

This subtle combination of sharp cheese and spicy curry powder helps lift the humble potato to new heights of flavour.

PREPARATION TIME:
25 MINUTES
COOKING TIME:
30 MINUTES
SERVES 6

- **6 medium potatoes**
- **30 g butter**
- **1/4 cup lemon juice**
- **3 teaspoons chicken stock powder**
- **2 tablespoons hot milk**
- **1/2 cup finely chopped fresh mint**
- **2 spring onions, finely chopped**
- **1/2 cup grated cheddar cheese**
- **1 teaspoon mild curry powder**

1 Wash the potatoes and prick with a fork or skewer. Place evenly around the turntable of the microwave. Cook the potatoes on High (100%) for 12 minutes and allow to stand for 10 minutes. Or cook potatoes on a rack in a moderate oven 180°C for about 30 minutes or until just tender. Cut the potatoes in half and scoop out the centres. Place the shells on a deep baking tray and the potato flesh into a bowl.

2 Mash the potato flesh and add the butter, lemon juice, chicken stock powder and milk. Mix until smooth. Add the chopped mint and spring onions. Spoon the mixture into the potato shells.

3 Combine the cheese with curry powder and sprinkle on top of the potato. Cover the tray with foil.

4 Place the tray on a preheated barbecue and cook over a moderate heat for about 15 minutes or until the potatoes are hot and the cheese is bubbly.

Jacket Potatoes

Jacket potatoes always go down well at a barbecue. Cook them alongside the other food or in the oven, and try them with one of the following toppings.

PREPARATION TIME:
10 MINUTES
COOKING TIME:
30–60 MINUTES
SERVES 4

4 large old potatoes

1   Wash and scrub the potatoes and pat them dry with absorbent paper.

2   Prick the potatoes all over with a fork or skewer and wrap them individually with foil.

3   Place the wrapped potatoes around the hot coals of the barbecue or on the top grill of a preheated kettle barbecue. Cook for 30–60 minutes (depending on the size of the potato). Insert a sharp knife or skewer in the centre to test if the potato is cooked.

4   When cooked, remove the foil from the potatoes and cut a large cross in the top of each. Squeeze to open and soften the potato flesh by mashing it gently with a fork. Mix a flavoured butter (see page 239) into the flesh and top with the topping of your choice. Serve hot.

Herbed Sour Cream Topping

PREPARATION TIME:
5 MINUTES
COOKING TIME:
NIL
SERVES 2–4

1 cup sour cream
1 tablespoon chopped chives
1 tablespoon chopped oregano
1 tablespoon chopped parsley
2 teaspoons chopped mint
salt and pepper, to taste
1 clove garlic, crushed (optional)

1   Combine all the ingredients in a bowl and mix well. Spoon over hot jacket potatoes and serve.

Jacket Potatoes with: Herbed Sour Cream Topping (above); Sweet Chilli Vegetable Topping (centre); Mushroom and Bacon Topping

Sweet Chilli Vegetable Topping

PREPARATION TIME:
10 MINUTES
COOKING TIME:
3–4 MINUTES
SERVES 1–2

1 tablespoon sesame oil
1 clove garlic, crushed
1 tablespoon soy sauce
2–3 teaspoons sweet chilli sauce
3 teaspoons plum sauce
1 small carrot, thinly sliced
1/2 red capsicum, thinly sliced
50 g small broccoli florets
1 small zucchini, thinly sliced
2 spring onions, sliced
salt and pepper, to taste

1   Heat the sesame oil in a wok or large frying pan and add the garlic, soy sauce, chilli sauce, plum sauce, carrot, capsicum, broccoli and zucchini. Cook for 2–3 minutes.

2   Add the spring onions and season with pepper and salt. Spoon over the hot jacket potatoes and serve.

Mushroom and Bacon Topping

PREPARATION TIME:
5 MINUTES
COOKING TIME:
5–6 MINUTES
SERVES 2–4

30 g butter
1 clove garlic, crushed
2 bacon rashers, finely sliced
10 large mushrooms, sliced
1/4 cup cream
1 tablespoon chopped chives
salt and pepper, to taste
shaved parmesan cheese, to serve

1   Heat the butter in a frying pan and add the garlic and bacon. Cook them for 1 minute.

2   Stir in the sliced mushrooms and cook a further 3–4 minutes until the mushrooms are soft.

3   Stir in the cream and chives, season with salt and pepper and cook for 1 minute.

4   Spoon the mixture over hot jacket potatoes and serve sprinkled with shaved parmesan cheese.

Baby Barbecued Potatoes

PREPARATION TIME:
20 MINUTES +
1 HOUR
STANDING
COOKING TIME:
20 MINUTES
SERVES 6

750 g baby potatoes
2 tablespoons olive oil
2 tablespoons fresh thyme leaves
2 teaspoons crushed sea salt

1   Wash the potatoes thoroughly under cold water. Cut any large potatoes in half so that all the potatoes are a uniform size for even cooking.

2   Boil, steam or microwave the potatoes until just tender. (Potatoes should remain whole and intact.) Drain and lightly dry with paper towels.

3   Place the potatoes in a large mixing bowl; add oil and thyme. Toss gently to coat potatoes and leave to stand for 1 hour. Prepare and heat the barbecue.

4   Place potatoes on a hot, lightly greased barbecue flatplate. Cook for 15 minutes, turning frequently and brushing with remaining oil and thyme mixture, until golden brown. Place in a serving bowl and sprinkle with salt and extra thyme sprigs, if desired.

Avocado, Mango and Walnut Salad

PREPARATION TIME: 15 MINUTES
COOKING TIME: 5 MINUTES
SERVES 6

3 bacon rashers
1 mignonette lettuce
2 mangoes
2 avocados
1/2 cup walnut halves

DRESSING
1/4 cup olive oil
2 tablespoons lemon juice
1 teaspoon French mustard
1 tablespoon thickened cream

1   Remove the rind from the bacon and roughly chop. Cook the bacon in a lightly oiled pan until crisp. Allow to cool on absorbent paper.

2   Wash the lettuce, separate the leaves, dry gently and place in a serving bowl.

3   A short time before required, peel and slice the mangoes and avocados. Arrange them over the lettuce and sprinkle with chopped bacon and walnut halves. Cover with plastic wrap but do not chill as the flavours are best at room temperature.

4   To make the dressing: Place the ingredients in a small bowl and whisk until well combined. Drizzle over the Avocado, Mango and Walnut Salad when ready to serve.

Avocado, Mango and Walnut Salad (above). Tomato and Mozzarella Salad (right). Five Bean Salad

Five Bean Salad

PREPARATION TIME:
10 MINUTES
COOKING TIME:
NIL
SERVES 8–10

1/3 cup mayonnaise
1 small purple onion
or 2 spring onions, chopped
ground pepper, to taste
250-g tub mung bean sprouts
750-g can four-bean mix,
   drained
440-g can corn kernels, drained
1/4 cup currants
2 tablespoons sultanas
1 red capsicum, diced
1/4 cup pecan pieces, toasted

1 In a large bowl mix together the mayonnaise, onion and pepper. Add all the other ingredients, except pecans, and mix well. Cover with plastic wrap. Chill.

2 Toss the salad just before serving. Sprinkle the top with pecans to garnish.

Note: Purple or Spanish onions are milder than their brown or white cousins, and ideal in salads.

Tomato and Mozzarella Salad

PREPARATION TIME:
10 MINUTES
COOKING TIME:
NIL
SERVES 8

6 firm, ripe tomatoes
250 g mozzarella cheese, thinly
   sliced
1 small purple onion, finely
   chopped
20 fresh basil leaves, finely
   chopped
1 tablespoon capers

DRESSING
3 tablespoons extra virgin
   olive oil
1 tablespoon lemon juice
salt and pepper, to taste

1 Slice the tomatoes 3 mm thick and alternate with slices of cheese in a large serving dish. Sprinkle with chopped onion, basil and capers.

2 To make the dressing: Combine all the ingredients in a small bowl. Drizzle over the salad when ready to serve.

Rice Salad with Lime

PREPARATION TIME:
10 MINUTES
COOKING TIME:
NIL
SERVES 6

4 cups cold cooked rice
2 seedless cucumbers, diced
1 red capsicum, finely diced
1 cup finely chopped fresh
    coriander

DRESSING
3 tablespoons olive oil
2 tablespoons lime juice
2 teaspoons grated lime rind
1 teaspoon ground sweet
    paprika
1/2 teaspoon salt
1 clove garlic, crushed

1   Place the rice in a bowl, add cucumbers, capsicum and coriander. Mix well.
2   To make the dressing: Combine all the ingredients and pour over the rice mixture. Toss lightly together and serve the rice salad immediately.

Note: Lime juice adds a particular flavour to this salad. As a second choice, lemon juice can be used if limes are not available.

Mixed Herb Tabouli

PREPARATION TIME:
20 MINUTES
COOKING TIME:
NIL
SERVES 8

3/4 cup burghul (cracked
    wheat)
3/4 cup hot water
2 bunches fresh parsley
1 bunch chives
1 1/2 cups fresh basil leaves
1/2 cup fresh mint leaves
4 spring onions, finely chopped
3 medium tomatoes, chopped
1/3 cup lemon juice
1/4 cup olive oil

1   Combine the burghul and hot water in a medium bowl and stand for 15 minutes or until all the water has been absorbed.
2   Remove the large stalks from the parsley and discard. Wash and dry the other herbs thoroughly. Chop well with a large, sharp knife or in a food processor. (If using a food processor, take care not to over-process.)
3   Place the burghul, parsley, chives, basil, mint, spring onions, tomatoes, juice and oil in a serving bowl; toss to combine. Refrigerate until required.

Chickpea Salad

PREPARATION TIME:
20 MINUTES

COOKING TIME:
NIL OR 2 HOURS
30 MINUTES (IF
USING DRIED
PEAS)

SERVES 6–8

1 3/4 cups (370 g) dried chickpeas, or 2 large cans chickpeas

3 1/2 litres water

1/4 cup olive oil

1 medium red onion

3 medium tomatoes

1 small red capsicum

4 spring onions

1 cup chopped fresh parsley

2–3 tablespoons chopped fresh mint leaves

DRESSING

2 tablespoons tahini (sesame paste)

2 tablespoons fresh lemon juice

2 tablespoons water

1/4 cup olive oil

2 cloves garlic, crushed

1/2 teaspoon ground cumin

salt and pepper, to taste

1   If using dried chickpeas, place in a medium pan. Cover with water and oil and bring to the boil. Partially cover and cook on a medium heat for 2½ hours or until tender. (Chickpeas will cook in about 30 minutes in a pressure cooker.)

2   Pour the chickpeas into a colander. Rinse them thoroughly with cold water and set aside to drain. If using canned chickpeas, drain well, rinse and drain again.

3   Peel the onion and slice it thinly. Cut the tomatoes in half and remove the seeds with a spoon. Cut the tomato flesh into small pieces. Slice the capsicum and spring onions into long thin strips.

4   Combine the onion, tomatoes, capsicum and spring onions in a bowl. Add the cooled chickpeas, parsley and mint.

5   To make the dressing: Combine the tahini, juice, water, oil, garlic, cumin, salt and pepper in a screw-top jar and shake vigorously to make a creamy liquid. Pour over the salad and mix through.

Greek Village Salad

PREPARATION TIME:
20 MINUTES
COOKING TIME:
NIL
SERVES 6–8

6 tomatoes, cut into thin wedges
1 red onion, cut into thin rings
2 Lebanese cucumbers, sliced
1 cup Kalamata olives
200 g feta cheese
1/2 cup extra virgin olive oil
dried oregano, to sprinkle

1 Combine the tomato wedges with the onion rings, sliced cucumber and Kalamata olives in a large bowl. Season to taste with salt and freshly ground black pepper.

2 Break up the feta into large pieces with your fingers and scatter over the top of the salad. Drizzle with the olive oil and sprinkle with some oregano.

Caesar Salad

PREPARATION TIME:
15 MINUTES
COOKING TIME:
20 MINUTES
SERVES 4

4 slices white bread, crusts removed, cubed
3 rashers bacon, chopped
1 cos lettuce
50 g Parmesan shavings, plus extra to serve

DRESSING
2–4 anchovies
1 egg
2 tablespoons lemon juice
1 clove garlic, crushed
1/2 cup olive oil

1 Preheat the oven to moderately hot 190°C (375°F/Gas 5). Spread the bread cubes on a baking tray and bake for 15 minutes, or until golden.

2 Cook the bacon over medium heat until it is crisp. Drain on paper towels.

3 Tear the lettuce leaves into pieces and put in a serving bowl with the bread cubes, bacon and Parmesan.

4 To make the dressing, process the anchovies, egg, lemon juice and garlic in a food processor for 20 seconds, or until smooth. With the motor running, add the oil in a thin stream until the dressing is thick and creamy. Drizzle over the salad, sprinkle with the extra Parmesan and serve immediately.

Gado Gado

6 new potatoes

2 carrots

250 g snake beans

2 tablespoons peanut oil

250 g firm tofu, cubed

100 g baby English spinach
  leaves

2 Lebanese cucumbers, cut
  into thick strips

1 large red capsicum, cut into
  thick strips

100 g bean sprouts

5 hard-boiled eggs

PEANUT SAUCE

1 tablespoon peanut oil

1 onion, finely chopped

2/3 cup peanut butter

1/4 cup kecap manis

2 tablespoons ground
  coriander

2 teaspoons chilli sauce

3/4 cup coconut cream

1 teaspoon grated palm sugar

1 tablespoon lemon juice

1   Cook the potatoes in boiling water until tender. Drain and cool slightly. Cut into quarters. Cut the carrots into thick strips and the beans into 10 cm lengths. Cook the carrots and beans separately in pans of boiling water until just tender. Plunge into iced water, then drain.

2   Heat the oil in a non-stick frying pan and cook the tofu in batches until crisp. Drain on paper towels.

3   To make the peanut sauce, heat the oil in a pan over low heat and cook the onion for 5 minutes, or until golden. Add the peanut butter, kecap manis, coriander, chilli sauce and coconut cream. Bring to the boil, then reduce the heat and simmer for 5 minutes. Stir in the sugar and lemon juice until dissolved.

4   Arrange the vegetables and tofu on a plate. Halve the eggs and place in the centre. Serve with the sauce.

Lemon, Fennel and Rocket Salad

PREPARATION TIME:
25 MINUTES
COOKING TIME:
5 MINUTES
SERVES 4

2 lemons
2 oranges
1 large fennel bulb or 2 baby fennel
200 g rocket
100 g pecans, chopped
1/2 cup stuffed green olives, halved lengthways

TOASTED SESAME DRESSING
1 tablespoon sesame oil
1 tablespoon sesame seeds
1/4 cup olive oil
2 tablespoons white wine vinegar
1 teaspoon French mustard

1 Peel the lemons and oranges, removing all the white pith. Cut into thin slices and remove any seeds. Thinly slice the fennel. Wash and dry the rocket and tear into pieces. Chill while making the dressing.

2 To make the dressing, heat the oil in a small pan over moderate heat. Add the sesame seeds and fry, stirring constantly, until lightly golden. Remove from the heat and cool. Pour into a small jug, whisk in the remaining ingredients and season with salt and ground black pepper.

3 Combine the fruit, fennel, rocket, pecans and olives in a shallow serving bowl. Drizzle with the dressing before serving.

Note: Blood oranges have a lovely tart flavour and, when in season, are delicious in this recipe.

Summer Bread Salad

PREPARATION TIME:
20 MINUTES
COOKING TIME:
15 MINUTES
SERVES 6–8

2 red capsicums
2 yellow capsicums
6 egg (Roma) tomatoes, cut into large chunks
100 g capers, drained
100 g anchovies, halved
100 g black olives
150 g bocconcini, halved
1 Italian wood-fired loaf
2 cups basil leaves

DRESSING
4 cloves garlic, finely chopped
1/4 cup red wine vinegar
1/2 cup extra virgin olive oil

1 Cut the capsicums into large pieces, removing the seeds and white membrane. Place, skin-side-up, under a hot grill, until the skin blackens and blisters. Cool in a plastic bag or under a tea towel, then peel away the skin and cut into thick strips.

2 Put the capsicum, tomato, capers, anchovies, olives and bocconcini in a bowl and toss to combine.

3 To make the dressing, put the ingredients in a screw-top jar and shake to combine.

4 Cut the bread into large pieces and place in a serving bowl. Drizzle with the dressing and mix until the bread is coated. Add the capsicum mixture and basil leaves, and toss gently.

Note: This salad is based on the Tuscan favourite which uses leftover crusty bread to make a salad.

Crunchy Haloumi Salad

PREPARATION TIME: 30 MINUTES +
2 HOURS MARINATING
COOKING TIME: 20 MINUTES
SERVES 6–8

2 red capsicums
300 g haloumi cheese
2 cloves garlic, crushed
1/4 teaspoon chilli flakes
1/4 cup olive oil
2 teaspoons chopped
    marjoram
1 small loaf fig and walnut
    bread or fruit bread,
    thickly sliced
250 g watercress, trimmed
250 g pear tomatoes, halved
2 avocados, sliced
375 g smoked tuna slices or
    tuna in brine, drained

DRESSING
2 tablespoons red wine
    vinegar
2 cloves garlic, crushed
1 teaspoon honey
1 tablespoon walnut oil
1/4 cup olive oil

1   Cut the capsicums into large pieces, removing the seeds and membrane. Place, skin-side-up, under a hot grill until the skin blackens and blisters. Cool under a tea towel or in a plastic bag, then peel away the skin and slice into thick strips.

2   Cut the haloumi cheese into thick slices and place in a shallow dish. Combine the garlic, chilli flakes, olive oil and marjoram, and pour the mixture over the haloumi. Cover the dish and refrigerate for 2 hours. Drain, reserving the marinade.

3   Toast one side of the fig and walnut bread slices until golden brown. Turn over and place a slice of the marinated haloumi on the untoasted side. Grill under high heat until the cheese is golden brown. Arrange the watercress on individual serving plates or a large platter, and top with the tomato, avocado, capsicum and tuna. Cut the haloumi croutons in half and arrange around the edge of the salad.

4   To make the dressing, put the reserved marinade, red wine vinegar, crushed garlic, honey, walnut oil and olive oil in a bowl and whisk to combine. Drizzle over the salad and serve immediately.

Papaya and Gorgonzola Salad

PREPARATION TIME:
20 MINUTES

COOKING TIME:
20 MINUTES

SERVES 4

1 cup orange juice
1 tablespoon oil
1 tablespoon soft brown sugar
1 fennel bulb, sliced
2 heads witlof, quartered
250 g watercress, ends trimmed
1 papaya, sliced
200 g Gorgonzola cheese, crumbled
1/2 cup hazelnuts, roughly chopped

DRESSING
1 cup loosely packed basil leaves
1/2 cup olive oil

1   Put the orange juice in a frying pan and cook over high heat until reduced by a third.

2   Stir the oil and brown sugar in a frying pan over low heat until the sugar dissolves. Add the fennel, witlof and orange juice, cover and cook for 15 minutes, or until the vegetables have caramelised. Check a couple of times during cooking; if it is looking too dry add a little water.

3   Divide the watercress among four serving plates, top with the papaya, caramelised vegetables, Gorgonzola and hazelnuts.

4   To make the dressing, process the basil and oil in a food processor until combined, then strain and drizzle over the salad.

Note: Gorgonzola is a blue-veined cheese with a strong, sharp flavour. It is named after the Italian town where it originated, and is made from pressed cows milk. If Gorgonzola cheese is not available, you can substitute Roquefort or Blue Castello in this recipe.

Coconut and Chickpea Salad

PREPARATION TIME:
15 MINUTES

COOKING TIME:
NIL

SERVES 6–8

1 green mango, diced
1 green chilli, finely chopped
2 x 380 g cans chickpeas, rinsed and drained
1/4 cup desiccated coconut
1/4 cup roughly chopped coriander

DRESSING
1 clove garlic, crushed
1/4 cup coconut milk
3 teaspoons fish sauce
2 tablespoons lime juice
1 teaspoon grated fresh ginger
1 teaspoon sugar

1 Combine the mango with the chilli, chickpeas, coconut and coriander.

2 To make the dressing, shake the ingredients together in a screw-top jar to combine.

3 Pour the dressing over the salad, cover and refrigerate for up to 3 hours to allow the flavours to develop.

Note: If green mango is not available, use a firm, underripe mango.

Snow Pea Salad

Sesame oil is a very strongly flavoured oil used in many Asian dishes. It should be used sparingly as its flavour tends to dominate.

PREPARATION TIME: 10 MINUTES
COOKING TIME: NIL
SERVES 6–8

150 g snow peas
1 bunch fresh asparagus
2 medium carrots, peeled
425-g can baby corn, drained
230-g can bamboo shoots, drained

DRESSING
1/4 cup vegetable oil
3 teaspoons sesame oil
1 tablespoon soy sauce

1   Trim the snow peas and cut in half. Remove the woody ends from the asparagus and cut them into 5-cm lengths. Cut carrots into matchsticks.

2   Place the snow peas and asparagus in a heatproof bowl and cover with boiling water. Stand for 1 minute, drain and plunge into iced water. Drain and dry thoroughly on absorbent paper.

3   Combine the snow peas, asparagus, carrots, corn and bamboo shoots in a serving bowl.

4   To make the dressing: Place the oils and sauce in a small screw-top jar; shake well to combine. Pour over the vegetables and combine well.

Fabulous Mixed Leaf Salad

Any variety of lettuce can be used in this salad.

PREPARATION TIME:
20 MINUTES
COOKING TIME:
NIL
SERVES 8

200 g snow peas, sliced diagonally
1 large red capsicum, sliced
4 leaves oak leaf lettuce
5 leaves white coral lettuce
1 punnet cherry tomatoes
50 g watercress sprigs
parmesan cheese, shaved, to serve

GARLIC CROUTONS
3 slices white bread
1/4 cup olive oil
1 clove garlic, crushed

DRESSING
2 tablespoons olive oil
1 tablespoon mayonnaise
1 tablespoon sour cream
2 tablespoons lemon juice
1 teaspoon brown sugar
cracked pepper to taste

1   Slice the snow peas and capsicum and wash the lettuce and tomatoes.

2   Combine the snow peas, capsicum, watercress, lettuce and tomatoes in a large mixing bowl.

3   To make Garlic Croûtons: Remove the crusts from the bread slices. Cut the bread into 1-cm squares. Heat the oil in a small, heavy-based pan and add garlic. Stir in the bread and cook until golden and crisp. Remove from the heat and drain on absorbent paper.

4   To make the dressing: Whisk all the ingredients in a small mixing bowl for 2 minutes or until well combined. Just before serving, pour the dressing over salad. Stir to combine. Top with Garlic Croûtons and shavings of parmesan cheese.

Apple and Pear Waldorf

When available use nashi fruit for this recipe. They are easy to purchase at most greengrocers. If nashi are out of season, use firm, crisp pears as an alternative.

PREPARATION TIME:
20 MINUTES
COOKING TIME:
NIL
SERVES 8–10

2 crisp red apples
2 pears or nashi fruit
1/4 cup lemon juice
1 stick celery, sliced
1/2 cup walnut or pecan pieces
1/2 cup mayonnaise
1 tablespoon shredded pickled ginger (optional)
1/2 teaspoon white pepper
1 tablespoon toasted sesame seeds (optional)

1   Core and dice the apples and pears. Toss in lemon juice to prevent the fruit from discolouring.

2   Reserving a teaspoon each of sesame seeds and ginger for the garnish, combine the remaining ingredients, mixing well. Add the fruit, stirring to coat the apples and pears with dressing. Sprinkle with sesame seeds and scatter with ginger.

Note: Shredded pickled ginger has a distinctive pink colour and sweet–salty flavour. It is available in Asian food stores.

Potato Salad

If you're using a store-bought mayonnaise, be sure to choose a sharp tasting one for the best result.

PREPARATION TIME:
20 MINUTES
COOKING TIME:
10 MINUTES
SERVES 8–10

8 medium potatoes, scrubbed well or peeled
1 medium orange sweet potato
1 medium white sweet potato
1/2 cup mayonnaise
3/4 cup sour cream
ground pepper, to taste
1 purple onion, finely chopped
1 red capsicum, diced
1 yellow or green capsicum, diced
250 g leg ham, cut into slivers

1   Peel and cut the potatoes and sweet potatoes into small cubes. Cook in boiling water for 5 minutes, or until tender but not mushy. Drain.

2   In a large bowl, mix the mayonnaise, sour cream, pepper and onion together. Add the cooked, drained potatoes while hot.

3   Gently stir in the capsicum and ham until just combined. Serve while warm or cover, refrigerate overnight and serve chilled.

Note: It is important to cut the potatoes into equal sizes for even cooking. This method of preparing the potatoes shortens the cooking time and ensures that the potatoes are not starchy in the middle, which sometimes happens when they are cooked whole.

Apple and Pear Waldorf (above). Potato Salad

Wild and Brown Rice Salad

PREPARATION TIME:
10 MINUTES
COOKING TIME:
1 HOUR 15 MINUTES
SERVES 6–8

1 cup brown rice
1/2 cup wild rice
1 medium red onion
1 small red capsicum
2 sticks celery
2 tablespoons chopped parsley
1/3 cup chopped pecans

DRESSING
1/4 cup orange juice
1/4 cup lemon juice
1 teaspoon grated orange rind
1 teaspoon grated lemon rind
1/3 cup olive oil

1   Cook the brown rice in a pan of boiling water for 25–30 minutes until just tender. Drain well and cool completely. Boil the wild rice for 30–40 minutes; drain well and cool.

2   Chop the onion and capsicum finely. Cut the celery into thin slices. Combine in a bowl with the parsley and cooked rices.

3   Place the pecans in a dry frying pan and stir over a medium heat for 2–3 minutes until lightly toasted. Transfer to a plate to cool.

4   To make the dressing: Place the juices, rinds and oil in a small screw-top jar and shake well.

5   Pour the dressing over the salad and fold through. Add pecans and gently mix through.

Red Cabbage Salad

PREPARATION TIME: 20 MINUTES
COOKING TIME: NIL
SERVES 8–10

1/2 red cabbage, shredded
3 medium carrots, grated
1 medium raw beetroot, peeled and grated
1 red capsicum, seeded and finely sliced
3 spring onions, chopped
1 orange, peeled and diced
440-g can unsweetened pineapple pieces in natural juice

DRESSING
1 egg, room temperature
1 teaspoon dry mustard
salt and pepper, to taste
1 tablespoon honey
1 tablespoon cider vinegar
1 tablespoon raspberry or white wine vinegar
1/4 cup vegetable oil

1 In a large bowl, combine the cabbage, carrots, beetroot, capsicum, spring onions and orange. Drain the pineapple pieces and add to the salad. Toss well.

2 To make the dressing: Place the egg, dry mustard, salt and pepper, honey and vinegars in a blender and process until smooth.

3 With the motor still running, gradually add the oil to the egg mixture. Blend until the oil is incorporated and the mixture is thick and creamy. Pour the dressing over salad, toss through and serve.

Savoury Cornbread

Whether hot off the barbecue or straight from the oven, the aroma alone of this superb bread will tempt the fussiest guest.

PREPARATION TIME:
15 MINUTES
COOKING TIME:
35 MINUTES
SERVES 8

60 g butter
2 tablespoons olive oil
1/2 cup finely chopped spring onions
1 clove garlic, crushed
2 canned jalapeño chillies, chopped
1/2 cup chopped fresh coriander
1 cup milk
1 egg, lightly beaten
1 cup self-raising flour
1 teaspoon salt
2 teaspoons baking powder
1 cup yellow cornmeal (polenta)
1/2 cup grated cheddar cheese
1/4 teaspoon ground sweet paprika

1 Melt the butter, and add the olive oil, spring onions, garlic, chillies, chopped coriander, milk and egg. Mix well.

2 Sift the self-raising flour, salt, baking powder and cornmeal into a bowl. Add the mixed ingredients and beat to a smooth batter.

3 Pour the mixture into a lightly greased and lined 23-cm square baking dish. Sprinkle with grated cheese and paprika. Bake in a preheated moderately hot oven 190°C for 30 minutes or until cornbread is golden brown.

Red Cabbage Salad. Savoury Cornbread (above)

4 To barbecue: Preheat kettle barbecue to medium high, then lower the heat. Place cornbread on a 5-cm rack which has been covered with a double layer of foil. Cook using indirect heat, hood down, for 35 minutes or until the cornbread pulls away from the sides of the pan. Cut the Savoury Cornbread into squares to serve.

Damper

Best cooked on a kettle barbecue.

PREPARATION TIME:
15 MINUTES
COOKING TIME:
30–35 MINUTES
SERVES 8

3 cups self-raising flour
1 teaspoon salt
80 g butter, chopped
250 ml milk
1 egg, lightly beaten
1 tablespoon sesame seeds
1/4 teaspoon ground sweet paprika

1 Sift the flour and salt into a large bowl. Rub the butter into the flour until the mixture resembles fine breadcrumbs.

2 Make a well in the centre and add the combined milk and beaten egg. Mix to a firm dough with a flat-bladed knife, bringing the mixture together with your hands if necessary.

3 Form the dough into a round and place on a baking tray lined with a double layer of heavy-duty foil, placed shiny side down. Pat out to 20 cm in diameter. Brush with a little water, sprinkle with sesame seeds and paprika.

4 Preheat the kettle barbecue to medium high. Cook the damper on indirect heat, hood down for 25–35 minutes, elevated on a 5-cm rack. The damper should be firm and hollow sounding when tapped. Reduce heat to medium if damper browns too quickly. Alternatively, bake in a preheated moderate oven 180°C for 20 minutes or until the loaf sounds hollow when tapped. Serve the damper immediately with butter (see photograph page 175).

Note: Damper can be made and shaped up to two hours in advance. Cover with plastic wrap and allow to stand at room temperature.

Chilli, Corn and Red Capsicum Muffins

PREPARATION TIME:
15 MINUTES

COOKING TIME:
25 MINUTES

MAKES 12 MUFFINS

1 cup plain flour
1/4 teaspoon salt
1 tablespoon baking powder
1 cup polenta
1 tablespoon soft brown sugar
1 egg
1/4 cup corn oil
2/3 cup milk or buttermilk
1 red chilli, finely chopped
1 small red capsicum, finely chopped
2 tablespoons chopped basil leaves
420 g can corn kernels, drained

1 Grease twelve 1/2-cup capacity muffin holes. Preheat the oven to moderately hot 200°C (400°F/Gas 6). Sift the flour, salt and baking powder into a bowl and mix in the polenta and sugar. Beat together the egg, oil and milk and add to the dry ingredients. Stir until just moistened, but do not overmix. Add the chilli, capsicum, basil and corn and mix briefly.

2 Spoon the mixture into the muffin tins. Bake for 25 minutes, or until the muffins are well risen. Leave for a few minutes, before turning out onto a wire rack to cool.

Fougasse

PREPARATION TIME:
20 MINUTES
+ 1 HOUR
30 MINUTES
RISING

COOKING TIME:
35 MINUTES

SERVES 4–6

7 g dried yeast
1 teaspoon sugar
3 cups plain flour
1 cup wholemeal plain flour
2 teaspoons salt

1 Mix the yeast, sugar and 1/2 cup of warm water in a bowl. Cover and set aside in a warm place for 10 minutes, or until foamy.

2 Sift the flours and salt, return the husks and make a well in the centre. Pour in 1 cup of extra warm water and the foamy yeast. Mix to a soft dough and gather into a ball. Turn out onto a floured surface and knead for 10 minutes, or until smooth.

3 Place in a large, lightly oiled bowl, cover loosely with greased plastic wrap and leave in a warm place for 1 hour, or until doubled in size.

4 Punch down the dough and knead for 1 minute. Press into a large, oval shape 2 cm thick and make several cuts on either side. Lay on a large, floured baking tray, cover with greased plastic wrap and leave to rise for 20 minutes. Preheat the oven to hot 210°C (415°F/Gas 6–7).

5 Bake for 35 minutes, or until crisp. After 15 minutes, spray with water to make the crust crispy.

Chilli, Corn and Red Capsicum Muffins (above). Fougasse

Savoury Scroll

PREPARATION TIME: 35 MINUTES
COOKING TIME: 35 MINUTES
SERVES 6

1 cup grated Cheddar
1/4 cup grated Parmesan
1 onion, chopped
1 red capsicum, chopped
100 g pancetta, chopped
1/4 cup chopped fresh
  parsley
3 cups self-raising flour
1 teaspoon salt
60 g butter, cubed
11/4 cups buttermilk
2 tablespoons olive oil

1 Lightly grease a baking tray. Preheat the oven to moderately hot 200°C (400°F/Gas 6). To make the filling, combine the Cheddar, Parmesan, onion, capsicum, pancetta and parsley. Season well with salt and pepper.

2 Sift the flour and salt into a large bowl. Add the butter and rub in with your fingertips until the mixture is crumbly. Make a well in the centre and pour in the buttermilk; mix to a soft dough and gather into a ball. Turn out onto a lightly floured surface and knead until smooth and elastic.

3 Roll out to a 50 x 25 cm rectangle. Sprinkle the filling over the top, leaving a 2 cm border, and press the filling down slightly. Roll up lengthways, enclosing the filling. Bring the ends together to form a ring and

brush the ends with some water. Press to seal.

4 Place on the prepared tray and snip the outside edge of the scroll with scissors at regular intervals, so the filling is exposed. Bake for 15 minutes, then reduce the temperature to moderate 180°C (350°F/Gas 4) and bake for a further 20 minutes, or until golden brown. Brush with the olive oil.

Grissini

PREPARATION TIME:
40 MINUTES +
30 MINUTES
RISING
COOKING TIME:
30 MINUTES
MAKES 18

7 g dried yeast
1 tablespoon caster sugar
2/3 cup milk
50 g butter
4 cups plain flour
1 teaspoon salt
sea salt flakes, sesame seeds
  or poppy seeds, to decorate

1 Grease three baking trays. Mix the yeast, sugar and 1/2 cup of warm water. Cover and set aside for 10 minutes, or until frothy. In a small pan, heat the milk and butter until the butter has melted.

2 Mix 3 1/2 cups of the flour and the salt in a bowl. Make a well in the centre and pour in the milk mixture and frothy yeast. Add enough of the remaining flour to mix to a soft dough, then turn out onto a lightly floured surface and knead for 10 minutes, or until smooth and elastic. Divide into 18 pieces.

3 Roll each piece to the thickness of a pencil and 30 cm in length. Place the grissini 3 cm apart on the baking trays. Cover loosely with greased plastic wrap and leave for 20 minutes.

4 Preheat the oven to hot 210°C (415°F/Gas 6–7). Brush the grissini with cold water and sprinkle with the sea salt or your choice of sesame or poppy seeds. Bake for 15–20 minutes, or until golden brown. Remove from the oven and cool on a wire rack. Reduce the temperature to moderate 180°C (350°F/Gas 4). Return the grissini to the trays, and bake for a further 5–10 minutes, or until crisp.

Ricotta and Dill Buns

PREPARATION TIME: 20 MINUTES
+ 1 HOUR 40 MINUTES RISING
COOKING TIME: 45 MINUTES
MAKES 8

7 g dried yeast
1 1/2 tablespoons caster sugar
250 g ricotta
30 g butter, softened
1/4 small onion, grated
1/4 teaspoon bicarbonate
  of soda
1 egg
3 3/4 cups plain flour
2 tablespoons chopped dill

1 Mix together the yeast, sugar and 1/4 cup of warm water in a bowl. Cover the bowl and set aside in a warm place for 10 minutes, or until frothy.

2 Put the ricotta, butter, onion, bicarbonate of soda and egg in a food processor with 1 teaspoon of salt and process until smooth. Add the frothy yeast and 3 cups of the flour. Add the remaining flour and mix to a smooth dough. Turn out the dough onto a floured surface and knead for 6–8 minutes, or until smooth. Add the dill during the last minute of kneading.

3 Put the dough in an oiled bowl, cover loosely with greased plastic wrap and set aside for 1 hour, or until doubled in size. Lightly grease a 20 x 30 cm baking tray.

4 Punch down the dough and divide into 8 pieces. Form into rounds and lay on the tray. Make 2 slashes on each bun. Cover with a damp tea towel for 30 minutes, or until well risen.

5 Preheat the oven to moderate 180°C (350°F/Gas 4). Bake the buns for 40–45 minutes, or until golden. Check after 20 minutes and reduce the oven to warm 170°C (325°F/Gas 3) if they are too brown.

Caramelised Onion Braids

PREPARATION TIME: 1 HOUR
+ 1 HOUR 35 MINUTES RISING
COOKING TIME: 1 HOUR 35 MINUTES
SERVES 8–10

2 1/2 cups plain flour
1 cup buckwheat flour
1 teaspoon salt
15 g fresh yeast or
**   7 g dried yeast**
1 1/4 cups warm milk
30 g butter
1 tablespoon oil
1 kg onions, thinly sliced
**   into rings**
1 egg, lightly beaten
2 teaspoons fennel
**   seeds**

1 Sift the flours and salt into a large bowl and make a well in the centre. Dissolve the yeast in 1/2 cup of the warm milk in a small bowl, then add the remaining warm milk. Pour into the well and mix to a dough. Turn out onto a floured surface and knead for 8 minutes, or until smooth. Place in a large oiled bowl, cover loosely with greased plastic wrap and leave in a warm place for 45 minutes–1 hour, or until doubled in size.

2 Melt the butter and oil in a frying pan, add the onion and cook over medium-low heat for 40–50 minutes, or until golden.

3 Punch down the dough, turn out onto a lightly floured surface and knead for 10 minutes, or until smooth and elastic.

4 Lightly grease 2 baking trays. Divide the dough in half. Working with 1 piece at a time, divide it into 3 pieces. Roll each piece out to a 30 x 10 cm rectangle. Divide the onion mixture into 6 portions and spread a portion along the middle of each rectangle, leaving a 2 cm border. Brush the edge with some of the beaten egg and roll over lengthways to enclose the filling.

5 Plait the 3 pieces together and place seam-side-down on a baking tray. Pinch the ends together. Repeat with the remaining dough and caramelised onion. Cover with a damp tea towel and leave in a warm place for 45 minutes, or until well risen.

6 Preheat the oven to moderate 180°C (350°F/Gas 4). Brush the top with the beaten egg and sprinkle with the fennel seeds. Bake for 35–45 minutes, or until well browned. Transfer to a wire rack to cool.

Bacon, Cheese and Onion Quickbread

PREPARATION TIME: 25 MINUTES
COOKING TIME: 1 HOUR 5 MINUTES
SERVES 6–8

1 tablespoon oil
3 onions, thinly sliced into
   rings
2 teaspoons soft brown
   sugar
4 rashers bacon, trimmed
   of excess fat and finely
   chopped
3 cups self-raising flour
100 g butter, chilled
3/4 cup grated Cheddar
1/2 cup milk

1   Heat half of the oil in a large, heavy-based frying pan. Add the onion and cook over medium heat for 10 minutes, stirring occasionally. Add the brown sugar and continue to cook for 10–15 minutes more, or until the onion is golden brown. Set aside and allow to cool. Heat the remaining oil in a small frying pan, add the bacon and cook over moderately high heat until the bacon is crisp. Drain on paper towels and add to the onion mixture.

2   Lightly grease a baking tray. Sift the flour into a large bowl, cut the butter into small cubes and rub into the flour with your fingertips until the mixture resembles breadcrumbs.

3   Add three-quarters of the onion mixture and 1/2 cup of the Cheddar to the flour mixture and mix well. Make a well in the centre and add the milk with about 1/2 cup of water (add enough water to bring the dough together). Using a flat-bladed knife, mix to a soft dough. Gently knead together to form a ball. Preheat the oven to hot 210°C (415°F/Gas 6–7).

4   Lay the dough on the tray and press out to form a 22 cm circle.

Using a sharp knife, mark the dough into quarters, cutting two-thirds of the way through. Sprinkle with the rest of the onion mixture and the remaining Cheddar. Bake for 15 minutes, then reduce the oven temperature to moderate 180°C (350°F/Gas 4). Cover the top loosely with foil if it starts getting too brown. Bake for a further 20–25 minutes, or until the base sounds hollow when tapped.

Mini Bagels

PREPARATION TIME:
50 MINUTES
+ 1 HOUR
25 MINUTES
RISING

COOKING TIME:
30 MINUTES

MAKES 22

15 g fresh yeast or
 7 g dried yeast
1 tablespoon sugar
2/3 cup warm milk
4 cups plain flour
1 teaspoon salt
30 g butter, melted
1 egg, lightly beaten
1 tablespoon poppy seeds

1 Lightly grease 3 baking trays. Combine the yeast, sugar and milk in a bowl. Cover and set aside in a warm place for 10 minutes, or until frothy. Sift the flour and salt into a large bowl. Make a well in the centre and add the butter, frothy yeast and 2/3 cup of warm water. Mix to a soft dough and gather into a ball. Knead for 10 minutes, or until elastic. Place

in a lightly oiled bowl, cover loosely with greased plastic wrap and leave for 1 hour, or until doubled in size. .

2 Punch down the dough and knead on a well-floured surface until smooth. Divide into 22 pieces. Working with 1 piece at a time (keeping the others covered with a damp tea towel) roll into tight balls. Poke a finger through the centre and gently enlarge the hole until it forms a doughnut. Lay on the baking trays, cover with the tea towel and leave for 10–15 minutes, or until risen.

3 Bring a large frying pan of water to the boil. Add 3–4 bagels at a time and cook for 1 minute. Remove with a slotted spoon and lay on the trays. They will be deflated at this stage.

4 Preheat the oven to moderate 200°C (400°F/ Gas 6). Brush the bagels with the egg and sprinkle with the poppy seeds. Bake for 25 minutes, or until browned.

Pesto Rolls

PREPARATION TIME:
10 MINUTES
COOKING TIME:
5–10 MINUTES
SERVES 6

6 small dinner rolls
1/4 cup toasted pine nuts
2–3 tablespoons freshly grated parmesan cheese
1–2 cloves garlic, peeled
2 tablespoons olive oil
50 g butter, chopped
3–4 teaspoons lemon juice
1 cup fresh basil leaves
salt and pepper, to taste
shaved parmesan cheese, to serve

1 Cut each dinner roll in half vertically.
2 Combine the rest of the ingredients in a food processor bowl and process for 20–30 seconds or until smooth. (Add a little more butter or oil if pesto is dry.)
3 Spread each half roll with the pesto and toast under a preheated grill for 5–10 minutes or until they have heated through. Serve with shaved parmesan cheese. Alternatively, place the roll halves together and wrap them in foil. Place them on a hot barbecue grill or flatplate, turning occasionally to ensure even cooking.

Savoury Bread

PREPARATION TIME:
10 MINUTES
COOKING TIME:
10–15 MINUTES
SERVES 6–8

1 Vienna loaf
1/2 cup grated cheddar cheese
2 tablespoons grated parmesan cheese
1 spring onion, finely sliced
2 bacon rashers, finely chopped
pepper, to taste

1 Across the top of the Vienna loaf, at 2-cm intervals, cut diagonal slits 1-cm deep in one direction. Make similar slits in the other direction to form a diamond pattern. Place the bread on a foil-lined baking tray.
2 Combine the rest of the ingredients in a small bowl and sprinkle it over the top of the loaf.
3 Bake the loaf in a preheated moderate 180°C oven for 10–15 minutes or until the cheese has melted and the bacon is crisp.

216

Garlic Bread

PREPARATION TIME:
10 MINUTES
COOKING TIME:
10–15 MINUTES
SERVES 6–8

1 French loaf
125 g softened butter
2–3 cloves garlic, crushed
1 tablespoon finely chopped parsley
pepper, to taste

1 Cut the French loaf into thick diagonal slices three-quarters of the way through.
2 Combine the other ingredients in a small bowl and beat them together until smooth.
3 Spread the mixture between each slice of bread, then wrap the loaf in foil and place it on a baking tray.
4 Bake in a moderate 180°C oven for 10–15 minutes or until the butter has melted and the bread is hot. Or place the wrapped bread on a hot barbecue grill or flatplate, turning occasionally to ensure even cooking.

Olive Bread

PREPARATION TIME:
10 MINUTES
COOKING TIME:
10–15 MINUTES
SERVES 6–8

1 French loaf
green or black olive paste, to spread
2 tomatoes
thin slices mozzarella or bocconcini
2–3 tablespoons finely shredded basil leaves
pepper, to taste

1 Cut the French loaf into 2-cm slices and spread each slice with a small amount of olive paste.
2 Thinly slice the tomatoes and place one or two slices on each slice of bread.
3 Top with mozzarella or bocconcini and sprinkle with basil and pepper.
4 Place the bread slices on a foil-lined tray and bake in a preheated moderate 180°C oven for 10–15 minutes or until the cheese has melted and the bread has heated through. Serve warm.

Savoury Bread (above left). Garlic Bread. Olive Bread. Pesto Rolls

Cheese Bread

Be creative with this recipe by using other combinations of cheese for variety. Best cooked on a kettle barbecue.

PREPARATION TIME:
15 MINUTES
COOKING TIME:
8 MINUTES
SERVES 8

1 crusty French loaf
1/3 cup olive oil
125 g butter, softened
1 clove garlic, crushed
2 tablespoons French mustard
1 cup grated cheddar cheese
1 cup grated mozzarella cheese
3 tablespoons sesame seeds

1   Slice the French loaf three-quarters of the way through, diagonally about 2 cm apart. Whip together the olive oil, softened butter, crushed garlic and mustard until creamy.

2   Spread the bread slices with the whipped mixture and place on a baking tray. Combine the cheeses, sprinkle the mixture between bread slices and top with sesame seeds.

3   Wrap the bread in heavy-duty or industrial-strength foil. Place in a baking tray or cake tin on the flatplate of a hot kettle barbecue. Cover and cook for 8 minutes or until the cheese bubbles. Alternatively, bake the bread in a moderate oven 180°C for about 10 minutes. Do not overcook.

Honey Garlic Dressing

Pour over a tossed green salad.

PREPARATION TIME: 5 MINUTES
COOKING TIME: NIL
MAKES 1 CUP

1/4 cup peanut oil
2 tablespoons lemon or lime juice
1 teaspoon grated lemon rind
6 teaspoons honey
1–2 cloves garlic, crushed
1 tablespoon chopped fresh chives
salt and pepper, to taste

1   Combine all the ingredients in a screw-top jar and shake until well combined.

Creamy Dressing

This dressing goes well with a Caesar Salad.

PREPARATION TIME: 5 MINUTES
COOKING TIME: NIL
MAKES 1/2 CUP

2 tablespoons olive oil
1 tablespoon mayonnaise
1 tablespoon sour cream
2 tablespoons lemon juice
1 teaspoon soft brown sugar
salt and cracked black pepper, to taste
1 clove garlic, crushed (optional)
1 tablespoon chopped fresh chives (optional)

1   Combine all the ingredients in a screw-top jar and shake until well combined.

Orange and Sesame Dressing

Delicious with a rocket and watercress salad.

PREPARATION TIME: 5 MINUTES
COOKING TIME: NIL
MAKES 1/2 CUP

1 tablespoon sesame oil
2 tablespoons orange juice
2 teaspoons toasted sesame seeds
1 teaspoon grated orange rind
1–2 teaspoons soy sauce
3/4 teaspoon grated ginger
salt and pepper, to taste

1   Combine all the ingredients in a screw-top jar and shake until well combined.

Vinaigrette Dressing

This classic dressing goes well with a fresh garden salad.

PREPARATION TIME: 5 MINUTES
COOKING TIME: NIL
MAKES 1/2 CUP

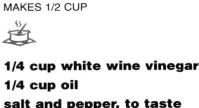

1/4 cup white wine vinegar
1/4 cup oil
salt and pepper, to taste
1–2 tablespoons freshly chopped herbs (optional)

1   Combine all the ingredients in a screw-top jar and shake until well combined.

Vinaigrette Dressing

Creamy Dressing

Orange and Sesame Dressing

Honey Garlic Dressing

Salsas and Dips

Once you have the main elements of the meal organised, it's time to think about the finishing touches. Dips served with fresh vegetables, breads and crackers can stave off any early pangs of hunger at the beginning of the barbecue, while refreshing salsas elevate the flavour of barbecued meats and seafood to new heights. All of the delicious recipes in this chapter are simple to make and, best of all, can be prepared ahead of time, leaving you free to enjoy the company of your friends.

Part of the charm of a barbecue is the casual and informal feeling it evokes. While the meat's on the hotplate and your guests are relaxing with a cool drink, tempt them with with some home-made dips, accompanied by chopped fresh vegetables, crackers and fresh crusty bread. If you have time, you could make up some crunchy dippers of your own. Crisp up thin slices of Lebanese bread, potato skins are always popular, or try making bagel chips with a little Parmesan and pesto sprinkled over the top. Just make sure your guests don't eat too much or they won't have room for all the other treats you have in store!

Salsas are a must at any barbecue. They are delicious (and decidedly more-ish) served as a dip with corn chips or toasted Turkish bread. When accompanying the main meal, salsas can transform an ordinary piece of barbecued meat or fish into an extraordinary taste sensation. Refreshing and light, they give a lift to the rich flavour of meat and chicken, and complement the subtlety of all types of seafood.

The secret to a good salsa or dip is to buy only the freshest ingredients. To enhance the refreshing quality of salsas, serve them chilled. Dips made with dairy products should also be kept refrigerated before use.

Peach, Red Capsicum and Ginger Salsa

Shown here with chargrilled chicken breast. Good with seafood and barbecued meats.

PREPARATION TIME:
20 MINUTES
COOKING TIME:
NIL
SERVES 4

- 3 tablespoons white wine vinegar
- 2 tablespoons caster sugar
- 2 teaspoons grated fresh ginger
- 1 clove garlic, crushed
- 1/2 teaspoon ground cumin
- 1/4 cup chopped coriander leaves
- 1/4 cup chopped mint
- 1 red capsicum, diced
- 1 small red onion, finely diced
- 1 small red chilli, finely chopped
- 3 canned or fresh peaches, diced

1 Combine the vinegar, sugar, ginger, garlic, cumin, coriander and mint.

2 Put the capsicum, onion, chilli and peaches in a large bowl. Gently stir through the vinegar herb mixture and serve at once.

Bocconcini, Tomato and Sun-dried Capsicum Salsa

Shown here with chargrilled beef steak. Also good with barbecued chicken or tuna steaks.

PREPARATION TIME:
20 MINUTES
COOKING TIME:
NIL
SERVES 6

- 180 g bocconcini, diced
- 200 g tomatoes, diced
- 1/3 cup drained sun-dried capsicum in oil, chopped
- 1 spring onion, finely sliced
- 1 tablespoon extra virgin olive oil
- 2 teaspoons red wine vinegar
- 1 tablespoon shredded basil leaves
- 1 tablespoon chopped flat-leaf parsley

1 Mix together the bocconcini, tomato, sun-dried capsicum and spring onion in a large bowl.

2 Whisk together the oil and vinegar until thoroughly blended. Stir through the basil and parsley.

3 Toss the dressing through the bocconcini and tomato mixture and season to taste with salt and black pepper. Serve at room temperature.

Roasted Red Capsicum, Tomato, Lime and Chilli Salsa

Shown here with chargrilled lamb steaks. Also good with veal, beef, chicken, fish and seafood.

PREPARATION TIME:
45 MINUTES
COOKING TIME:
35 MINUTES
SERVES 6

2 red capsicums
2 tomatoes
1/2 small red onion
1–2 small red chillies
2 limes
2 tablespoons olive oil
1 teaspoon sugar

1   Preheat the oven to moderate 180°C (350°F/ Gas 4). Cut the capsicums into quarters and discard the membrane and seeds. Place in an oiled baking dish and bake for 30 minutes, turning regularly. If the capsicum begins to burn, add 2 tablespoons of water to the baking dish. Allow to cool and then chop into small cubes.

2   Score a cross in the base of each tomato. Place in a bowl of boiling water for 10 seconds, then plunge into cold water and peel the skin away from the cross. Cut the tomatoes in half and scoop out the seeds with a teaspoon. Cut the tomato flesh into thin strips.

3   Finely chop the onion and chilli. Peel the limes, then cut off the pith and carefully cut the flesh into fine segments.

4   Mix together the capsicum, tomato, onion, chilli, lime segments, olive oil and sugar in a bowl. Season well with salt and freshly ground black pepper. Cover and leave to stand for at least 15 minutes for the flavours to blend, before serving.

Chilli Avocado Salsa

Shown here with lamb chops. Also good with corn chips, pita bread, chargrilled meats and any Mexican food.

PREPARATION TIME:
30 MINUTES
+ 3 HOURS REFRIGERATION
COOKING TIME:
NIL
SERVES 6

3 tomatoes, seeded and diced
1 small red onion, finely chopped
1–2 jalapeno chillies, seeded and very finely chopped
1/3 cup flat-leaf parsley, chopped
1–2 cloves garlic, crushed
3 tablespoons light olive oil
1 ripe avocado
2 limes, to garnish

1   Mix together the tomato, onion, jalapeno, parsley, garlic and olive oil. Season to taste, cover and refrigerate for 3 hours.

2   Just before serving, halve the avocado, remove the stone and gently mash the flesh with a fork while still in the skin. Scoop out the avocado and stir into the salsa. Serve with lime wedges.

Papaya and Black Bean Salsa

Shown here with chargrilled white fish cutlets. Also good with salmon or tuna steaks, chicken, beef and lamb.

PREPARATION TIME:
25 MINUTES
COOKING TIME:
NIL
SERVES 4

1 small red onion, finely chopped
1 papaya (about 500 g), peeled, seeded and cubed
1 birds eye chilli, seeded and finely chopped
1 tablespoon salted black beans, rinsed and drained
2 teaspoons peanut oil
1 teaspoon sesame oil
2 teaspoons fish sauce
1 tablespoon lime juice
1 tablespoon chopped coriander leaves
2 teaspoons shredded mint

1   In a bowl, gently toss together the onion, papaya, chilli and black beans with your hands.

2   Just before serving, whisk together the peanut oil, sesame oil, fish sauce and lime juice. Pour over the salsa and gently toss. Add the coriander and mint and serve immediately, at room temperature.

Mexican Layered Dip

PREPARATION TIME: 50 MINUTES
COOKING TIME: NIL
SERVES 12

450 g can refried beans
35 g packet taco seasoning
   mix
300 g sour cream
200 g ready-made salsa sauce
1/2 cup grated Cheddar
2 tablespoons chopped pitted
   black olives
200 g corn chips
1 tablespoon chopped
   coriander

GUACAMOLE
3 ripe avocados
1 tomato
1–2 red chillies, finely
   chopped
1 small red onion, finely
   chopped
1 tablespoon chopped
   coriander
1 tablespoon lime or lemon
   juice
2 tablespoons sour cream
1–2 drops habanero sauce or
   Tabasco sauce

1   Using a fork, mix the refried beans and taco seasoning together in a small bowl.
2   To make the guacamole, cut the avocados in half, peel and discard the skin and stone (chop into the stone with a sharp knife and lift it out). Roughly chop the avocados and place in a bowl, then mash lightly with a fork. Cut the tomato in half horizontally, scoop out the seeds with a teaspoon and discard. Finely dice the flesh and add to the avocado. Stir in the chilli, onion, coriander, lime or lemon juice, sour cream and habanero or Tabasco sauce. Season with freshly cracked black pepper.
3   To assemble, spread the bean mixture in the middle of a large serving platter (the dish we used was 30 x 35 cm), leaving a clear border for the corn chips. Spoon the sour cream on top, leaving a small border of bean mixture showing. Repeat with the guacamole and salsa sauce so that you can see each layer. Sprinkle with cheese and olives.
4   Arrange the corn chips around the edge of the platter and garnish with the coriander.

Note: Habanero sauce is a very hot condiment sauce made from habanero chillies. Use sparingly to add extra zing to the dip. It is available from delicatessens and speciality stores.
Hint: Always wear rubber gloves when you are chopping chillies. If this isn't possible, remember to scrub your hands thoroughly with warm soapy water after chopping. Don't touch your eyes or any other delicate skin or you will cause burning and skin irritation.

Taramasalata

PREPARATION TIME:
25 MINUTES
COOKING TIME:
NIL
SERVES 8

4 slices white bread, crusts removed
1/4 cup milk
100 g smoked cod's roe (tarama)
1 egg yolk
1 clove garlic, crushed
1 tablespoon grated onion
1/4 cup olive oil
1/3 cup lemon juice

1   Soak the bread slices in the milk for 5 minutes, then remove and squeeze out the excess liquid.
2   Process the cod's roe and egg yolk in a food processor for 10 seconds. Add the bread, garlic and onion and process for 20 seconds, or until the mixture is well combined and smooth.
3   With the motor running, gradually add the olive oil in a thin stream. Process until all the oil is absorbed.
4   Add the lemon juice in small amounts, to taste. Transfer to a bowl and serve with bread and black olives. Store in the refrigerator in an airtight container for up to 1 week, and return to room temperature before serving.

Asparagus, Apple and Avocado Dip

PREPARATION TIME:
40 MINUTES
+ 2 HOURS
REFRIGERATION
COOKING TIME:
5 MINUTES
SERVES 10–12

2 bunches asparagus
3 green apples
2 tablespoons lemon juice
3 ripe avocados
300 g sour cream
4 drops Tabasco sauce

1   Wash and trim the woody ends from the asparagus. Steam or microwave until just cooked, then plunge into iced water and drain. Chop off the tips and set aside, to serve. Finely chop the remaining asparagus stalks.
2   Peel and grate the apples and sprinkle with 1 tablespoon lemon juice to prevent browning. Add the asparagus and mix together. In a separate dish, mash the avocado flesh. Mix in the remaining lemon juice and stir into the apple and asparagus. Add the sour cream and mix well. Add the Tabasco, cover with plastic wrap and refrigerate for 2 hours. Serve with the asparagus tips for dipping.

Moroccan Sweet Carrot and Honey Dip

PREPARATION TIME:
20 MINUTES +
OVERNIGHT
SOAKING
COOKING TIME:
1 HOUR
SERVES 6

150 g dried chickpeas
50 g butter
1/2 teaspoon ground cumin
1/2 teaspoon ground coriander
1/2 teaspoon ground cinnamon
1/4 teaspoon chilli powder
200 g carrots, chopped
1 tablespoon honey
1/3 cup thick natural yoghurt
2 tablespoons chopped parsley
2 tablespoons olive oil
1 tablespoon olive oil, extra

1   Place the chickpeas in a bowl, cover with water and soak overnight. Drain and rinse well, then place in a pan and cover with cold water. Bring to the boil, then reduce the heat and simmer for 45 minutes, or until tender. Skim off any scum that rises to the surface. Drain, rinse and mash well.

2   Melt the butter in a heavy-based frying pan; add the cumin, coriander, cinnamon, chilli and carrots. Cook, covered, over low heat for 5 minutes, turning the carrots to coat them in the spices. Drizzle with honey. If the carrots start to stick add a tablespoon of water. Cover and cook for 20 minutes until the carrots are very tender and a caramel brown colour. Cool slightly and mash in the frying pan to include all the bits on the base of the pan.

3   Combine the mashed chickpea and carrot with the yoghurt, parsley and olive oil, and season well with salt and pepper. Spoon into a serving bowl and drizzle with extra oil. Serve with celery sticks or blanched green beans.

Hummus

PREPARATION
TIME:
15 MINUTES
COOKING TIME:
NIL
SERVES 4–6

425 g can chickpeas
2–3 tablespoons lemon juice
2 tablespoons olive oil
2 cloves garlic, crushed
1/4 cup tahini

1   Place the drained chickpeas, lemon juice, olive oil and garlic in a food processor. Season with salt and pepper. Process for 20–30 seconds, or until smooth. Add the tahini and process for a further 10 seconds. Delicious served with Lebanese bread or toasted pita bread.

Prawn, Corn and Sweet Chilli Dip

PREPARATION
TIME:
1 HOUR
+ 2 HOURS
REFRIGERATION
COOKING TIME:
3 MINUTES
SERVES 8

1 kg cooked prawns
juice and grated rind
   of 3 limes
100 g frozen corn kernels
250 g soft cream cheese
1/4 cup finely chopped chives
1 tablespoon sweet chilli
   sauce
4 cooked king prawns,
   to garnish

1   Peel, devein and rinse the prawns; pat them dry and place in a bowl. Add the lime juice to the prawns, cover and refrigerate for 10 minutes.
2   Cook the frozen corn kernels in boiling water for 2–3 minutes, or until tender. Drain and plunge the kernels into iced water to prevent further cooking, then drain and pat dry with paper towels.
3   Place the prawns and lime juice in a food processor and process in short bursts for 2–3 seconds, or until the prawns are chopped into small pieces but not minced.
4   Transfer the chopped prawns to a bowl and mix in the cream cheese, corn kernels, lime rind and chives. Add the chilli sauce and mix well. Cover the dip with plastic wrap and refrigerate for at least 2 hours. Just before serving, peel and devein the king prawns, leaving the tails intact. Transfer the dip to a serving bowl and garnish with the peeled prawns. Serve with cooked king prawns, for dipping.

Guacamole

PREPARATION TIME:
30 MINUTES
COOKING TIME:
NIL
SERVES 6

3 ripe avocados
1 tablespoon lime or lemon juice
1 tomato
1–2 red chillies, finely chopped
1 small red onion, finely chopped
1 tablespoon finely chopped coriander leaves
2 tablespoons sour cream
1–2 drops Tabasco or habanero sauce

1 Roughly chop the avocado flesh and place in a bowl. Mash lightly with a fork and sprinkle with the lime or lemon juice to prevent the avocado discolouring.

2 Cut the tomato in half horizontally and use a teaspoon to scoop out the seeds. Finely dice the flesh and add to the avocado.

3 Stir in the chilli, onion, coriander, sour cream and Tabasco or habanero sauce. Season with freshly cracked black pepper.

4 Serve immediately or cover the surface with plastic wrap and refrigerate for 1–2 hours. If refrigerated, leave at room temperature for 15 minutes before serving.

Hint: You will need 1–2 limes to produce 1 tablespoon of juice, depending on the lime. A heavier lime will probably be more juicy. To get more juice from a citrus fruit, prick it all over with a fork and then heat on High (100%) in the microwave for 1 minute. Don't forget to prick it or the fruit may burst.

Marinated Roasted Vegetable Dip

PREPARATION TIME:
55 MINUTES +
4 HOURS
MARINATING
COOKING TIME:
50 MINUTES
SERVES 8

1 small eggplant, sliced
2 zucchinis, sliced
3 red capsicums
1/2 cup extra virgin olive oil
2 cloves garlic, sliced
2 Roma tomatoes
200 g canned, drained
   artichoke hearts
1/4 cup oregano leaves
250 g ricotta cheese
1/4 cup sliced black olives

1   Place the eggplant and zucchini in a colander over a bowl and sprinkle with the salt, then leave for 15–20 minutes. Cut the capsicums into large flat pieces, removing the seeds and membrane. Brush with a little olive oil and place, skin-side-up, under a hot grill until the skin blackens and blisters. Cool in a plastic bag, then peel away the skin. Reserve about a quarter of the capsicum to garnish and place the rest in a large non-metallic bowl.

2   Place half the olive oil in a bowl, add 1 clove garlic and a pinch of salt and mix together well. Rinse the eggplant and zucchini and pat dry with paper towels. Place the eggplant on a non-stick or foil-lined tray and brush with the garlic oil. Cook under a very hot grill for 4–6 minutes each side, or until golden brown, brushing both sides with the oil during grilling. The eggplant will burn easily, so keep a close watch. Allow to cool while grilling the zucchini in the same way. Add the eggplant and zucchini to the capsicum in the bowl.

3   Slice the tomatoes lengthways, place on a non-stick or foil-lined baking tray and brush with the garlic oil. Reduce the temperature and grill for 10–15 minutes, or until soft, then add to the other vegetables.

4   Cut the artichokes into quarters and add to the bowl. Mix in any remaining garlic oil along with the remaining olive oil. Stir in the fresh oregano and remaining garlic. Cover with a tight-fitting lid or plastic wrap and refrigerate for at least 2 hours.

5   Drain the vegetables and place them in a food processor. Add the ricotta and blend for 20 seconds, or until smooth. Reserve 1 tablespoon of olives to garnish and add the remainder to the food processor. Mix together in a couple of short bursts, then transfer to a non-metallic bowl and cover with plastic wrap. Chill for at least 2 hours.

6   Slice the reserved capsicum into fine strips and arrange on top of the dip with the reserved olives.

Baba Ganouj (Eggplant Dip)

PREPARATION TIME:
15 MINUTES
+ 20 MINUTES STANDING
COOKING TIME:
35 MINUTES
SERVES 6–8

2 medium eggplants
3–4 cloves garlic, crushed
2 tablespoons lemon juice
2 tablespoons tahini
1 tablespoon olive oil
sprinkle of paprika, to garnish

1 Halve the eggplants lengthways, sprinkle with salt and leave for 15–20 minutes. Rinse and pat dry with paper towels. Preheat the oven to moderate 180°C (350°F/Gas 4).

2 Bake the eggplants for 35 minutes, or until soft. Peel away the skin and discard. Place the flesh in a food processor with the garlic, lemon juice, tahini and olive oil and season to taste with salt and pepper. Process for 20–30 seconds. Sprinkle with paprika and serve with Lebanese bread.

Note: We sprinkle eggplants with salt and leave them before using because they can have a bitter taste. The salt draws the bitter liquid from the eggplant. Slender eggplants do not need to be treated before use.

Chilli Crab and Tomato Dip

PREPARATION TIME:
25 MINUTES
COOKING TIME:
NIL
SERVES 6

2 x 170 g cans crab meat, drained
200 g neufchatel cheese (see Note)
2 tablespoons chilli sauce
2 teaspoons tomato paste
1 teaspoon grated lemon rind
2 teaspoons lemon juice
1 small onion, finely grated
3 spring onions, finely sliced
1 tomato, seeded and finely chopped

1 Squeeze any remaining liquid from the crab meat. Beat the neufchatel until smooth, then add the crab meat, chilli sauce, tomato paste, lemon rind, lemon juice and onion. Season well with salt and pepper. Mix together well and spoon into a serving bowl.

2 Scatter the spring onion and chopped tomato over the top and chill before serving.

Note: Neufchatel is a smooth, mild, good-quality cream cheese available from delicatessens.

Marinades, sauces and butters

*t*ransform the most ordinary meal into something different and delicious with marinades. They not only add flavour to the dish, but also help to tenderise your meat. Because food is cooked quickly on the barbecue, marinating it beforehand gives it a head start.

Acidic-based marinades containing vinegar, citrus juice or wine break down and tenderise meat fibres and are particularly good for tougher meats. Oil-based marinades will moisturise the meat and are suitable for chicken and pork, which have a tendency to dry out when cooked. Try a yoghurt-based marinade for chicken or lamb. The marinade will form a delicious crust over the meat when it is cooked. Dry marinades are usually a combination of salt and ground spices or dried herbs. Pastes are made by adding a little oil to the dry mixture to allow it to adhere more easily to the meat.

If you barbecue regularly, it's a good idea to have a couple of your favourite marinades made up and stored in the refrigerator. Remember also, to use any leftover marinade to baste the food occasionally while you are cooking; but don't use a plastic or nylon bristled brush as it may melt onto the food. Any marinade that contains sugar or honey (or hidden sugar like tomato sauce) should only be brushed over almost at the end of the cooking, or the sugar will caramelise and become very dark and bitter.

Ideally, large cuts of meat and whole chickens should be marinated for some hours in the refrigerator, turning occasionally to allow for as much penetration of flavour as possible. Cubed meats and smaller portions require less marinating time. Don't marinate seafood for longer than one hour, particularly when using an acidic ingredient in the marinade.

Fresh relishes or a delicious sauce can really dress up simple meat or seafood dishes. Some of those featured here also make good dipping sauces for finger food like barbecued king prawns or satays.

If you have no time to prepare a sauce you could always make a selection of flavoured butters and store them in the freezer. Use them to liven up barbecued vegetables or a steak, or use them to flavour bread rolls or jacket potatoes. They are all simple to prepare and make a real difference to the look and flavour of your meal.

Lemon and Wine Marinade

Use to marinate lamb or chicken.

PREPARATION TIME: 5 MINUTES
COOKING TIME: NIL
MAKES 1 CUP

2 tablespoons lemon juice
2 teaspoons grated lemon rind
1 clove garlic, crushed
1/4 cup white wine
1/4 cup olive oil
2 tablespoons soft brown sugar
1 tablespoon chopped rosemary
1 tablespoon lemon thyme

Combine all the ingredients in a bowl and mix well.

Teriyaki Marinade

Use to marinate lamb or beef.

PREPARATION TIME: 5 MINUTES
COOKING TIME: NIL
MAKES 1/2 CUP

1/4 cup soy sauce
2 tablespoons teriyaki sauce
3 teaspoons grated fresh ginger
1–2 cloves garlic, crushed
2 tablespoons soft brown sugar
1/4 cup chicken or beef stock
2–3 tablespoons sweet sherry

Combine all the ingredients in a bowl and mix well.

Spiced Yoghurt Marinade

Use to marinate lamb or beef.

PREPARATION TIME: 5 MINUTES
COOKING TIME: NIL
MAKES 1 CUP

1 cup plain yoghurt
1 onion, finely chopped
3/4 teaspoon ground coriander
3/4 teaspoon ground cumin
3/4 teaspoon garam masala
3/4 teaspoon ground cinnamon
1/2 teaspoon ground ginger
1 teaspoon sugar
1 clove garlic, crushed
salt and pepper, to taste
pinch cardamom

Combine all the ingredients in a bowl and mix well.

Apricot and Onion Marinade

Use to marinate pork or chicken.

PREPARATION TIME: 5 MINUTES
COOKING TIME: NIL
MAKES 1 CUP

1/3 cup apricot nectar
1 teaspoon Worcestershire sauce
1 tablespoon oil
1 tablespoon malt vinegar
1–2 tablespoons French onion soup mix
2–3 spring onions, finely sliced
1/4 cup red or white wine (optional)

Combine all the ingredients in a bowl and mix well.

Mustard and Herb Marinade

Use to marinate beef or lamb.

PREPARATION TIME: 5 MINUTES
COOKING TIME: NIL
MAKES 1/2 CUP

1/4 cup olive oil
2 tablespoons balsamic vinegar
2 teaspoons soft brown sugar
2–3 teaspoons Dijon, German or wholegrain mustard
1–2 teaspoons mixed dried herbs
1 tablespoon chopped fresh parsley
salt and pepper, to taste

Combine all the ingredients in a bowl and mix well.

Horseradish Cream Sauce

Serve this sauce with fish or beef.

PREPARATION TIME: 10 MINUTES
COOKING TIME: NIL
MAKES 1 CUP

125 g cream cheese
1 tablespoon mayonnaise
1 tablespoon sour cream
1–2 teaspoons minced horseradish or horseradish cream
1 tablespoon chopped chives, lemon thyme or parsley

1   Using electric beaters, beat the cream cheese until soft and creamy.

2   Add the rest of the ingredients and beat until well combined.

Tartare Sauce

Serve this sauce with seafood.

PREPARATION TIME: 5 MINUTES
COOKING TIME: NIL
MAKES 1 CUP

- **1/2 cup whole egg mayonnaise**
- **1 tablespoon sour cream**
- **1–2 tablespoons halved capers**
- **3 teaspoons finely chopped gherkins**
- **1 tablespoon chopped fresh dill (optional)**

Combine all the ingredients in a small bowl and mix well.

Chilli Barbecue Sauce

Serve this sauce with lamb or beef.

PREPARATION TIME: 5 MINUTES
COOKING TIME: 1 MINUTE
MAKES 1/2 CUP

- **20 g butter**
- **1 teaspoon ground cumin**
- **1/2 teaspoon ground coriander**
- **1/2 teaspoon ground paprika**
- **1 tablespoon sweet chilli sauce**
- **1/3 cup bottled barbecue sauce**
- **2 teaspoons Worcestershire sauce**

1   Heat the butter in a small pan. Add the cumin, coriander and paprika and cook for 30 seconds.
2   Stir in the sweet chilli sauce, barbecue sauce and Worcestershire sauce and mix well.

Creamy Mustard Sauce

Serve this sauce with beef or chicken.

PREPARATION TIME: 5 MINUTES
COOKING TIME: NIL
MAKES 1/2 CUP

- **2 tablespoons whole egg mayonnaise**
- **1/3 cup sour cream**
- **2–3 tablespoons Dijon or wholegrain mustard**
- **1 tablespoon of your favourite chopped fresh herbs (optional)**
- **salt and pepper, to taste**

Combine all the ingredients in a small bowl and mix well. If the sauce is too thick, add a little cream to achieve the required consistency.

Coriander Mayonnaise

Serve this sauce with chicken, seafood or veal.

PREPARATION TIME: 15 MINUTES
COOKING TIME: NIL
MAKES 1 CUP

3 egg yolks
3/4 cup light olive oil
2 tablespoons lemon juice
1–2 tablespoons chopped fresh coriander
salt and pepper, to taste
1 clove garlic, crushed (optional)

1 Place the egg yolks in a food processor bowl or blender. With the motor constantly running, add the olive oil in a thin stream and process until thick and creamy.
2 Add the lemon juice and coriander and process until combined. Season the mixture with salt and pepper and the garlic, if using.

Tomato Sauce

Serve this sauce warm or cold with burgers, sausages, steak or fish.

PREPARATION TIME: 10 MINUTES
COOKING TIME: 10 MINUTES
MAKES 1 CUP

1 tablespoon olive oil
20 g butter
1 small onion, finely chopped
1 clove garlic, crushed
1–2 teaspoons Italian mixed dried herbs
2 large tomatoes, skinned and chopped
1/2 cup tomato purée
2 teaspoons balsamic vinegar
salt and pepper, to taste

1 Heat the olive oil and butter in a small pan and add the onion, garlic and herbs. Cook for 2–3 minutes or until the onion is soft.
2 Stir in the tomatoes, tomato purée and vinegar and cook for 3–4 minutes. Remove from the heat.
3 Place the mixture in a food processor and process until smooth, seasoning with salt and pepper.

Garlic Herb Hollandaise

Serve this sauce with seafood, chicken or beef.

PREPARATION TIME: 15 MINUTES
COOKING TIME: NIL
MAKES 1 CUP

2 egg yolks
160 g melted butter
2–3 tablespoons lemon juice or white wine vinegar
1 tablespoon chopped chives
1 tablespoon chopped basil
1 tablespoon chopped oregano
1 clove garlic, crushed
salt and pepper, to taste

1 Place the egg yolks in a food processor bowl or blender. With the motor constantly running, add the melted butter in a thin stream. Process until thick and creamy.
2 Add the lemon juice or vinegar, chives, basil, oregano and garlic and season with salt and pepper. Process for 10 seconds to combine.

Smoky Cajun Barbecue Sauce

Use this as a dipping sauce or accompaniment to beef, pork or chicken.

PREPARATION TIME: 10 MINUTES
COOKING TIME: 15 MINUTES
MAKES 1 1/2 CUPS

1 medium onion, grated
1 cup tomato sauce
1/3 cup sweet chilli sauce
1 tablespoon cider vinegar
1/3 cup brown sugar
5 cloves garlic, crushed
3/4 teaspoon ground pepper
1 tablespoon liquid hickory smoke (optional)

1   Place all the ingredients except the liquid smoke in an enamel-lined or flameproof glass pan.
2   Stir over a low heat until the sugar dissolves, then simmer for 12 minutes, stirring occasionally. Remove from the heat, allow to cool and add the liquid smoke, if using.
3   Stir well and store in a glass jar in the refrigerator.

Note: If using liquid smoke, add one teaspoon at a time at the end of cooking, so you can adjust the quantity to suit your particular taste.

Tomato and Coriander Relish

Serve this relish with satays, kebabs, vegetable dishes, breads and seafood.

PREPARATION TIME: 10 MINUTES
COOKING TIME: NIL
MAKES ABOUT 3 CUPS

3 firm ripe tomatoes, chopped
2 cups coriander leaves, chopped
juice of half a lime
1 teaspoon salt
1 teaspoon chilli powder (optional)
1 medium onion, finely chopped

Combine all the ingredients in a bowl and mix thoroughly.

Note: This makes an appealing salad combination as well. Slice tomatoes and onions and arrange on a platter, sprinkle with the salt, chilli powder and coriander leaves. Combine lime juice with a little olive oil and drizzle over the salad to serve.

Sweet and Sour Sauce

Use as a dipping sauce or accompaniment to seafood or chicken.

PREPARATION TIME: 5 MINUTES
COOKING TIME: 5 MINUTES
MAKES 1 1/2 CUPS

1/2 cup water
1/2 cup pineapple juice
1/4 cup white vinegar
1 tablespoon brown sugar
1/4 cup tomato sauce
1 tablespoon cornflour
1 tablespoon water

1   Place the water, pineapple, vinegar, brown sugar and tomato sauce in a small pan.
2   Mix the cornflour and water to a smooth paste. Add to the pan, stirring constantly over a medium heat until the sauce boils and thickens. Cool slightly before serving.

Rosemary Butter

Use with lamb and other meats.

PREPARATION TIME: 10 MINUTES
COOKING TIME: NIL
MAKES 1/2 CUP

125 g butter, softened
2 tablespoons chopped fresh rosemary
squeeze lime juice
1/4 teaspoon ground pepper

Combine the butter with the other ingredients and beat until smooth. Place in a butter container or, using plastic wrap, form into a log shape and refrigerate. Slice into 1-cm thick rounds to serve.

Herb Butter

Use with steaks, chicken, seafood, vegetables and hot breads or rolls.

PREPARATION TIME: 10 MINUTES
COOKING TIME: NIL
MAKES 3/4 CUP

125 g butter, softened
1 tablespoon finely chopped spring onions
2 tablespoons chopped fresh parsley
1 tablespoon snipped fresh chives
or 2 teaspoons dried mixed herbs
1/4 teaspoon white pepper

Combine the butter with the other ingredients and beat until smooth. Place in a butter container or, using plastic wrap, form into a log shape and refrigerate. Slice into 1-cm thick rounds to serve.

Lime and Chilli Butter

Serve with chicken or seafood.

PREPARATION TIME: 10 MINUTES
COOKING TIME: NIL
MAKES 1 CUP

125 g butter
1 tablespoon lime juice
1 teaspoon grated lime rind
1 teaspoon chopped chilli
2 teaspoons chopped fresh coriander

Beat the butter until it is light and creamy. Add the rest of the ingredients and beat again until smooth. Place in a butter container or, using plastic wrap, form into a log shape and refrigerate. Slice into 1-cm thick rounds to serve.

Savoury Anchovy Butter

Serve with beef.

PREPARATION TIME: 10 MINUTES
COOKING TIME: NIL
MAKES 1 CUP

200 g butter
4 anchovy fillets, drained
2 spring onions, chopped
1 clove garlic, peeled
1 tablespoon grated lemon rind

1 Place all the ingredients in a food processor bowl and process for 20–30 seconds or until the mixture forms a smooth paste.
2 Transfer the mixture to small serving pots and refrigerate.

Make interesting shapes with different nozzles

Serving pots can be stored in the refrigerator for several weeks

Shape flavoured butter into a log. Freeze and slice rounds as required

239

Desserts

*n*o matter how much your guests have enjoyed their main meal, they can usually be persuaded to squeeze in a little dessert. Served with coffee, liqueur coffee or perhaps a dessert wine, a sweet offering, whether it be light and refreshing or sinfully rich, is the perfect end to a successful barbecue.

There's no better way to finish a meal than with something sweet. But it's not much fun for you to have to disappear into the kitchen to slave over dessert while everyone else relaxes outside. Fortunately, all the recipes in this chapter can be prepared ahead of time, so that you can have them on the table in minutes.

When entertaining, you need to feel confident that what you are serving will look and taste as good as the recipe suggests, so here are a few tips to help you achieve sweet perfection. If you are making the Fresh fruit pavlova or Berry nests, for example, you will want the meringue to be perfect. There are several methods for making meringue, but you must start with a clean, dry mixing bowl. It's best to have your egg whites at room temperature and, if possible, use caster sugar as it dissolves faster

than any of the larger crystal sugars. Beat the egg whites to soft, firm or stiff peaks, as the recipe requires— the aim is to reach maximum volume without overbeating. When you think the meringue is ready, take a little mixture and rub it between your thumb and forefinger. It should feel smooth and slightly gritty; if it's too gritty it will need extra beating.

Cheesecakes can also be an uncertain entity, and it's often difficult to tell whether they are cooked through. A simple test is to gently wobble the cheesecake with the oven door slightly ajar, leaving the cheesecake in the oven. It should have a slight wobble. If you remove the cheesecake from the oven before it is properly cooked, it will sink. Allow to cool completely before refrigerating overnight for a firm, rich and creamy texture.

Fresh Fruit Pavlova

PREPARATION TIME:
30 MINUTES
COOKING TIME:
40–45 MINUTES
SERVES 6–8

4 egg whites
1 cup caster sugar
1 1/2 cups cream, whipped
1 banana, sliced
250 g punnet strawberries, sliced
2 kiwi fruit, sliced
pulp from 2 passionfruit

1 Preheat the oven to slow 150°C (300°F/Gas 2). Line a large oven tray with non-stick baking paper and draw a 20 cm circle on the paper. Beat the egg whites with electric beaters in a large dry bowl until soft peaks form. Gradually add the sugar, beating well after each addition. Beat for 5–10 minutes until all the sugar has completely dissolved.

2 Spread the meringue mixture onto the tray inside the marked circle. Shape the meringue evenly, running the flat side of a palette knife along the edge and over the top. Run the knife up the edge of meringue mixture, all the way round, making furrows. This strengthens the pavlova, stops the edge crumbling and gives it a good, decorative finish.

4 Bake for 30 minutes, or until pale and crisp. Reduce the heat to very slow 120°C (250°F/Gas 1/2) and bake for a further 10–15 minutes. Turn off the oven and leave the pavlova inside to cool, using a wooden spoon to keep the door ajar. Top with whipped cream and arrange with fruit. Drizzle with passionfruit pulp.

Coconut Cake with Lemon Syrup

PREPARATION TIME:
10 MINUTES

COOKING TIME:
1 HOUR
45 MINUTES

SERVES 8–10

250 g butter
1 3/4 cups caster sugar
7 eggs, lightly beaten
1 2/3 cups self-raising flour
4 cups desiccated coconut

SYRUP
2 cups caster sugar
1/2 cup lemon juice
2 teaspoons finely grated
  lemon rind
1 small lemon, finely sliced
icing sugar, for dusting

1 Preheat the oven to moderate 160°C (315°F/Gas 2–3). Grease a 26 cm springform tin and line the base with baking paper. Place the butter and sugar in a large bowl and beat on high speed until light and fluffy. Add the eggs gradually, beating well after each addition.

2 Gently fold the sifted flour and coconut into the egg mixture. Pour into the prepared tin and bake for 1 1/2 hours, or until just firm. (The cake may dip slightly in the centre.)

3 Combine the sugar, lemon juice, lemon rind and 1/2 cup water in a heavy-based pan. Cook over low heat, stirring constantly until the sugar dissolves. Boil the syrup without stirring for 12 minutes, or until slightly thickened.

4 Remove the cake from oven, and pour the hot syrup evenly over hot cake, reserving about 1/2 cup of syrup. Leave in the tin to cool completely. Add the sliced lemon to the remaining syrup and cook over low heat for 5 minutes. Decorate the cake with the glazed lemon slices, and dust with icing sugar before serving.

Cassata

PREPARATION TIME: 50 MINUTES +
2 HOURS + OVERNIGHT FREEZING
COOKING TIME: NIL
SERVES 20

FIRST LAYER
2 eggs, separated
1/3 cup icing sugar
3/4 cup cream
50 g flaked almonds, toasted
almond essence

SECOND LAYER
130 g dark chocolate,
  chopped
1 tablespoon dark cocoa
2 eggs, separated
1/3 cup icing sugar
3/4 cup cream

THIRD LAYER
2 eggs, separated
1/4 cup icing sugar
1 cup cream
60 g glacé cherries, halved
2 tablespoons chopped
  preserved ginger
220 g glacé fruit (pineapple,
  apricot, fig and peach),
  finely chopped
1 teaspoon vanilla essence

1 Line the base and sides of a deep 20 cm square tin with foil.
2 To make the first layer: Beat the egg whites with electric beaters until soft peaks form. Add the icing sugar gradually, beating well after each addition. In a separate bowl, beat the cream until firm peaks form. Using a metal spoon, fold the yolks and beaten egg whites into the cream. Add the almonds and a few drops of essence. Stir until combined. Spoon into the tin and smooth the surface. Tap the tin gently on the bench to level the surface of the mixture. Freeze for 30–60 minutes, or until firm.
3 To make the second layer: Place the chocolate in a heatproof bowl over a pan of simmering water, and stir until melted. Add the cocoa, and stir until smooth. Remove from heat, and cool slightly. Proceed as for step 2, beating the egg whites and icing sugar and then the cream. Using a metal spoon, fold the chocolate into the cream. Fold in the yolks and beaten egg whites, and stir until smooth. Spoon over the frozen first layer. Tap the tin on the bench to level the surface. Freeze for 30–60 minutes, or until firm.
4 To make the third layer: Proceed as for step 2, beating the egg whites and icing sugar and then the cream. With a metal spoon, fold the yolks and egg white into the cream, then stir in the fruit and vanilla essence. Spoon over the chocolate layer in the tin. Freeze overnight. Slice and serve. Wrap the remainder in foil and return to the freezer.

Berry Nests

PREPARATION TIME:
30 MINUTES
+ COOLING

COOKING TIME:
1 HOUR
15 MINUTES

MAKES 12

4 egg whites
small pinch of cream of tartar
1 cup caster sugar
1 1/4 cups cream
2 teaspoons icing sugar
1 tablespoon brandy
fresh mixed berries

1   Line a large baking tray with non-stick baking paper and preheat the oven to slow 150°C (300°F/Gas 2). Beat the egg whites and cream of tartar until soft peaks form then gradually add the sugar. Beat until stiff and glossy.

2   Fit a piping bag with a medium-sized star nozzle and use to pipe tightly coiled spirals of meringue (about 8 cm across) onto the prepared tray. Pipe rings on the top edges of the rounds to form nests.

3   Bake for 30 minutes. Reduce the oven to very slow 120°C (250°F/Gas 1/2) and bake for a further 45 minutes. Turn the oven off and allow the nests to cool in the oven with the door ajar. Whip the cream with the icing sugar and brandy. Pile into the nests and top with mixed berries of your choice.

Note: The cream of tartar will help to dry the meringues, making them crisp and crunchy.

Tiramisu

PREPARATION TIME:
20 MINUTES
COOKING TIME:
NIL
SERVES 6–8

3 cups strong black coffee, cooled
1/4 cup dark rum
2 eggs, separated
1/4 cup caster sugar
250 g mascarpone
1 cup cream, whipped
20 large sponge finger biscuits
2 teaspoons dark cocoa powder

1 Combine the coffee and rum in a glass or jug.

2 Using electric beaters, beat the egg yolks and sugar in a small bowl for 3 minutes, or until the mixture is thick and pale. Add the mascarpone and beat until the ingredients are just combined. Using a metal spoon, fold in the whipped cream.

3 Using electric beaters, beat the egg whites until soft peaks form; then fold quickly and lightly into the cream mixture with a metal spoon.

4 Dip half the biscuits, one at a time, into the coffee mixture. Drain off any excess and arrange in the base of a serving dish about 20 x 25 cm and 6 cm deep. Spread half the cream mixture over the biscuits.

5 Dip the remaining biscuits into the coffee mixture and repeat layering with the biscuits and cream mixture. Smooth the surface with a spatula and dust with cocoa powder. Refrigerate for at least 2 hours to allow the flavours to develop (best refrigerated overnight). Serve with fresh fruit.

Summer Berry Tart

PREPARATION TIME:
35 MINUTES
+ 20 MINUTES
REFRIGERATION
COOKING TIME:
35 MINUTES
SERVES 4–6

1 cup plain flour
90 g butter, chopped
2 tablespoons icing sugar

FILLING
3 egg yolks
2 tablespoons caster sugar
2 tablespoons cornflour
1 cup milk
1 teaspoon vanilla essence
250 g strawberries, halved
125 g blueberries
125 g raspberries
1–2 tablespoons apricot jam

1   Sift the flour and icing sugar into a bowl and add the butter. Rub the butter into the flour and icing sugar with your fingertips until it resembles fine breadcrumbs. Make a well in the centre, add 1–2 tablespoons water and mix with a flat-bladed knife, using a cutting action, until the mixture comes together in beads. Add more water if necessary. Gently gather the dough together and lift out onto a lightly floured surface. Press together until smooth.

2   Roll out the pastry to fit a 20 cm round fluted flan tin. Line the tin with the pastry, trim the edges, and refrigerate for 20 minutes. Preheat the oven to moderate 180°C (350°F/Gas 4). Cut a sheet of greaseproof paper to cover the pastry-lined tin. Spread a layer of dried beans or rice evenly over the paper and bake for 15 minutes. Remove from the oven, and discard the paper and rice. Return to the oven for 15 minutes, or until lightly golden.

3   To make the Filling: Place the egg yolks, sugar and cornflour in a bowl, and whisk until pale. Heat the milk in a small pan until almost boiling, then remove from the heat. Add the milk gradually to the egg mixture, beating constantly. Strain into the pan, and stir constantly over low heat for 3 minutes, or until it boils and thickens. Remove from heat, and add the vanilla essence. Transfer to a bowl, cover with plastic wrap, and leave to cool.

4   Spread the filling in the cooled pastry shell and top with the berries. Gently warm the apricot jam until it liquefies, then sieve. Brush the warmed jam over the fruit with a pastry brush before serving.

Banana Caramel Tart

PREPARATION TIME: 35 MINUTES
+ 50 MINUTES REFRIGERATION
COOKING TIME: 40 MINUTES
SERVES 8

1 1/4 cups plain flour
2 tablespoons icing sugar
3/4 cup ground walnuts
80 g butter, chopped
1/4 cup iced water

FILLING
400 g condensed milk
30 g butter
1 tablespoon golden syrup
4 medium bananas, sliced
1 cup cream, whipped
1/2 cup pure thick cream
50 g dark chocolate, melted

1 Sift the flour and icing sugar into a mixing bowl and add the walnuts and butter. Rub the butter into the flour until fine and crumbly. Add almost all of the iced water, and mix with a flat-bladed knife to a firm dough. Add more water if needed. Turn out onto a lightly floured surface, and press together until smooth. Roll out the pastry and ease it into a 23 cm flan tin, then trim the edges. Cover and refrigerate for 20 minutes.

2 Preheat the oven to moderate 180°C (350°F/Gas 4). Cover the pastry-lined tin with a sheet of greaseproof paper, and spread dried beans or rice over the paper. Bake for 15 minutes, then remove the paper and beans.

Return the pastry to the oven for 20 minutes, until lightly golden. Cool completely.

4 To make the Filling: Place the condensed milk, butter and syrup in a heavy-based pan. Stir constantly over medium heat for 5 minutes, until the mixture boils and thickens and turns a light caramel colour. Cool slightly.

Arrange half the banana slices over the pastry, then pour on the caramel. Smooth with the back of a spoon. Chill for 30 minutes.
5 Using a metal spoon, gently fold the creams together. Drop dollops of cream over the caramel, and top with the remaining banana slices. Drizzle on the chocolate.

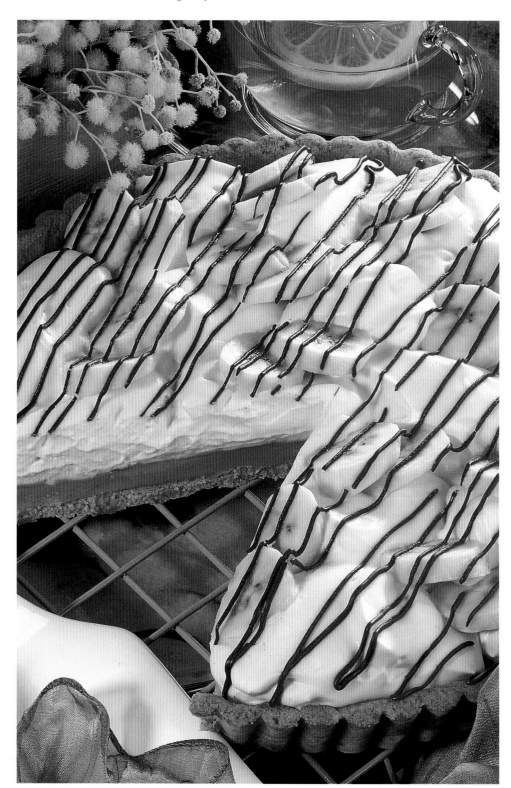

New York Cheesecake

PREPARATION TIME: 1 HOUR + CHILLING
COOKING TIME: 1 HOUR 50 MINUTES
SERVES 10–12

1/2 cup self-raising flour
1 cup plain flour
1/4 cup caster sugar
1 teaspoon grated lemon rind
80 g butter, chopped
1 egg

FILLING
750 g cream cheese, softened
1 cup caster sugar
1/4 cup plain flour
2 teaspoons grated orange rind
2 teaspoons grated lemon rind
4 eggs
2/3 cup cream

CANDIED RIND
1 cup caster sugar
rind of 3 limes, 3 lemons and
   3 oranges, shredded
1 1/2 cups cream

1 Sift the flours into a large bowl, and add the sugar, lemon rind and butter. Rub in the butter with your fingertips until the mixture resembles fine breadcrumbs. Make a well in the centre and add the egg. Mix with a flat-bladed knife, using a cutting action, until the mixture comes together in beads. Gently gather the dough together and lift out onto a lightly floured work surface. Press together, wrap in plastic wrap and refrigerate for 20 minutes, or until firm.

2 Preheat the oven to hot 210°C (415°F/Gas 6–7). Roll the pastry between 2 sheets of baking paper until large enough to fit the base and side of a greased 23 cm round springform cake tin. Ease into the tin and trim the edges. Line with a piece of crumpled baking paper and pour in some baking beads. Bake for 10 minutes, then remove the baking paper and beads and flatten the pastry lightly with the back of a spoon. Bake for a further 5 minutes. Allow to cool.

3 To make the Filling: Reduce the oven to slow 150°C (300°F/Gas 2). Beat the cream cheese, sugar, flour and rinds until smooth. Add the eggs, one at a time, beating after each addition. Beat in the cream, pour the filling over the pastry and bake for 1 hour 25–35 minutes, or until almost set. Cool, then refrigerate.

4 To make the Candied Rind: Put the sugar in a pan with 1/4 cup water and stir over low heat until dissolved. Add the rind, bring to the boil, reduce the heat and simmer for 5–6 minutes. Allow to cool and drain the rind (you can save the syrup to serve with the cheesecake). Whip the cream, spoon over the cold cheesecake and top with Candied Rind.

Chinese Fortune Cookies

PREPARATION TIME:
15 MINUTES

COOKING TIME:
ABOUT 5 MINUTES EACH TRAY

MAKES ABOUT 30

3 egg whites
1/2 cup icing sugar, sifted
45 g unsalted butter
1/2 cup plain flour

1 Preheat the oven to moderate 180°C (350°F/ Gas 4) and line an oven tray with baking paper. Draw three 8 cm circles on the paper.

2 Place the egg whites in a clean, dry bowl and whisk until they are just frothy. Add the icing sugar and butter and stir until the mixture is smooth. Add the flour, mix until smooth then set the mixture aside for 15 minutes. Using a flat-bladed knife, spread 1 1/2 level teaspoons of the mixture over each circle. Bake the cookies for 5 minutes, or until they are slightly brown around the edges.

3 Working quickly, remove the cookies from the trays by sliding a flat-bladed knife under each round.

4 Place a written or typed fortune message in the centre of each cookie. Fold the cookie in half, then in half again over a blunt-edged object. Set aside to cool on a wire rack. Cook the remaining mixture the same way.

Storage time: Fortune Cookies may be stored for up to 2 days in an airtight container.

Hint: Make only two or three cookies at a time, or they will harden before you have time to fold them and will break during folding.

Note: Fortune cookies make a great after-dinner talking point and guests will be impressed if you make your own. It also allows you to have some fun personalising the messages.

Amaretti

PREPARATION TIME:
25 MINUTES +
1 HOUR
STANDING
COOKING TIME:
15 MINUTES
MAKES 40

1 tablespoon plain flour
1 tablespoon cornflour
1 teaspoon ground cinnamon
3/4 cup caster sugar
1 teaspoon grated lemon rind
1 cup ground almonds
2 egg whites
1/4 cup icing sugar

1 Line two 32 x 28 cm biscuit trays with baking paper and preheat the oven to moderate 180°C (350°F/Gas 4).

2 Sift the plain flour, cornflour, cinnamon and half the caster sugar into a large bowl. Stir in the lemon rind and ground almonds.

3 Place the egg whites in a small, dry mixing bowl. Using electric beaters, beat until firm peaks form. Add the remaining caster sugar gradually, beating constantly until the mixture is thick and glossy and all the sugar has dissolved. Using a metal spoon, fold the egg white mixture into the dry ingredients until just combined and a soft dough forms.

4 With wet or oiled hands, roll 2 level teaspoons of the mixture at a time into a ball, and arrange on the prepared tray, allowing room for spreading. Sift icing sugar liberally over the biscuits, and bake for 15 minutes, or until the biscuits are lightly browned. Transfer to wire rack to cool.

Sugar and Spice Palmiers

PREPARATION TIME:
20 MINUTES
COOKING TIME:
20 MINUTES
MAKES 32

1 sheet frozen butter puff pastry
2 tablespoons raw sugar
1 teaspoon mixed spice
1 teaspoon ground cinnamon
40 g butter, melted
icing sugar, to dust

1 Brush two flat oven trays with melted butter or oil and line with baking paper.

2 Thaw the pastry sheet as directed on the packet. Meanwhile, combine the sugar and spices in a small bowl. Cut the sheet of pastry in half and brush each piece with melted butter. Sprinkle generously with the sugar mixture, reserving 2 teaspoons.

3 Fold the long edges of pastry inwards, then fold again so that the edges almost meet in the centre. Fold once more, then place the pastry rolls on a tray and refrigerate for 15 minutes. Preheat the oven to hot 210°C (415°F/Gas 6–7). Using a small, sharp knife, cut the pastry rolls into 32 slices.

4 Arrange the palmiers cut-side-up on the prepared trays, brush with butter and sprinkle lightly with the reserved sugar mixture. Bake for 20 minutes, or until golden. Cool on a wire rack and dust lightly with icing sugar before serving.

Mixed Nut Biscotti

PREPARATION
TIME:
30 MINUTES
COOKING TIME:
45 MINUTES
MAKES
ABOUT 50

25 g almonds
25 g hazelnuts
75 g unsalted pistachios
3 egg whites
1/2 cup caster sugar
3/4 cup plain flour

1   Preheat the oven to moderate 180°C (350°F/
Gas 4). Brush a 26 x 8 x 4.5 cm bar tin with oil
or melted butter and line the base and sides with
baking paper. Spread the almonds, hazelnuts and
pistachios onto a flat baking tray and place in the
oven for 2–3 minutes, or until the nuts are just
toasted. Allow to cool.

2   Place the egg whites in a small, clean, dry mixing
bowl. Using electric beaters, beat the egg whites
until stiff peaks form. Add the sugar gradually,
beating constantly until the mixture is thick and
glossy and all the sugar has dissolved.

3   Transfer the mixture to a large mixing bowl.
Add the sifted flour and nuts. Using a metal spoon,
gently fold the ingredients together until well
combined. Spread the mixture into the prepared tin
and smooth the surface. Bake for 25 minutes. Remove
from the oven and cool completely in the tin.

4   Preheat the oven to moderately slow 160°C
(315°F/Gas 2–3). Using a sharp, serrated knife, cut
the baked loaf into 5 mm slices. Spread the slices
onto oven trays and bake for about 15 minutes,
turning once halfway through cooking, until the
slices are lightly golden and crisp. Delicious dipped
into coffee, or served with a sweet dessert wine.

Index

USEFUL INFORMATION

The recipes in this book were developed using a tablespoon measure of 20 ml. In some other countries the tablespoon is 15 ml. For most recipes this difference will not be noticeable but, for recipes using baking powder, gelatine, bicarbonate of soda, small amounts of flour and cornflour, we suggest that, if you are using the smaller tablespoon, you add an extra teaspoon for each tablespoon.

The recipes in this book are written using convenient cup measurements. You can buy special measuring cups in the supermarket or use an ordinary household cup: first you need to check it holds 250 ml (8 fl oz) by filling it with water and measuring the water (pour it into a measuring jug or even an empty yoghurt carton). This cup can then be used for both liquid and dry cup measurements.

Liquid cup measures

1/4 cup	60 ml	2 fluid oz
1/3 cup	80 ml	2 1/2 fluid oz
1/2 cup	125 ml	4 fluid oz
3/4 cup	180 ml	6 fluid oz
1 cup	250 ml	8 fluid oz

Spoon measures

1/4 teaspoon	1.25 ml
1/2 teaspoon	2.5 ml
1 teaspoon	5 ml
1 tablespoon	20 ml

Cup conversions

1 cup plain/self-raising flour	125 g (4 oz)
1 cup grated Parmesan cheese	100 g (3 1/2 oz)
1 cup grated Cheddar cheese	125 g (4 oz)
1 cup breadcrumbs (fresh)	80 g (2 3/4 oz)
1 cup breadcrumbs (dry)	100 g (3 1/2 oz)
1 cup dried chickpeas	220 g (7 oz)
1 cup grated chocolate	125 g (4 oz)
1 cup rice, uncooked	200 g (6 1/2 oz)
1 cup rice, cooked	185 g (6 oz)
1 cup sugar, caster/granulated	250 g (8 oz)
1 cup icing sugar	125 g (4 oz)
1 cup fresh basil/coriander/mint leaves, firmly packed	30 g (1 oz)
1 cup chopped fresh basil/coriander/mint leaves, firmly packed	60 g (2 oz)

Alternative names

bicarbonate of soda	—	baking soda
capsicum	—	red or green (bell) pepper
chickpeas	—	garbanzo beans
cornflour	—	cornstarch
fresh coriander	—	cilantro
cream	—	single cream
dark chocolate	—	plain/bittersweet chocolate
eggplant	—	aubergine
flat-leaf parsley	—	Italian parsley
golden syrup	—	light corn syrup
hazelnut	—	filbert
heat bead	—	barbecue briquette/ barbecue charcoal
icing sugar	—	confectioners' sugar
plain flour	—	all-purpose flour
prawns	—	shrimp
sambal oelek	—	chilli paste
snow pea	—	mange tout
spring onion	—	scallion
thick cream	—	double/heavy cream
tomato paste (US/Aus.)	—	tomato purée (UK)
Weber barbecue	—	Kettle grill/Covered barbecue
zucchini	—	courgette

Weight

10 g	1/4 oz	220 g	7 oz	425 g	14 oz
30 g	1 oz	250 g	8 oz	475 g	15 oz
60 g	2 oz	275 g	9 oz	500 g	1 lb
90 g	3 oz	300 g	10 oz	600 g	1 1/4 lb
125 g	4 oz	330 g	11 oz	650 g	1 lb 5 oz
150 g	5 oz	375 g	12 oz	750 g	1 1/2 lb
185 g	6 oz	400 g	13 oz	1 kg	2 lb

Published in 1999 by Merehurst Limited, Ferry House, 51–57 Lacy Road, Putney, London SW15 1PR

Editor: Sally Feldman **Designer:** Michelle Withers **CEO & Publisher:** Anne Wilson **International Sales Director:** Mark Newman
ISBN 1 897730 61 6

A catalogue record of this book is available from the British Library.

Printed by Tien Wah Press, Singapore. PRINTED IN SINGAPORE.